A JOURNEY THROUGH THE YEMEN

BAZAAR AT DHAMAR.

A

JOURNEY THROUGH THE YEMEN

AND

SOME GENERAL REMARKS UPON THAT COUNTRY

BY

WALTER B. HARRIS, F.R.G.S.

AUTHOR OF

'THE LAND OF AN AFRICAN SULTAN ; TRAVELS IN MOROCCO'

ILLUSTRATED FROM SKETCHES AND PHOTOGRAPHS
TAKEN BY THE AUTHOR

DARF PUBLISHERS LIMITED
LONDON
1985

First Edition 1893
New Impression 1985

ISBN 1 85077 036 0

Printed and bound in Great Britain by
A. Wheaton & Co. Ltd

TO

MY FATHER AND MOTHER

I DEDICATE THIS BOOK.

PREFACE.

BUT very few words are necessary as a preface to this book, as more than once in its pages its objects are stated.

An account of my journey through the Yemen appeared last autumn in a series of articles in the 'Illustrated London News,' and it is with kind permission of the proprietors of that paper that some of the illustrations reappear here. Many of the illustrations, however, have not seen the light of day before.

The chapter on the Yemen rebellion was published as an article in 'Blackwood's Magazine' for February last.

The remainder of the book consists of entirely new matter.

I cannot attempt to thank here the many persons who aided me and rendered me services during the time I was in the Yemen. Without their assistance my journey would probably have failed. To them I am most grateful.

W. B. H.

Sept. 1893.

CONTENTS.

APPENDIX.

ILLUSTRATIONS.

FULL-PAGE ILLUSTRATIONS.

PART I.

SOME GENERAL REMARKS ON THE YEMEN

A JOURNEY THROUGH THE YEMEN.

CHAPTER I.

THE YEMEN.

THE Yemen may be described as forming the south-
west corner of Arabia. So little is known of the
geography of the interior, and to such a slight extent
do even the natives define the boundaries between
their own land and the surrounding provinces, that
any exact description of the country is impossible.
The same may be said of nearly all oriental frontiers,
except where, taking an example from European
customs, a clear line of demarcation has been agreed
upon; for, as a rule, limits depend far more upon
tribal position and inheritance than upon any natural
features of the land in question; and in many cases
in the settlement of frontier questions with oriental
Powers, even European Governments have been

obliged to follow upon these lines. This is especially clearly exemplified in the case of the Algerian and Moroccan frontier, in the southern parts of which no absolute boundary has been fixed, certain tribes, whether in French or Moorish territory, belonging to whichever of the two nationalities under which they are enrolled.

How infinitely difficult it is, then, in the case of the Yemen, to state where that province begins and ends, will be appreciated.

As to two of its limits, the task of definition is simple; for on the west the Red Sea, and on the south that portion of the Indian Ocean known as the Gulf of Aden, allow of no question. On the north and east far more serious difficulties arise. Without attempting to delineate any exact frontier, which, with our present geographical knowledge of the country, would fail at the best to be anything more than roughly correct, more general terms must be used than would be justifiable in a more pretentious work than the present.

It may be stated, then, that the province of Arabia known as the Yemen is bounded on the east by the Hadramaut tribes, and on the north by the Asir, although some authorities include the latter, making the north frontier of the Yemen adjacent with the southern limit of the Hejaz, the province of Arabia in which are situated the holy cities of Mecca and Medina. As far as the writer was able to gather, however, from the natives themselves, the Asir is considered to be an entirely different district, although its inhabitants are nearly related to the Yemenis by blood. In fact, it may be said without much exaggeration that the present divisions of Arabia as marked upon the maps are but little in advance geographically of the ancient Greek and Roman arbitrary distinctions of Arabia Felix, Arabia Petræa, and Arabia Deserta. Even allowing for the widest limits claimed for the Yemen, the whole country lies between 42° and 46° east longitude and 12° and 20° north latitude.

Although no natural formation of the Yemen can assist one in correctly determining its inland frontiers, the same cannot be said of the two great divisions into which the country is split up. These are so apparent that, from the earliest geographers to the present day, they have remained unchanged and fully recognised. But in order to appreciate this, a few words must be said as to the formation of the country. While the interior consists of vast mountain-ranges and elevated plateaux, some of which lie at an altitude of over eight thousand feet above the sea-level, the seaboard consists, both on the west and south, of low-lying sandy deserts and plains, varying in breadth from thirty to nearly a hundred miles. The only exception where a spur of the mountains approaches the sea is at the headland of Sidi Sheikh, the south-west corner of the

Red Sea—a spur of land a few miles in width exactly
opposite the island of Perim, from which it is divided
by a narrow channel. It may be remembered that
only a few years back there was a false report that
France had purchased this advantageous spot from
the Turkish Government.

The formation of these maritime plains is such that
it may be safely surmised that a very considerable
portion, at least of what is now desert, was at one
time covered by the sea. So fast, indeed, has been
the silting action, that more than one former port
now lies well inland. As an example of this, Sir R.
L. Playfair, in his excellent 'History of the Yemen,'
mentions the town of Muza, once a flourishing seaport, now over twenty miles inland. In many places,
too, shells and chips of coral are to be found at great
distances from the coast. The same retrograde action
of the sea can be traced, too, at Aden, which was, no
doubt, at one time an island, and is now joined to
the mainland by a low isthmus, formed by the silting
of sea-sand upon a submarine basis of rock.

The name Teháma is applied to these plains of the
Yemen. It is a district exceedingly subject to
drought, and with a very small rainfall. What
water-supply it boasts, with the exception of oases,
is principally due to the mountain torrents, which,
originating in the highlands, rush impetuously down
the steep slopes, usually to be entirely exhausted by
the desert before reaching the sea. It is said, how-

ever, that even in the driest seasons water may be found by sinking wells in the river-beds. Although the supply thus obtained is sufficient to maintain the lives of Bedouins and their flocks and herds, it is far from proving of any great utility to cultivation, in such spots where, even in good years, cultivation is possible. However, fortunately for the inhabitants, there are scattered over these deserts many oases, where cereals can be reared with tolerable certainty of reaping the crops. The poor quality of the soil as a rule renders agriculture, except in the most favourable positions, an unprofitable pursuit. The plains serve, too, for the breeding of camels,—those of the Abdali and Foudtheli country, lying to the north and north-east of Aden, being especially famous for their swiftness and carrying capabilities.

The Jibál, or highlands, display entirely opposite features. Enormous ranges of mountains rise abruptly from the Teháma to great altitudes, in places probably 14,000 and 15,000 feet. These ranges for the most part take a general south-easterly direction, and are split up into a series of wide, fertile, parallel valleys. It was doubtless the luxuriance and agricultural wealth, added to the attractiveness of the climate, of this portion of Arabia, that won for the Yemen in former days the title of Arabia Felix. In these great valleys the coffee is grown, sharing with the production of the indigo-plant and other dye-giving species the attention of the mountaineers. Added

to this, the climate is such as to allow nearly all
European vegetables to grow and flourish, and also
many varieties of fruit-trees. The nature of the
country renders necessary for cultivation the terracing of the steep mountain-sides, and over this
laborious task an almost incredible amount of work
and time is expended. But of this I shall have
opportunity of speaking anon.

There is, as might be expected, a vast difference in
the temperature of the highlands and the plains.
While at Aden and the surrounding country the
thermometer averages all the year round some 85°
Fahrenheit, it probably does not rise above a mean
of 61° or 62° in the shade at Sanaa, the capital of
the Yemen, where, as in all the elevated country,
frosts are by no means uncommon in winter. Nor
is it solely in temperature that great differences are
apparent with regard to the low and high elevations;
for whereas also in the former the rainfall is uncertain
and sometimes almost nil,[1] the mountain country
boasts two regular wet seasons — in spring and in
autumn respectively. In this respect the seasons
may be said to correspond with those of the plateaux
of Harrar and the Galla country. In both cases the
rain is said to be of almost daily occurrence, but
lasting only a short time, the showers being broken
by periods of bright sunshine.

Nothing can be imagined more beautiful than the

[1] In 1871 the rainfall at Aden was only one-fourth of an inch.

COFFEE PLANTATION ON TERRACES AT ATTARA, NEAR MENAKHA.

scenery of the mountains of the Yemen. Torn into all manner of fantastic peaks, the rocky crags add a wildness to a view that otherwise possesses the most peaceful charms. Rich green valleys, well timbered in places, and threaded by silvery streams of dancing water; sloping fields, gay with crops and wild-flowers ; the terraced or jungle-covered slopes,—all are so luxuriant, so verdant, that one's ideas as to the nature of Arabia are entirely upset. Well known as is, and always has been, the fertility of this region, its extent is almost startling, and it can little be wondered at that Alexander the Great intended, after his conquest of India, to take up his abode in the Yemen, had not death cut short his career.

Thus briefly described, it will be seen that the Yemen consists of two entirely different systems of country, influenced by two entirely different climates : the one arid plains, without much appreciable rain-fall ; the other a mountainous district, producing cereals, dyes, aromatic gums, coffee, and other rich produce—a country of valleys and plateaux, well watered withal, and enjoying a climate that for salubrity may be said to equal any in the tropics. Having now pointed out in a general way the differ-ence of the two districts, I purpose to enter a little more definitely into the description of each.

To commence with the Teháma, as being the sea-board. It consists, as already stated, of plains varying from thirty to a hundred miles in breadth,

and separating the highlands from the sea, both on
the west and south. These, for the sake of distinction, I shall call respectively the western and
southern Tehàma. The former contains some five
cities of importance, situated either on the coast
of the Red Sea or in that district which divides
it from the mountains. Almost in the Asir country
lies Lohaya, a small town on the coast, to which
I shall refer more particularly in a chapter on the
Yemen rebellion. Proceeding south, the next coast
town of importance is Hodaidah, to-day the capital
of that portion of the Yemen, and still farther
south Mokha. As it was my lot to spend a week
in the fever - stricken town of Hodaidah, I shall
reserve anything I have to say about it for another
opportunity; but as it was my ill fortune to see
Mokha only from the sea and not to land there,
and as I shall therefore not have to narrate any
personal experiences in reference to it, I shall add
some description of the place and its history at
this juncture.

There is certainly no name of any city in the
Yemen as familiar to Englishmen as that of Mokha,
with the exception of Aden. This it owes to its
having for a long time enjoyed almost the sole
reputation of the export city of the coffee-berry.
However, it is not generally known that no coffee
grows at all in the immediate vicinity of Mokha,
and that all that was shipped from there was previ-

ously carried to the city by caravans from the mountains, often over very great distances. Almost as suddenly as Mokha rose to fame has it fallen again. Before the arrival in the Red Sea of the English and Portuguese traders it scarcely existed at all, the outlets for the trade of this portion of the Yemen being Okelis and Muza. It was not, in fact, until the fifteenth century A.D. that Mokha became a place of resort for ships, and it owes its origin more to the discovery of coffee than to any advantages or attractions of its own. In the early part of the seventeenth century the English and Dutch founded trading "factories" there, and from that time for a period of some two hundred years its fame and wealth were renowned. Van den Broeck describes the place as it existed at the time of his visit in 1616, and notes that to such an extent has its trade recently augmented that goods from Hungary and Venice were found in the market, which had been carried by caravans the whole length of Arabia, to be exchanged for the produce of the far east.[1] He further describes the town as a most flourishing community, containing within its walls numbers of numerous nationalities who had flocked there on hearing of its fame and renown.

A century after the Dutch and English had founded their factories the French followed their example, while in 1803 the Americans commenced

[1] Hist. gen. des Voyages, vol. xxxi. p. 438.

to trade direct with the Red Sea ports. On the British occupation of Aden in 1839, the immense superiority of that place as a port, and the security and advantages assured by British rule, drew the commerce from Mokha thence, the former celebrated city fast falling to decay and ruin.[1] Before this period, however, serious outrages had been offered to British subjects, and during the first twenty years of this century there had been constant trouble brewing between the fanatical natives and the Christians, augmented no doubt by the jealousy felt by the former for the manner in which the Europeans had annexed their trade. More extraordinary still than these outrages was the manner in which their perpetration was looked upon by the British Government, and it was not until things became unbearable that forcible means were taken to punish the offenders, and in 1820 a force under Captain Bruce, who had been sent thither to enforce a treaty with the Imam's Amir, and Captain Lumley of H.M.S. Topaz, bombarded Mokha, and succeeded in forcing an entry into the town. The result of this long-delayed act of reparation on the part of the Indian Government was the placing upon an honourable footing of the British "factory," and the carrying through of a treaty of commerce with the Government of the Yemen.[2]

Although the author did not land in Mokha, the

[1] Playfair's Yemen, p. 22.   [2] Ibid., pp. 135-139.

captain of the steamer on which he proceeded from Hodaidah to Aden very kindly approached as near the shore as was compatible with the ship's course, and with the aid of glasses a very good view of the place was obtained. From a distance it still has the appearance of being a flourishing town, but on nearer approach one can see that, although the walls of the houses are still standing, the roofs and floors have for the most part fallen in, and Mokha is to-day little more than a vast ruin, from which a few tall minarets still rise to tell of its former beauties. A handful of Turkish soldiers and a few Bedouins are all that remain of its once heterogeneous population; and where once the streets were filled with richly robed merchants, goats feed to-day on the coarse weeds.

As Lohaya and Hodaidah are more particularly mentioned elsewhere in this book, little more remains to be said of the ports of the western Teháma. Some mention must be made, however, of the islands of Kamaran and Perim, the two most important of the many that lie on the eastern side of this part of the Red Sea. The former owes its importance to-day from the fact that it is a British possession, and serves as the quarantine station of the pilgrims going to and returning from Jeddah, en route to and from Mecca. It is situated in latitude 15° 20′ N. and longitude 42° 30′ E., and is about ten miles in length, varying from two to four wide. In some parts it is little more than a swamp, in others some low hills allow of the growth of palm-trees; but the inhabitants are nearly all engaged in the pearl and turtle fisheries.[1]

The other island which may be included in a description of the Teháma is Perim. It is situated in the Straits of Bab el - Mandeb, a mile and a half from the Arabian and about ten miles from the African shores. It is formed of dark volcanic igneous rock and plains of sand on which a few sand-loving flowers grow. The highest point of the island is between two and three hundred feet above the sea-level. What, however, compensates for its aridness and hideous character is the grand harbour it possesses. This bay is a mile long by half a mile wide, well sheltered, and averaging a depth of five fathoms in the good anchorages. In 1799, in consequence of the invasion of Egypt by the French, a British naval force, under Admiral Blanket, proceeded to the Red Sea, while the Bombay Government, acting in conjunction with the other force, seized Perim in the name of the East India Company. No fresh water, however, being procurable, it was during the next year abandoned as a station for troops. To-day, under the hands of the Perim Coal Company not only offices but a hotel has been erected there, and the place promises to become a flourishing coaling-station. All the water is, of course, produced by condensers. A few British troops are habitually

[1] Sailing Directions for the Red Sea.

quartered there, being sent from time to time for that purpose from Aden, and there is telegraphic communication both with that port and Hodaidah.

Two cities of importance lie in the interior of the western Teháma—namely, Zebeed and Beit el-Fakih. The former has throughout all the medieval history of the Yemen played a part of great importance; for not only has Zebeed been a seat of learning and art, but also has been inseparably connected with all the great civil wars and religious differences that have from time to time shaken the Yemen to its very foundations. Before the invasion of the Turks it was the capital and seat of government of the Teháma, though to-day Hodaidah has usurped its position as such.

The foundations of Zebeed were laid by Ibn Ziad after his conquest of the Teháma in 204 A.H.[1] The city is described not only by Omarah but also by many other native historians, who one and all make mention of its political importance as well as of its size. The account most to the point, perhaps, is that of El Khasraji, who states that the city is circular in form; that near it to the south flows the river of the same name, while to the north is the Wadi Rima, the two ensuring a fertile situation and a constant water-supply. He adds that it stood midway between the mountains and the sea, and almost equidistant from both, the time taken

[1] Kay's translation of Omarah's Yemen, 1892.

to reach either the one or the other being half a day.

Of Beit el-Fakih little need be said here, as to-day it is a place of but slight importance. Like all these cities of the Tehǎma, it is irregularly built of sun-dried mud bricks. Its name, " The House of the Scholar," is derived from its being the place of burial of a certain Seyed Ahmed ibn Musa, whose tomb is still much reverenced and visited as a place of veneration. The town possesses no claim to interest either politically or commercially.

The next portion of the Yemen of which notice must here be taken are the plains commencing from the Straits of Bab el-Mandeb, and extending to some sixty miles east of Aden. These plains are included in the Tehǎma, but in order to distinguish them from that part already noticed, I describe them as the southern Tehǎma. Like the western Tehǎma, they separate the mountains from the sea, and in many respects these two portions of desert bear great re-semblance. The southern Tehǎma varies from fifty to a hundred miles in breadth, and is inhabited by wild tribes, the most important of which are the Subaiha, the Abdali, and the Foudtheli, the first being nomad in character. These plains boast no cities of any size except Howta, the capital of the Sultan of Lahej, chief of the Abdali tribe, which lies some twenty-seven miles north-west of Aden, and Taiz,—though the latter, from its situation on a spur of the mountains, may be said rather to dominate than to belong to these southern plains. Ibn Khaldun, in his geography of the Yemen, refers to Taiz as an important city overlooking the Tehâma, and mentions that it had at all times been a royal residence. Without much further mention of this city, which the author did not visit, a few remarks may be made upon its later history. Owing to jealousies between members of its ruling family, a certain Seyed Kassim, uncle to the then ruling Imam, Ali Mansur, treacherously sold the place to the Egyptians in 1837, and it was taken without resistance by Ibrahim Pasha, a general in the service of the famous Mahammed Ali Pasha, who held it until in 1840 a fanatical Mahdi el - Fakih Saïd took the town, only to have it wrested from him in 1841 by the Imam Seyed Mahammed el - Hadi. During the late Yemen rebellion it fell into the hands of the Arabs, for formerly it lay within the limit of Turkish influence, and has probably by this time been reoccupied by the Osmanli troops.

With these few remarks upon the plain districts of the Yemen, scanty as they are, notice may now be taken of the mountainous districts. Such parts as the author travelled through will be more minutely treated of in the narration of his journey, together with the towns of Yerim, Dhamar, and Sanaa, the three principal cities of the Yemen plateaux. However, there are other places of importance to which reference must be made here, and which, although not situated upon the plateau, must by their position be included in this division of the Yemen. Of these the most important are Ibb and Jiblah. Both of these mountain - fortresses are of some antiquity, and have played no mean part in the history of the country. Ibb is mentioned by Omarah as being situated upon the great pilgrim-road built by Huseyn ibn Salaamah, a slave-vizier, which led from the Hadramaut, east of Aden, to Mecca itself, which was constructed about the year 400 A.H. After leaving Aden this great pilgrim - route was split up into two parts, one proceeding *viâ* Ibb and the mountains, joining the author's route at Kariat en-Nekil, north of Dhamar; the other following the Tehâma. The road which leads *viâ* Ibb proceeds through Sanaa, and thence *viâ* Sadah and Taif to the Holy City.

Jiblah, or Dhu Jiblah, as it was formerly called, owes its name to the fact that it was built upon the site of a pottery belonging to a Jew, Jiblah by name. It lies some ten miles to the south-west of Ibb. Ibn Khaldun gives a short description of the place. It is, he says, a fortress, and was founded by Abdullah, the Sulayhite, in the year 458 A.H. Like Taiz, it was a royal residence.

The other cities of the mountain district, lying principally north of Sanaa, the capital, and therefore not coming under that portion of the country which

VIEW OF MOUNTAIN-RANGES NEAR SÔK EL-KHAMIR.

On the road from Sanaa to Hodaidah.

it was the author's lot to travel over, will be noticed anon.

Rough as these notes are, they will, I venture to think, help to illustrate the map. To attempt here the task of identifying the ancient sites with modern names would be not only a task of great difficulty, but also one unsuitable to the present book. Mr Kay, in his most able translation of Omarah's History, has pointed out how extremely laborious and uncertain has been his attempt to do so, even with such maps as to-day exist of the country. The author, after consideration, thought it more advisable to avoid entering into discussions that bear but little relation to his work, and would, he fears, but prove uninteresting to the general reader. He has therefore confined his geographical notes to such portions of the country as he himself passed through, supplemented by a few remarks upon places that demand some notice, either from their importance to-day or from historical interest. In the chapter relating to the history of the country the same course has been pursued, a few pages of print being put aside for what would fill volumes were it taken in hand.

Having now treated of the Yemen as it appears from a cursory glance at the map, it is intended to enter a little more fully into its description, unconnected with its natural formation of plains and highlands.

Ibn Khaldun, in the preface to his Geography,

states that the Yemen is divided into seven royal
seats of Government ;[1] but Niebuhr gives a larger
list of provinces, which is again added to by Sir
Lambert Playfair. These divisions of the country,
it must be understood, are entirely Arab in origin,
and to-day have been more or less altered to suit the
Turks. However, on inquiry from the natives, the
writer found that, although disregarded by the
Osmanli conquerors, the names are still in common
use amongst the indigenous peoples.

The author gives the list of these provinces in
the order in which they are printed in Playfair's
' Yemen ' :—

Aden.	Khaulán.
The Teháma.	Sahán (including Sadah).
Sanaa.	Nejrán.
Lahej.	Nehm.
Kaukeban.	East Khaulán (several small
Beled el-Kabail (Hashid wa	principalities).
Bakil).	Beled el-Jehaf (or Mareb),
Abou Arish.	and
A district lying between	Yaffa.
Abou Arish and the	
Hejaz, inhabited by Bed-	
ouins, &c.	

" These are," says Playfair, " as nearly as they can
be classified, the great political divisions of the
country ; but numerous smaller states and tribes
exist which cannot be classed with propriety in

[1] Ibn Khaldun, Kay's translation, 1892.

any of the above districts, yet which are too insignificant to require a separate notice." [1]

The first two of these provinces, the *Teháma* and *Aden*, are described elsewhere. The third is *Sanaa*, taking its name from the city, the capital of the Yemen. On account of continued wars and struggles, its boundaries have for ever been shifting. Within the province are situated the cities of Dhamar, Yerim, Rodaa, Ibb, Jiblah, Kátaba, Taiz, and Hais.

Lahej is described more fully elsewhere, so there is little further need to make mention of it here, except to roughly indicate its limits ; for under this title are contained not only the tribe-lands of the Abdali Sultan, but also the Subaiha, Akrabi, Foudtheli, and Houshabi tribes. The country inhabited by these Arabs of the Plains may be said to extend from the Straits of Bab el-Mandeb to about eighty miles east of Aden. The country is poor, and boasts but one or two towns, but many large villages.

The next province is *Kaukeban*, which, with *Beled el-Kabail*, *Abou Arish*, and *Beni Hallel*, may be taken altogether. The latter tribe inhabit a strip of plain country along the borders of the Red Sea, while the three former include that portion of the country lying to the north-east and east of Beni Hallel, and extending as far east as a line drawn from Sanaa due north.

[1] Playfair's Yemen, p. 4.

North again of Abou Arish, and between that
country and the Hejaz, is the Asir, part of which is
mountainous and part plains—the former inhabited
by dwellers in fixed abodes, and the latter by wild
Bedouins.

North of Sanaa, and upon the road connecting
that city with Mecca, the continuation of the pilgrim-
road of Huseyn ibn Salaamah mentioned elsewhere,
is the province of *Khaulán,* east of which again is
Sahán, included in the province and former princi-
pality of Sadah.   This forms one of the richest
portions of the Yemen, being famous for fruits,
honey, and cattle.   It consists of large valleys well
watered, and at such an elevation as to render them
not only suitable for the growing of fruit-trees, but
also exceedingly healthy.   Niebuhr mentions these
tribes as hospitable but inclined to robbery, and as
speaking as pure Arabic as is anywhere in use.

The next province is still more mountainous, and,
on account of its inaccessibility, has remained almost
unconquered.   It is known as *Nejran,* and consists
of wide fertile valleys reaching nearly to the desert
of Akhaf.   Like Khaulán, it is renowned for its
cattle and fruit, the breed of horses, too, being celebrated.   They are said to be of the famous Nejed
strain.

The province of *Kahtan,* situated eleven days'
journey north of the valley of Nejran, is another
example of the difficulties of fixing any reliable

frontier to the Yemen. Evidently it is inhabited by Yemeni people, as it takes its name from the founder of that stock, Kahtan, who is said to be no other than Joktan of the Jewish Scriptures.

Eastern Khaulán lies to the north-east of the capital Sanaa. It possessed formerly a celebrated city of the Jews, which is now said to be almost entirely deserted. Although generally known by the name of Eastern Khaulán, it in reality consists of a number of small principalities.

Beled el-Jehaf may be said to form the extreme eastern division of the northern portion of the Yemen, but whether it should be considered as part of that country is open to doubt. It extends from a few days' journey east of Sanaa as far as the desert that divides Oman from Western Arabia. It is in this district that is situated the city of Mareb, otherwise known as Saba or Sheba, whence the celebrated queen visited Solomon. The natives have traditions of a Queen Balkis, whom they affirm to have been the lady in question. However, this has been proved impossible, as the dates do not correspond. It was at Saba that the celebrated dam was built, the destruction of which, about one hundred years A.D., wrought such widespread destruction. A few words about this prodigious building will be found in reference to the tanks at Aden in the chapter upon that possession.

The last of the list of provinces is *Yaffa*, which lies between the Hadramaut on the east and south, and the districts of Lahej and Sanaa on the north and west. It became independent some two centuries ago, up to that time having been under the rule of the Imams of Sanaa.[1] It is a rich fertile country, producing gums, cereals, and coffee. It possesses three towns—Yaffa, Medinet el-Asfal, and Gharrah. Living in close conjunction with the Yaffai tribe are the Oulaki, divided into the upper and lower, their capitals being respectively Nisáb inland, and Howr on the coast.[2]

These, then, are the principal provinces into which the Yemen is considered by the natives to be divided, though to define exactly their boundaries, as in the case of the frontiers of the whole country, would be an impossible task.

With regard to the geography of the Yemen but few more words are needed, in order to render clear the following pages of the narrative of the author's journey. Although an account is given elsewhere of the Turkish dominion of the Yemen, it may be as well to delineate the present frontier since the Osmanli occupation of the country, although again it is almost an arbitrary one.

To commence from the south. The division between the Arab tribes of the southern Teháma and Turkish Yemen commences some ten miles east of the Straits of Bab el-Mandeb, and so includes the promontory of Sidi Sheikh, which projects toward Perim

[1] Niebuhr, vol. ii. p. 68. [2] Playfair's Yemen, pp. 43, 44.

Island, from which it is divided by a narrow strait a
mile and a half in width. From thence the frontier
runs in a north-easterly direction, passing a little to
the east of Taiz, from which it again turns more
directly east, passing to the south of Mavia, and,
skirting the territory of the Amir of Dhala, includes
the town of Kátaba. From this spot it turns almost
due north, keeping well to the east of Yerim and
Dhamar, although these towns, as a matter of fact,
form practically the eastern boundary of the Turkish
Yemen. From Dhamar to Sanaa the frontier runs
almost due north and south, and may be said to exist
about forty to fifty miles east of a straight line drawn
between these two cities.

From Sanaa to the north the Turks claim authority
as within their limits over all the country lying to the
west of a line drawn from Sanaa to the south-eastern
corner of the province of the Hejaz, although over the
Asir and other inaccessible mountain tribes their authority is purely nominal, and has never been acknowledged to any extent.

It must not be thought that all the country lying
within the frontier thus described is securely under
Turkish rule, for there are whole tribes which do not,
nor ever have done so, acknowledge anything more
than a nominal subjection to the Sublime Porte.

That these notes upon the geography of the Yemen
will prove of but little value to *savants* the writer
knows only too well; but if his journey was unpro-

ductive of any scientific or historical discoveries, it must be borne in mind the period at which it was undertaken : that not only was a rebellion still taking place, that a month or two before had shaken the whole country to its very foundations, but also that the author was by the Turks treated as a spy, and was more than once in great personal danger from the Arabs. Under these circumstances he feels that he cannot be blamed if his journey was devoid of any great results. All that he can boast to have brought back with him is a story of travel and adventure, and numerous photographs and notes, that will tend to throw light upon the present condition of the Yemen, especially on what has been taking place in that country since the Turkish occupation of the highlands in 1872. His narrative of travel tells a story of long night marches, and of days spent in hiding; of a sojourn in a Turkish prison ; and this story, he trusts, will prove sufficient evidence that he had little or no opportunity for research. It was owing to a mere chance that his notes and photographs were saved from destruction by the Turkish authorities at Sanaa.

If these pages tend to throw some light upon this most interesting corner of Arabia, and help to show what the country and its inhabitants are like, the author will be well satisfied with the result.

CHAPTER II.

HAVING in the last chapter briefly sketched the principal geographical features of the Yemen, it remains now to make mention of its history. The same remarks as were made as to the geography are applicable here, that with the exception of certain periods which have been made the study of archæologists and orientalists, there is but very little known of the history of the Yemen, and there are long periods existing between the times of which something has been written or translated that are almost blanks. Nor is it on this account alone that the task of compiling in two chapters so many centuries of historical matter is a difficult one, for many of the times and dynasties of which there exists some trustworthy account are all but unimportant in treating of the country in general, what knowledge we possess in very many cases being simply the genealogies of local princes and rulers. However, it is only by a study of these shreds of history that we are able to gain

any facts concerning the condition of the country
during the early centuries after the introduction of
Islam, for instance ; and if they in themselves appeal
almost solely to the student of things oriental, they
yet tend to throw more light upon the inner life of
the people than it would be possible to gather elsewhere.

But the history of the Yemen is by no means confined to such a brief period as that which has passed
between the birth of Islam and to-day. There exists
a far more ancient and more wonderful history, of
which, unhappily, we know as yet but little, but
which, should it even be possible to make thorough
examination of its monuments and records, may
prove that many of the existing civilisations sprang
from the Yemen and Hadramaut, and that the ancient
Egyptians themselves, owed the foundations of their
arts and learning to the inhabitants of Southern
Arabia. Some light has been thrown lately upon
the old civilisation of Southern Arabia by the successful excavations carried on by Mr Theodore Bent in
Mashonaland, which have proved most clearly that
the Arabs of Southern Arabia were in touch with
that distant quarter of Africa, and not only in touch,
but even so firmly rooted there as to erect forts and
temples, to build and to decorate, and to work the
mines of that country.

At present scientific exploration of the Yemen and
the other divisions of Southern Arabia has been,

for many reasons, so seldom undertaken that there remains to be discovered there more than is probably to be found in any part of the world. How rich the country is in archæological remains may be judged from the quantity of inscriptions, &c., brought back by the enterprising and scholarly Austrian Dr Glaser, to whom we owe nearly all that is known of the earlier periods of Yemenite history. It was through the extensive researches of this *savant* that any conclusive data have been given not only to individual sovereigns but to whole dynasties, with the result that although far from perfect knowledge, very considerable light has been thrown upon the early days of the Yemen.

Before, however, entering into any precise account of the historical records of the Yemen, it may be as well to briefly mention a few well-founded traditions generally accepted amongst the natives and believed by themselves to be undisputable. In this they are, no doubt, mainly right in the origin ; but in attempting to trace their descent, through periods later than those of the earliest times, they have to some extent become confused. This is most apparent in the cases of the two great divisions, or nations, which inhabited the Yemen, the weaker of which, at times, finding similarity between names, claimed descent from a common ancestor with the stronger, until by force of time no clear line of division was possible in many cases.

Although there can be little doubt of a prehistoric and almost pretraditional race inhabiting Southern Arabia, the only record worthy of acceptance from native sources of their existence is their mention in the Koran. No traditions exist as to them amongst the people to-day, or even amongst those Arab historians of the middle ages who made special studies of the subject.

The inhabitants of Southern Arabia may be divided into two great stems, to which the names of Yemenite and Ishmaelite tribes have been very properly given.

The Yemenite nation are the direct descendants of Kahtan, generally identified with Joktan of the Jewish Scriptures, of the line of Shem, the son of Noah, another of whose descendants, Hazarmaveth, gave his name to what is to-day known as Hadramaut.

The second great division into which the inhabitants of the Yemen may be divided are the descendants of Adnan, who was of the family of Ishmael, son of Abraham : although unfortunately the connecting links are absent, yet in spite of this there can be no doubt as to the fact. This Adnan is said to have been the contemporary of Bukht Nasser, in other words Nebuchadnezzar ;[1] and it was the fierce wars waged by this monarch, tradition relates, that drove the Ishmaelite tribes to seek refuge amongst the Yemenite peoples. If this be the case, it is a marvel-

[1] Kay's Omarah. London, 1892.

lous fact that two nations inhabiting the same country for such an enormous period of time, and for the last twelve or thirteen hundred years united in religious ideas, are able to-day to speak with any certainty as to which branch they belong. Yet such is the case, with the exception of certain Arab tribes who claim descent from Kahtan, the mistake arising through certain similarities of names to be found amongst his descendants and those of Adnan.

Each of these two divisions of the population are again split up into sections, though in the case of the Yemenites such is not to be found until the days of Himyar, son of Abd esh-shems and great-grandson of Kahtan. It is unnecessary here to enumerate the tribes still existing which claim to have sprung from the family of Himyar, more than to mention the three principal ancestors on which their claims are based. These are respectively Himyar himself, and Malik and Arib, sons of Zayd, son of Kahtan, son of Abd esh-shems.

The family of Ishmael are likewise split up into many tribes, claiming descent from three separate members of the posterity of Abraham—namely, El-Yas, Kays Aylan, and Rabiah.

There yet remains another section which cannot be passed over without notice, as commentators differ as to from which stem they originated. These are the descendants of Kudaah. While some protest that their ancestor was Himyar, son of Abd esh-shems, others claim that they are of Ishmaelite descent, and ought to be enrolled under the heading of Arab tribes. It is more than possible that in their case an early amalgamation took place between the two stocks, and individuals adopted as their ancestor whichever of the founders of the parties it best suited their interests to put forward.

Such, then, was the origin of the two nations which to-day, still to be distinguished from one another by their traditions of ancestry, form the population of the Yemen.

Although there is no reason to doubt the genuineness of these traditions, and in fact everything points to their being authentic, the next period with which we come in contact is no longer a traditional one, but has been handed down to us in monuments and inscriptions still existing. The knowledge we have upon this period of the history of the Yemen is due to the aforementioned Dr Edouard Glaser, who has successfully translated over a thousand inscriptions, with the result of practically proving the existence of two separate great dynasties that in succession held sway over the country. In so doing, what was commonly believed to have been the fact until his discoveries were made has been disproved, and an entirely new epoch in the history of the world brought to light. I refer to the dominion of the Minæan and Sabæan kings. It is, too, from these records that there has been found to have existed, contemporarily with early Egyptian times, a remarkable state of civilisation and commerce in the Yemen, and what was wrongly believed to have been in early pre-Islamic days a country of savagery, has been proved to have contained a cultured population, skilled in art and excelling in commerce. This fact doubtless to no small degree influenced the history of the civilisation of the ancient world.

The earlier of the two great dynasties which at different epochs held sway over the Yemen, if not also over the surrounding coasts of Africa, was that of the Minæans, who are known in tradition as the Maïn. Thirty-two names of kings of this dynasty have already been discovered; and as a proof of the immense power they must have held, tablets commemorative of their wars have been found as far removed from the seat of their government as Teima, on the road from Damascus to Sinai; while an inscription from Southern Arabia renders thanks to Astarte for their escape from the ruler of Egypt and their safe return to their own city of Quarnu. This votive tablet was erected by the governors of Tsar and Ashur, which again speaks for the immense tract of country owing allegiance to the Minæan king; for of these places one has been identified as being situated near where the Suez Canal now passes. This extension of frontier was doubtless owing to the great importance of the trade-routes from East to West, the possession of which in later times brought the otherwise unimportant Jewish kingdom so much to the fore. But more important, perhaps, than the discovery that these peoples were living in a state of considerable civilisation, and carrying on most profitable commerce, is the fact of their knowledge of writing; for many of the recently discovered inscriptions in the Yemen date from a period contemporary with Egyptian hieroglyphics and Chaldæan cuneiform, and earlier than any known inscription in the Phœnician characters.

Following upon the Minæan dynasty, of which, as before stated, thirty - two kings are known by name, is that of the Sabæans : yet the nature of the inscriptions shows that a very considerable period of time must have elapsed between the two ; for whereas, in the earlier specimens of writing, full grammatical forms are found, the latter is not nearly so complete. Yet the Sabæan dynasty can be traced back with certainty to the time of Solomon, one thousand years B.C., and there is every reason to believe that they had been in power at that time for a very considerable period. How very remote, then, must be the antiquity of the preceding dynasty, which we know to have been separated from the latter by a sufficient lapse of years to have allowed of radical changes in the formation and grammar of their written language ! Besides which, although comparatively few inscriptions have been discovered of this period, we have a list of no less than thirty-two

Minæan sovereigns. Professor Sayce, in an able article upon this subject, states that he believes that it is quite possible that inscriptions may be discovered which will prove Southern Arabia to have been in a state of civilisation in the days of Sargon I., or even of Menes, who is supposed to have lived some five thousand years B.C. : nay more, he expresses his opinion, which many traditions tend to prove, that all civilisation may have sprung from the Yemen and its adjacent provinces.[1]

Apart from the great interest attending this alone, another point must at once attract our attention— namely, the existence of an alphabet earlier than that of the oldest discovered Phœnician inscriptions. Until these researches into the writings of the Yemen, it was believed that the Phœnician formation of letters was an abridgment of the hieroglyphics of Egypt; but there seems now to be reason to suppose that this still more ancient writing of Southern Arabia may prove to be not only the source from which the Phœnicians derived their alphabet, but also the origin of those of all modern nations, including Greece and Rome. What may be said almost to prove this theory, says Professor Sayce, is the fact that while the Phœnician letters, described by name as animals and things, have but little resemblance to the object from which the name is taken, this still older form of

[1] Professor Sayce's "Ancient Arabia" and "Results of Oriental Archæology," in the Contemporary Review.

Semitic writing bears a decided resemblance to the objects described in the names of the Phœnician letters.

Probable as all this is, it must remain for the time at least only a theory, until further discoveries are forthcoming ; but apart from all suppositious matters, it may safely be stated that, be the Aryan origin what it may, it is to Southern Arabia that we must look for the home of the Semitic peoples. Referring back to the earlier paragraphs of this chapter, in which mention is made of the two great divisions of the inhabitants of the Yemen, it will be seen that the tradition existed in the time of Mahammed, and is mentioned in the Koran, of an older population, whom it may be inferred were the original Semitic stock,— for it must be remembered that the present geographical position of the Semitic races is almost entirely owing to the spread of Islam, and it is to Arabia, and Arabia alone, that we must look for their origin,—at a time preceding the first Minæan kings, and probably at a period when the stone age was passing into that of metal, and fishers and hunters were becoming traders and agriculturists.[1] But of all the incidents of the ancient history of the Yemen, there is one that will especially appeal to all. I refer to the visit of the Queen of Sheba to Solomon about the year one thousand B.C. Sheba has always been identified with Saba, the capital of the Sabæan empire, a city lying

[1] Human Origins. S. Laing, 1892. P. 94.

some seven days' journey to the north-east of Sanaa, the present capital of Turkish Yemen. The story is too well known to need any comment here; it need only be noticed that the point it is written from is that of a Jewish historian, who would naturally tend to magnify the glories of Solomon and the admiration of the queen at his wonderful city, palace, and temple. Yet, as a matter of fact, it is not at all improbable that Saba possessed buildings as fine as any of those of Solomon; and certainly, whereas no ruins remain of the latter, the great dam, built some seventeen hundred years B.C. at Saba, still stands, though of course in ruins, to tell the tale of the vast building powers of the Sabæan architects. Nor do we in the gorgeous description of Solomon's works find reference to anything that could possibly have compared in size and structure with this extraordinary *barrage*, of which it is sufficient to say that it measured three hundred cubits thick, one hundred and twenty feet high, and two *miles* in length.[1] The presents which the Queen of Sheba brought to Solomon tend as much as anything to prove that she was a native of Southern Arabia, for her offerings will be found either to be produce of that country, or such articles as could, owing to the enormous commerce of Saba, find an outlet in that direction from farther south and east.

Although the already discovered inscriptions point to Saba having been the capital of a great and civil-

[1] These measurements were made by Mons. D'Arnaud in 1843.

ised empire eight hundred years B.C., the existence of the great dam, which may be attributed to Lokman, who lived 1750 years B.C., and the visit of the Queen of Sheba to Solomon, speak of greater antiquity.

The religion of the Sabæans is too large a question to attempt here, more especially as there are evidences that during the long periods of the Minæan and Sabæan dynasties it underwent many changes, merging from a primitive idolatry into worship of the planets and stars, and even, in cases, to the recognition of a supreme deity. They believed in the immortality of the soul, a future state of reward or punishment, and many also in transmigration. The gradual change of doctrine appreciable in the religion, besides being due to the natural outcome of increased civilisation and culture, was no doubt largely influenced by the astronomers and astrologers of Chaldæa. Doubtless, too, there existed in their religious traditions a sort of hero-worship, for we read in various authorities of certain names as being those of deities and of men. Thus we find the city of Saba was called after a god of that name, while again the founder is mentioned as being Saba the son of Abd esh-shems, the father of the so-called Himyaric dynasty.

Any attempt, with the space at disposal here, to draw conclusions from the traditions existing as to the earliest inhabitants of the Yemen, is out of the question; and rather than do so, it will better suit

ANCIENT TANK AT MENURA, NEAR DHAMAR.

our purpose to keep to what have been proved to be facts—the existence of the Minæan and later the Sabæan dynasties; the high state of culture and commerce in Southern Arabia at a very remote period; and the existence of a written language that was possibly, if not probably, the origin of Phœnician, and so of all European forms of writing; and the still greater idea that Southern Arabia may be proved to be the land of " Punt," and the birthplace of the Egyptian race, and their arts and culture.

Shortly before the commencement of the Christian era Egypt became a Roman province, and a few years later an expedition under Ællius Gallus was sent to explore Arabia and Ethiopia. How difficult would be the task was evidently realised, for when the expedition started from Cleopatris, near the modern Suez, it consisted of no less than eighty vessels of war and a hundred and thirty transports, with ten thousand Roman troops and fifteen thousand mercenaries.[1] But the expedition was destined to disaster, for although it penetrated as far as Southern Arabia —probably Nejran—the troops were decimated by famine and disease, and only a small handful ever returned.

In looking through these early pages of the history of the Yemen, one cannot but be struck with the important part that women played in politics; and even after the introduction of Islam, and the women

[1] Vincent's Periplus, vol. i. p. 53.

had been assigned a lower position, the old custom crops up again and again, and we find women seizing the reins of government.

The first example that we find of the power exercised by women is without doubt the Queen of Sheba; while a second example follows within a few years after the failure of the expedition of Ællius Gallus, in the person of Queen Balkis, whose real name was Belkama or Yalkama, and who was sufficiently strong-minded to amalgamate two kingdoms by marrying her rival, whom she immediately removed by poison.

About A.D. 120 the great dam of Saba or Mareb burst, spreading wholesale destruction throughout the wide fertile valley below it. About this period, too, an expedition was carried by the then King Tubba el-Akran as far as Samarcand, and thence into China; and in A.D. 206, Abou Kariba, one of the most illustrious of all the Himyaric kings, invaded Chaldæa and defeated the Tartars of Adirbijan. He started on a second expedition to conquer Syria, but returned after taking the Hejaz to the Yemen, where he is said to have renounced idolatry and embraced Judaism.

A legend, quoted by Sir Lambert Playfair in his ' History of the Yemen,' tells of the introduction of the Jewish faith into the Yemen during the reign of this Sultan. It savours of the priests of Baal; for, wishing to put to the test the merits of Judaism and idolatry, the priests of either creed proceeded to a certain spot whence fire emerged from the ground. Pushed on by the crowd, the test was tried, and while the Jewish priests passed through the flame unscathed, the idolaters perished. But the feeling between the two was by no means destined from this fact to become a cordial one, and constant fights occurred between the two parties. Although Christianity seems to have appeared in the Yemen previous to the year 297 A.D., it was not until that date that it became a religion of importance in the country. It was during the reign of the king Tubba ibn Hassan, who held the throne at this period, that Christianity was introduced into Abyssinia; and about the middle half of the fourth century the Emperor Constantius sent a certain bishop, Theophilus Indus, to convert the Yemenis, of whom the king was so far tolerant, even if he did not himself embrace Christianity, to allow the building of churches. One was erected at Zafar, near Yerim; another at Aden; and a third at a port in the Arabian Sea, supposed generally to be Hormuzd.

So king succeeded king with the usual rapidity of oriental countries, until in 478 A.D. a certain Lakhnia (or Lakhtiaa) Tanú usurped the throne, whose cruelties to the surviving members of the royal family are recorded by more than one historian. However, it remained for one of these, a youth by name Asaad abou Karib, or Dhu Nowas, to revenge his relations by stabbing the usurper with a dagger, he himself being unanimously elected to the throne.

He embraced Judaism, and adopted the name of
Yusef (Joseph). However, like many converts, he
became a fanatic, and his cruelties toward the
Christians are perhaps unparalleled in history. Dhu
Nowas attacked them in Nejran, and having foully
broken his promise that no harm should befall them,
gave them the choice between death or Judaism.
Twenty thousand, it is said, were burned alive in
huge pits filled with blazing wood. The Koran com-
mends these people who died for their religion, and
calls a curse upon their persecutor.[1]

But the cruelty of Dhu Nowas was to reap its
reward. A few Christians who escaped fled to the
Court of the Christian emperor of the East, who
presented them with letters to the Christian king of
Abyssinia, requesting him to punish the perpetrator
of these cruel outrages.

In A.D. 525, accordingly, the Abyssinians invaded
the Yemen, and Dhu Nowas was defeated, being
drowned, purposely, it is said, after the first battle.
From that moment the Abyssinian general Aryat met
with but futile resistance, and pushed into the heart
of the country, destroying and razing the cities as he
went along.

Thus was overthrown, never to rise again, the
Himyaric dynasty, which had held the throne of the
Yemen for over two thousand years. Many of the
kings had been celebrated both for war and culture,

---

[1] Koran, chap. lxxxv.

but their ancestors were now, on account of their fanatical persecution of the Christians, in return to suffer from cruelties and oppression as severe as any they themselves had ever practised.

It is but one of the many examples of the terrible bloodshed consequent upon diversity of opinion on religious subjects,—for with bloodshed did Christianity force itself into the Yemen, and with bloodshed was it destined a few years later to disappear. Aryat, having conquered the Yemen, was appointed Viceroy of the King of Abyssinia in that country, and reigned until nearly the middle half of the sixth century, being succeeded by Abrahá, in fighting with whom Aryat was slain.

Meanwhile, by every means of cruelty and oppression Christianity had been pushed forward; but at length a bishop was appointed at Zafar, whose name is to-day included in the calendar of saints as St Gregentius, who persuaded Abrahá to adopt more lenient measures than those of his predecessor; and even the Arab authors acknowledge him to have been a just and compassionate prince. That he was, however, a fanatic is certain; for the church at Sanaa having been defiled by an Arab from Mecca, where for centuries the Kaabah had been a place of pilgrimage, he vowed to destroy that place, and at the head of a great army marched into the Hejaz. Approaching Mecca, the inhabitants fled; but Abrahá, mounted upon his famous white elephant Mahmoud, failed,—for it is said not only did the huge pachyderm refuse to turn toward the city, but that a miraculous flight of birds dropped pebbles upon the heads of the invading army, killing both men and elephants. This miracle is generally explained as an epidemic of smallpox : however, be it what it may, it ended in the total rout and flight of the Abyssinian troops, who in a miserable plight resought the Yemen, where shortly afterwards Abrahá died.

This "battle of the elephant," as the Arab historians called it, is doubly famous, as it happened in the year of the birth of Mahammed.

But the Abyssinian rule was soon to end. Acts of tyranny and cruelty hurried on its termination, and Jaskum, the last sovereign, died in 575 A.D., when the ancestors of the Himyaric dynasty, certain of being unable to regain the throne for themselves, and having failed to persuade the Romans to take up their cause, implored the aid of the Persian monarch Kesra, who after many delays fitted out an expedition, formed for the most part of convicts from the prisons, which reached Aden, under the personal conduct of a descendant of Himyar, Maadi Karib, and a Persian general of the name of Wahraz. A battle ensued with the Abyssinians, in which their monarch—for the Viceroys had by this time taken imperial rights—was killed. Sanaa was reached, and the gates broken down to allow the Persian conqueror to enter with uplifted banners, and Maadi

Karib was proclaimed viceroy, paying tribute and owning allegiance to the Persian sovereign.

The event of the return of a descendant of Himyar to power is celebrated by many an Arab historian and poet.

Amongst many other ambassadors and men of repute who flocked to the court at Sanaa, after the overthrow of Christianity, was the grandfather of Mahammed, Abd el-Mutalib, who was received with special honours, as belonging to the powerful tribe of the Koreish, lords of Mecca. But Maadi Karib was destined to fall a victim to Abyssinian treachery, being murdered by his body-guard, which consisted of javelin-throwers of Habesh. A state of anarchy ensued, in which the natives struggled with the Abyssinians for the supreme power; and finally the Persian monarch Kesra Paruiz was forced to send an expedition, which proved entirely successful. But bloodshed was the result, and the Abyssinians were put to the sword with great cruelty, even the half-breed children being slaughtered.

Great as was the number of the slain, both the Abyssinian and Persian occupation has left its mark in the Yemen, and a particular and despised race exists there to-day known as the Akhdam.[1] Authorities differ as to whether they are the descendants of the Abyssinians or Persians; but so closely did

[1] Akhdam, plural of Khedim, a word usually employed for a slave to-day.

one occupation follow upon the other that it may be reasonably supposed that, owing to the youth of the children at the time, and the rapidity with which both nationalities died out of the country, but little distinction would exist, in spite of diversity of colour, between the two.

Meanwhile the Persian rule was for a time fairly established, though many tribes were almost entirely governed by their own local chiefs. All religions were tolerated, and Christianity maintained its ground, principally in Nejran, and we find mention amongst early authorities of a Christian bishop of that province, Kos by name. It was probably in his time that a Christian Church was erected in Nejran.

At this period a great change was to take place in the religion and government of Arabia, for there had arisen at Mecca a prophet, Mahammed by name, of the tribe of the Koreish, who was destined to influence not only all Arabia but the whole history of the world.

CHAPTER III.

THE YEMEN SINCE THE HEJIRA.

MAHAMMED was destined to overthrow the whole social and religious status of Arabia. But the Yemen was by no means anxious at the first to accept the new doctrine, and for a time remained steadfast to the Persian cause and religion, under the viceroyalty of Budhan, who, though eventually he accepted the faith of Islam, hesitated until pressure was brought to bear upon him, and until he had obtained, to him, satisfactory evidence of the Prophet's miracles.

The dissensions at this period existing amongst the Christians of the Yemen added not a little to the success of the spread of the new religion. Yet in these first days of conversion every leniency was shown to the Christians, and a treaty was made between the princes of Nejran, which, it may be remembered, was the stronghold of Christianity in the Yemen, and Mahammed himself, very advantageous to the former, one of the clauses stipulating that

JTY-E

tolerance was to be allowed, and no Christians forcibly converted to Islam.

But the Prophet had fixed his heart on the conversion of Arabia Felix, and for this purpose, in the
tenth year of the Hejira, Ali ibn Abou Taleb, his
son - in - law and nephew, was despatched thither.
Failing by moderate means to bring over the people,
the sword was resorted to ; but in spite of this fact,
authorities state that Islam was grafted in the country
with the loss of only some twenty lives.

But its course was to be by no means a smooth
one, for amongst several other pretenders two arose
at the same period, 632 A.D., who laid claim to the
prophetic office. Both had been converts to Islam,
and one at least had actually seen Mahammed, and
it was no doubt the report of his enormous success
that stirred these men to rival his claims.

The first, Mosailma by name, was a chief of the
tribe of Hanífa. Being of a diplomatic turn of mind,
he thought to make an alliance with Mahammed, and
a correspondence took place between the two, worthy
of repetition here. The letters ran as follows :—

" From Mosailma, the Prophet of God, to Mahammed, the Prophet of God ! Let the earth be half
mine and half thine."

Mahammed's answer was short but to the point :—

" From Mahammed, the Prophet of God, to Mosailma, the Liar. The earth belongs to God. He
giveth it as an inheritance to such of his servants as

pleaseth him, and the happy issue shall attend such as fear him."

But Mosailma was not to be discouraged by this reply, and continued his career until, shortly after the death of Mahammed, his successor the Caliph Abou Bekr sent an expedition under a certain general Khalid to attack him. In a battle near Akriba Mosailma was slain, and his followers disbanded; who, seeing their leader die, once more reverted to Islam.

The second impostor was El-Aswad, chief of the tribe of Anis. He had previously been an idolater, but had become a convert to the Mahammedan faith. Meeting at first with every success, he installed himself at Sanaa, and nearly the whole of the Yemen acknowledged his authority. But at the instigation of Mahammed, who was at this time still alive, he was treacherously slain by his wife and accomplices.

These two impostors, although their career did not to any extent permanently affect the history of the Yemen, are celebrated throughout Arab traditions, in which they are known as "The Liars."

But the troubles in the Yemen were by no means at an end. Every preceding dynasty had left dissension and rival blood in the country, and for a long period, during the reign of the early Caliphs, the country was constantly disturbed with war and bloodshed. Pretender to the throne followed pretender, and it was not for a period of some years that any tranquillity was restored to the Yemen.

In A.D. 655 Ali succeeded to the Caliphate on the death of Othman, and having to quell many disturbances and dissensions at home, he did not for some time turn his attention to the Yemen, where, after a lapse in the war between Muavia, governor of Syria, and the Caliph, a large band of the troops of the former, under the leadership of Bashir ibn Ardeb, carried out the most horrible atrocities on the partisans of the cause of Ali. But revenge was near, and a short time later—39 A.H.—troops to the number of four thousand were despatched by Ali from Kufa, who equalled perhaps the cruelties of Muavia's adherents; but they succeeded in stamping out the cause of Othman, the lately assassinated Caliph, and Ali's son was proclaimed governor of the Yemen. Islam had by this period made such a firm footing in the country, that, in spite of the dissensions between Christians, idolaters, and Jews, we find the troubles confined almost entirely to the many sects of Islam itself. Some of the most important of these will be found mentioned elsewhere, so that no reference is necessary to them here, except as showing how firm a hold the acceptance of the new religion had gained amongst the inhabitants of the Yemen.

The country after the death of Ali became subject to the Omeyyad dynasty of Caliphs, until in A.D. 749 the Abbasides exterminated them, with unparalleled bloodshed and cruelty, the conquest of the Yemen being carried out by Mahammed Abousi Mahammed. The typical cruelty of this man is well exemplified by a paragraph in Sir R. L. Playfair's 'History of the Yemen.' Finding the inhabitants suffering from what is now known as "Yemen boils," an exceedingly common complaint in that country, he ordered all those who showed any signs of the sickness to be buried alive as unclean. Happily his own death prevented this cruel order from being carried out. Sharing the ups and downs of the Abbaside dynasty, to whom the Yemen acknowledged a varying system of vassalage, in 811 A.D. the inhabitants declared for El-Mamun, son of Harun el-Rashid, the great Caliph of the East, who was sharing with his brother Amin the government. Under this Caliph the governor of the Yemen was Mahammed, son of Ziad. He conquered the Tehámâ, or western plains, and became sovereign of the whole country.

There remained at this period a tribe of the name of Beni Yafur, descendants of the old Himyaric kings, who lived at Sanaa. Acknowledging the Abbaside Caliphs, they were by force obliged to fall under the jurisdiction of Ibn Ziad; but Asaad ibn Yafur, the last of the family, took advantage of the Karmathian rising throughout the Yemen to usurp the power, which he held until his death. He was the last prince of the Himyaric people; and although his family held the throne for a few years they never

arrived at any great power, their position being
materially weakened by insurrections and family
strifes.

Ibn Ziad having died, and been succeeded by
several members of his family, Abou'l-Jaysh his
grandson came to the throne. On the death of the
Caliph El-Mutawakil and the abdication of El-
Mustain, he disclaimed all allegiance to the Caliphate, and took to himself regal honours, though
there seems to be some apparent discord as to dates,
for the assassination and abdication of the Caliphs
occurred before Abou'l-Jaysh came to the throne.
Probably he was the first to assume regal power,
although his immediate predecessors had ceased paying tribute to the Caliphs.[1]

Apparently Abou'l-Jaysh was a man of great power,
and by the time of his death he was master of the
whole of the Yemen, while his revenues reached an
enormous sum. It was during his reign that the
Zaidite dynasty sprang up. The foundation of
what afterwards was the principal line of the Imams,
or Sultans of the Yemen, is not without interest.
Although to-day ousted from power by the Turks,
the leader of the late rebellion was no less a personage than a descendant of the great family who in
A.H. 288 (A.D. 901) founded at Sadah the Zaidite
dynasty. As of the direct family of the prophet
Mahammed, it may be interesting to trace the line

[1] Ibn Khaldun, Kay's translation, 1892.

from the founder of Islam to Yahya, who returned
to the Yemen from India in 288 A.H. to announce
the supremacy of the Zaidis. This is best done by
a short genealogical tree.

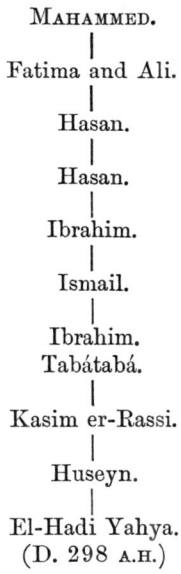

MAHAMMED.
|
Fatima and Ali.
|
Hasan.
|
Hasan.
|
Ibrahim.
|
Ismail.
|
Ibrahim.
Tabátabá.
|
Kasim er-Rassi.
|
Huseyn.
|
El-Hadi Yahya.
(D. 298 A.H.)

Although Yahya succeeded in wresting Sanaa from
Asaad ibn Yafur, he was unable to hold it, and eventually returned to Sadah, where descendants of his family
are to-day living.

From this period we find a constant rise and fall
of dynasties. While Imams alternately held and
lost authority, there were springing up, generally
to disappear, princes in many parts of the country,
so that at times the Yemen was divided into a

number of principalities. Celebrated amongst these
were the Sulayhites and the Zurayites, of whom the
latter for centuries held possession of the southern
province of Aden. But, meanwhile, in the north the
Imams were succeeding one another with the usual
rapidity of oriental sovereigns, and with very varied
authority. In the fifth century A.H. we find the
Abyssinian line again in possession of Zebeed, at
this time the principal city of the Teháma.

Meanwhile the Zaidi family of Rassites continued
to govern at Sadah without serious interruption.

In 1173 A.D. the then reigning Sultan of Sanaa
surrendered his power to Turan Shah, brother of
Salah ed-din (Saladdin), the Ayyubite Caliph of
Egypt; and Ali, son of the Sultan El-Mansur Hatim,
was nominated governor of that city.

It would be out of place here to trace the long
lines of governors and rulers who dominated the
Yemen during the next two centuries. A few
names, however, are remembered to-day, and mentioned by authorities as being men of great power
or culture. The first is El-Muzaffer, who united
for the time at least all the Yemen under his
sway, and who died at the end of the thirteenth
century; and again, Abdul-Wahab, who reigned
early in the sixteenth century, and founded many
colleges at Sanaa, Taiz, and Zebeed, and built a
number of cisterns and aqueducts at places where
water was scarce.

During the next period of the history of the Yemen, we come in contact for the first time with European traders and the Turks, who were destined in no small degree to influence the future of the country.

About the year 1445 A.D. the Christian king of Abyssinia sent a mission to Florence, and a famous missive to the priests of Jerusalem. This king is well known to history from these two acts alone, and to-day is celebrated as Prester John. Whether his embassy stirred the religious zeal or the cupidity of Europe it is difficult to say, but it resulted, whatever its cause may have been, in a Portuguese expedition to the far East, which eventually ended in the leader, De Covilham, marrying and settling in Shoa.

I think there is but little need here to repeat the adventures of many European expeditions that were sent at various periods to visit this portion of the globe. Such as refer more immediately to Aden will be found mentioned in the chapter on that possession, while I have elsewhere referred to the "factories" at Mokha.

Early in the sixteenth century the Mamlook power in Egypt was overthrown by the Sultan Selim I., upon which event the larger portion of the Arabian states went over to the new cause. This Selim was desirous of himself leading an expedition for the conquest of Arabia, but was obliged to abandon the idea on account of ill health; nor did he ever recover sufficiently to carry out his purpose. His son, Suleiman the Magnificent, was equally intent upon the conquest of India, and for this purpose fitted out a fleet in A.D. 1520. On the 27th June 1538 the fleet left Suez, and Aden was reached a few months later, and the town was taken. Proceeding to India, Suleiman Pasha was forced to retire on being attacked by the Viceroy of Goa, and returned to Aden, where he left sufficient troops to garrison the town, and proceeded to Mokha, whence messengers were sent to Zebeed with the demand that the governor of that city should at once proceed to the coast. The Arab's refusal to comply with this order cost him his life, for a few months later Zebeed was taken, and a number of its inhabitants put to the sword. This completed the conquests of Suleiman the Magnificent, and all the coast of Arabia acknowledged the Turkish rule, Sanaa itself becoming the seat of the Pasha of the Yemen. But although firmly rooted in the country, the Turkish forces were unable to extract tribute from the numerous tribes, many of which remained practically independent. A revolt occurred at Aden in 1551, which was, however, put down by Peri Pasha, who wrested the town from the Portuguese, to whom it had been handed over by its Arab inhabitants.

Eight years later a still greater rebellion broke out throughout the whole of the Yemen. However, the Turks, under Hasan Pasha, were able to quell it, and continue their rule in the country.

At the beginning of the seventeenth century the English appear for the first time in this part of the world, the first ship to trade in the Red Sea being the East India Company's vessel Ascension, Captain Sharpey, who, however, failed in his desire to establish commercial relations between the two countries. This voyage was followed by several others, but of these mention will be found in the chapter relating to Aden.

In 1630 the Turks withdrew from the Yemen, and the government fell into the hands of a descendant of Ali ibn Abou Taleb, who married Fatima, the daughter of the Prophet Mahammed. This man was by name Kasim, whose full titles were Mansur el-Kasim el-Kebir. His ancestor, El-Hadi Yahia, had founded the Rassite dynasty in 284 A.H. The family of Kasim, which now commenced to hold the government of the Yemen, continued until the conquest of Sanaa by the Turks in 1872 to fill the posts of Imams.[1] A few words are necessary in explanation of this title, by which the rulers of the Yemen have been so long known. The word Imam literally means the leader of prayer in the mosque. Thus it will be seen that the office was not merely a temporal one, but was also imbued with religious rights, enjoyed on account of their descent

---

[1] A list of the Imams of Sanaa will be found at the end of the book.

from the Prophet. Not daring to assume the title
of "Caliph," they preferred the minor one " Imam,"
though practically by carrying out the old-established
customs, such as changing their names on succeeding
to power, they took upon themselves the position
enjoyed by the direct successors of Mahammed himself. The office was a hereditary one, and generally
succeeded to by primogeniture, provided the eldest
son was of an age and character suitable to his
being able to carry out the necessary duties.

Niebuhr gives an interesting account of the principal officers in the service of the Imams, a portion
of which may be mentioned here.[1] The various
provinces were, he says, under the governorship of
a " Dowla," or military governor, who was responsible
for his district, collected the taxes, commanded the
troops, and regulated all local affairs. It was custom-
ary for a man only to hold the office for a few years,
in order to prevent his acquiring great wealth
or influence. Their position was always an uncertain one, as they necessarily made many enemies,
who were ready to do them some ill turn at headquarters. The Bas-Katéb was secretary, appointed
by the Imam, under each, whose principal work
was to spy upon and report to their lord and
ruler the actions of the " Dowla." As ordained by
the tenets of Islam, all cases relating to laws laid
down in the Koran were tried by the Cadi, or

[1] Niebuhr's Travels, vol. ii. p. 85.

chief judge. The ports were under the rule of three officers,—an Amir el-Bahr, or captain of the port; an Amir es-Sôk, whose duty lay in regulating the markets ; and a Sheikh el-Beled, who collected the taxes. El - Kasim was succeeded by his son El-Muayyad Mahammed, who in turn was succeeded by his brother Ismail, who lived a life of supreme simplicity, and died after a long reign, mourned by the whole country.

So Imam succeeded Imam with all the changing fortunes of oriental rulers, and without apparently performing any deeds which redound to their own praise or raised the splendour of their country. In all probability their lives were simply spent in Eastern uxoriousness, and in keeping in order the turbulent tribes by which they were surrounded.

In 1709 the French appeared for the first time in the Red Sea, and carried out a treaty with the governor of Mokha, on behalf of the then Imam El-Mehdi. The principal clauses referred to religious toleration, the duties on merchandise, and that re-dress should be given for any insults offered to French subjects.[1] In spite of this treaty in 1738 Mokha was bombarded by the French, on account of debts owing to the traders by the governor of that city. The town was taken, but handed back to the Imam on the payment of the debt. This ended in the drawing up of a second treaty, some-

[1] Playfair's Yemen, pp. 113, 114.

what reducing the duty chargeable on the imports and exports.

For the next twenty years affairs in the Yemen remained in a state of tolerable peace. From time to time tribes raised the standard of independence; but there seems to have been no organised attack upon the Imams, although the family was continually engaged in intrigue as to the succession. However, in 1758 a serious rebellion broke out, under a certain Abd er-Rabi ibn Ahmed, who had been governor of a small province in the service of the Imam. Abd er-Rabi had made enemies in the household of the Imam, and at their instigation was recalled. He refused, however, to obey, whereupon the Imam sent a force of some three thousand men to bring him. Nevertheless, he was able to hold out within the walls of Kátaba for no less a period than nearly a year, and eventually made his escape by night to his followers in the tribe of Hajeriya. Finding it impossible to capture Abd er-Rabi, the Imam made overtures to the Sultan of Aden to assist him. Abd er-Rabi hearing of this, entered Lahej and blockaded Aden. He was destined, however, to fall a victim to an act of treachery. The Imam was at this period attacking the city of Taiz, which he was unable to capture, and, hoping to kill two birds with one stone, invited Abd er-Rabi to join him. This the latter did, and the city was taken. The Imam, delighted with his success, under the most solemn protestations of friendship invited him to

HOWTA, THE CAPITAL OF LAHEJ.

Sanaa, where on his arrival he was, after every ignominy had been showered upon him, decapitated.[1]

In 1762 King Frederick V. of Denmark organised
an expedition for the exploration of Arabia under the
leadership of Karsten Niebuhr. With him were asso-
ciated three other Danes, who all died either during
the expedition or immediately upon its termination.
In spite of the fact that more than a century has
elapsed since this expedition took place, we have
never since been given a clearer or more interesting
and valuable account of the Yemen. The social
state of the country is particularly well described,
and no one can overestimate the value of Niebuhr's
work. He twice interviewed the Imam during his
stay at Sanaa, and the second time greatly interested
his royal host by exhibiting and explaining his scientific instruments. Niebuhr's account of the Imam
and his surroundings is most interesting, but unfortunately space does not allow of my giving any
extracts here.

In 1770 an attack was made upon the British factory at Mokha. However, two British men-of-war
were sent to the spot, and an indemnity was paid,
which it was found out eventually had been extracted
from Indian merchants, who were, of course, British
subjects ! The Yemen at this time had attracted a few
European adventurers, who had become Moslems and
entered the service of the Imam. Amongst these was

[1] Playfair's Yemen, pp. 118, 119.

a certain Scotchman of the name of Campbell, who was commanding the artillery of El-Mehdi Abbas, the then Imam. A rebellion had burst out in the country, and the rebels had seized upon a stronghold in the vicinity of Sanaa, in which was water, and where they had collected a quantity of provisions. Such, however, was the fear of the natives for the ingenuity of these European renegades, that they surrendered on hearing that Campbell and his companions were engaged upon the manufacture of shells—a task they had neither the means nor the knowledge of carrying to a successful end. The episode is merely interesting as showing the acknowledgment of the Arabs of the superiority of the European over themselves in such things—an allowance readily made to-day by nearly all classes of the Arab world.

In 1799 a British force was sent to cruise in the Red Sea, on account of the French having taken possession of Egypt; and Perim, an island situated in the straits of Bab el-Mandeb, was occupied, though, on account of the scarcity of water, it was only held for a period of four months.

The trade of the Red Sea with India had up to this period been a very considerable one, but owing to the misgovernment of the Imams, and their inability to offer security to traders, it had greatly diminished in the last few years. On this account Sir Home Popham was sent on a special mission to the Yemen in 1801, and was nominated Ambassador to the Southern

Arabian states. He arrived at Mokha on his return from Calcutta in 1802, and set out for Sanaa. However, he reached only as far as Taiz, and there, as had been the case along the entire route, he was treated with every ignominy. The Imam protested that the treatment of the Ambassador had been carried on without his knowledge and contrary to his orders, and he promised to punish the offenders. In all probability Ali Mansur, who then held the throne at Sanaa, was entirely unable to cope with the turbulent tribes, and it is known for certain that from his extravagances he was always in arrears with the subsidised chiefs of the neighbouring districts.

I have briefly mentioned elsewhere the Wahabi sect, which, under the leadership of Abd el-Wahab en-Nejdi, sprang up in the eighteenth century. It had not, however, seriously made itself felt in the Yemen until this period, its progress being no doubt largely influenced by the Wahabi conquest of Mecca and Medina. During the years 1804 and 1805 the Yemen suffered from continual raids of the Wahabi leaders, for the most part chiefs of the Beni Asir, the tribes lying between the Hejaz and the Yemen proper. But treachery was on foot, and certain Shereefs nominally owing allegiance to the Wahabi doctrine were really working in the interests of the Imam of Sanaa, and in this manner the marauders were held more or less in check. Meanwhile the Imam Ali Mansur had been deposed by his son Ahmed, who

had seized the reins of government. But the city of
Mokha refused to acknowledge Ahmed while the old
Imam was still alive, and on that account Ahmed
put an expedition into the field against the Dowla
of that town. Happily for the country Ali Mansur
died, and the people of Mokha were then able to acknowledge his son as Imam, and so a disastrous war
was staved off.

So great had become the power of the Wahabis that
in 1813 Mahammed Ali Pasha invaded the Hejaz in
the name of Turkey, and restored Mecca and Medina
to the Osmanli Sultan. Thence an envoy was sent to
the Imam at Sanaa, requesting his co-operation in
the stamping out of the Wahabis. This was readily
granted, for the Imam evidently saw that Mahammed
Ali's eyes were turned in the direction of the Yemen ;
and although he protested that he himself was devoid
of means to carry on warfare, he gave the envoy
letters to the Dowla of Mokha to supply him with
vessels and material, knowing full well that he
possessed neither.[1]

In 1814 Mahammed Ali's troops took the town of
Konfoda, north of Lohaya ; but the Asir tribes surprised it a few months later, drove the Turks out, and
seized an enormous quantity of booty and supplies.
So worn out were the Turkish troops with their long
campaign that Mahammed Ali was obliged to abandon
his scheme for the taking of the Yemen, and retired to

[1] Playfair's Yemen, p. 131.

Cairo, leaving Ibrahim Pasha to continue the campaign, which ended in the downfall of the Wahabis. The viceroyalty of Ibrahim was marked with every kind of cruelty and despicable corruption, and his departure from Jeddah in 1819 was the signal for great rejoicings. Mahammed Ali then carried out a treaty with the Imam, who, on the condition of paying one hundred thousand dollars a-year, was to be restored several provinces which he had lately lost, including Konfoda and Lohaya, which the Turks themselves had taken.

On account of a brutal attack that was made upon Lieutenant Dommicetti, at the time confined to his bed with fever, and upon the employees of the British factory, a force was sent to that place in 1819 to demand reparation, and a treaty from the Imam, in which certain privileges were granted to British subjects. Difficulties arose, and in December 1820 Mokha was bombarded by Captain Bruce, and full reparation made by the governor.

The Porte meanwhile had become uneasy at the great success attending the campaigns of Mahammed Ali Pasha; and on a Mamlook, Mahammed Agha, generally known as Turkchee Bilmas, rebelling against Mahammed Ali, the Sultan of Turkey, hoping to profit through his agency, installed him governor of the Hejaz. Marching south, Turkchee Bilmas took Hodaidah in 1832. Zebeed was the next city to fall, whence he marched upon Mokha, which also surrendered; but the tide changed, and

a year later Mokha alone remained in Turkchee
Bilmas' hands, where he was attacked by a large
force by sea, under Ahmed Pasha, and by some
20,000 of the Asir tribes by land. In the attack
upon the city Turkchee Bilmas escaped to the East
India Company's vessel Tigris, and was conveyed
in her to Bombay.

In 1837 the Imam's uncle, Seyed Kasim, treacherously sold Taiz to the Egyptians; but their power
there was of short duration, for in 1840 the
Egyptians evacuated the Yemen, which thereupon
became distracted with strife. Although Ibrahim
Pasha had previously agreed to hand over the
Tehâma to Mahammed ibn Oun, Shereef of Mecca,
he was not successful, for a Shereef of the Abou
Arish disputed its possession. The Shereef of Mecca
therefore despatched troops to the coast, who occupied Hodaidah the very day the Pasha left it, but
only to hold it for a very short time, for a month
later the Asir tribe entered the town. Shereef
Huseyn, brother of Mahammed el-Meccawi, assumed
the governorship of Mokha, and commenced to ill-
treat the British subjects there, at the same time
demanding, in an insulting letter, the surrender of
Aden.[1]

The Imam was not at first able to attend to these
matters, as a religious rebellion had broken out
under the leadership of a fanatic, El-Faki Saïd, who

[1] Playfair's Yemen, p. 147.

called himself " Medhi el-Mantether." But as soon as this impostor had been attacked and killed, the Imam turned his attention to the Tehâma. Failing in obtaining the aid of the British, it appears that both he and her Majesty's Government referred the matter to Constantinople, with the result that a commissioner was sent by the Porte to confer with the Shereef. However, he appears, says Playfair in his notes upon the subject, to have been bribed by Shereef Huseyn, and returned to Constantinople with but little accomplished. The result, however, of his mission became apparent a year later, when the Sultan appointed him Pasha of the Tehâma, on the understanding that he paid a tribute of 70,000 dollars per annum to the Porte.

The Imam, El-Hadi Mahammed, died in 1844, and was succeeded by Ali Mansur, who had been formerly deposed, and whose great idea seemed to be to retrieve the losses his predecessors had suffered. Fighting at once commenced, but the Imam's troops met with but little success, and smallpox carried off a very considerable number. A rebellion broke out a few months later, the Imam was deposed, and his cousin, Mahammed Yahya, placed on the throne in his stead. Desirous of carrying out the scheme of his predecessor for the recovery of the Tehâma, he took the field and finally routed the Shereef Huseyn at Bajil, near Hodaidah, the Shereef himself being taken prisoner. Hodaidah, Zebeed, and

Beit el-Fakih were handed over to the Imam, and shortly afterwards he captured Mokha, where he learned that another division of the Shereef Huseyn's

A Native of the Teháma.

army had retaken Zebeed. The Imam fled to Sanaa, and a few weeks later Mokha fell once more into the hands of Huseyn. The Turks, seeing the opportunity a suitable one to push their interests in Southern Arabia, sent an expedition to Hodaidah, on the arrival of which the Shereef Huseyn handed over the place to the new-comers. The Imam was compelled to visit the Pasha at Hodaidah, and a treaty was signed, the principal clauses of which were as follows :—

1. The country governed by the Imam was to continue under his jurisdiction, but he was himself to be considered as a vassal to the Porte.

2. The revenues of the country were to be equally divided between the Porte and the Imam.

3. Sanaa was to be garrisoned with a thousand regular Turkish troops.

4. The Imam was to receive 37,000 dollars per month from the revenue previous to its division.[1]

Both the Turks and the Imam suffered, however, from the results of this treaty—the former by being almost annihilated on their arrival at Sanaa, the latter by being deposed and murdered. The power of the Imams was gone ; the Turks, although driven out of the highlands of the Yemen, retained their footing on the coast, and carried on desultory warfare in many directions. The country, after years of war and bloodshed, remained in a state of anarchy, and the descendants of the great Imams seemed to lose all spirit and authority. They sank into private life at Sanaa, giving themselves up to luxury and vice ; and the greatness of the Yemen was finished.

[1] Playfair's Yemen, pp. 153, 154.

CHAPTER IV.

THE INFLUENCES OF ISLAM IN THE YEMEN.

BEFORE entering upon any account of the various religious influences that have since the time of Mahammed disturbed the Yemen, it may be as well to put aside a few pages for some general remarks upon the religion of Islam, the tenets of which are well known enough to those who have made any study of the subject, but are to the general world almost a closed book. It is this disregard of religions other than our own which so weakens the constant cry of their inferiority. Rather it should be the desire of such as wish to uphold Christianity to carefully study and compare its doctrines with those of the beliefs they are so ready to cry down. The world has arrived at a stage when people are not satisfied with a mere assertion, but demand to hear both sides of the question and to reason for themselves ; and to those who have taken up or made even a small study of Islam it is a pain, or perhaps at times an amusement, to listen to the rabid cries as to its inferiority, issuing from the throats of men who base their action upon a few what they call " practical results." It is not the author's purpose here to enter into a long discussion upon the subject, or to point out at any length the many fallacies which are believed to be doctrines of Islam by a large proportion of the British public.

But of all the arguments used to show the inferiority of the Mahammedan religion, there is none so loved and so often brought into use as the present condition of countries practising its belief. How little real value this argument possesses it will not take long to prove ; and it may be generally stated that the backward condition of Mahammedan states is not owing to their form of religion to nearly so great an extent as it is owing to the nature of the people who profess it ; in other words, the low standpoint of most Islamic countries can be traced to the origin of its inhabitants rather than to their beliefs. Strong as is this statement, there is at least one very good example to prove its truth—namely, that under similar circumstances of breed and climate we find Christian nations sunk deeper in degradation and vice than their Moslem neighbours. Take, for example, Abyssinia, into which Christianity was introduced between the years 300 and 320 A.D. Why then, since from that period they have been pursuing the Christian belief, do we not find them to-day in a state infinitely superior to the surrounding Moslem countries—in fact, living in a state of civilisation equalling that of the European nations, or even of the Yemenite Arabs or the Turks? Why do we find Abyssinia to-day a country given over to drink and debauchery, when they are regular attendants at church? Why do we find them living in the circular thatch-huts and wearing the same apparel that they did probably when Christianity first made its appearance amongst them? Because, I say, their nature is such that it is untouchable by any religion, no matter how lofty be its aims and aspirations. "Can the Ethiopian change his skin, or the leopard his spots?" Certainly not, no matter how much he may be painted over with gaudy colours. Again, why in Egypt do we not find the Kopts in a far higher state of civilisation and intellectual superiority than their neighbours? It may be argued that their Christianity is not an example of true Christianity, just as it may be argued that the Islam of to-day is not the true Islam. Yet it strikes one that Islam is very much nearer its original ideal than we are to ours, who have turned our religion round and round and inside out to make it fit the requirements of modern progress and personal comforts. Before, Christian reader, you turn to smite your neighbour the Moslem, look round you. Before you begin to pull the mote out of his eye, pay a little attention to the beam that is in your own. Look at the great armies of Europe ready to tear one another to pieces! Look at the

streets of the great cities flocked with prostitutes!
Look at the swarming drunken population of our
towns! Look at the financial robberies and the un-
charitableness of our own lands,—and when you have
mended that, then you may turn to show your
brotherly love, which is so engrafted in the Christian's
heart, and rend your neighbour.

Justice, I say! If it be one's desire to take up
the cudgels against what millions hold most dear,
then let it not be done until the cudgels can be taken
up and victory assured by making a careful study of
what one is going to fight against. Religious tolerance is one of the boasts of Englishmen; let it be
their care that the boast is not a vain one.

Again, it is often said that by its so carefully lay-
ing down the laws, Islam has prevented any material
change from taking place in the condition of those
that profess it. How about Judaism? The laws are
as equally, if not more specifically, laid down in their
books than even they are in the Koran, and yet we
find to-day the Jews in all material matters almost
the leaders of the world.

There can be no doubt that Christianity is a far
finer religion than Islam. Christianity is beautiful
in its simplicity—beautiful in that it touches so little
upon affairs of worldly importance; but it is doubtless a religion founded for Western and Northern
people. There is no doubt that, coming from Pales-
tine, it chose its natural course when it proceeded to

Europe. Why was it not embraced by the Arabs and peoples of the south, who at that time, with the exception of such as were Jews, were professing the foul rites of idolatry? The southerner, wild turbulent son of the desert, is unsuited to Christianity; he must have some belief that touches him deeper, that inspires his ardour by teaching something he can understand,—some religion that regulates his course of life, as well as offers him hereafter a future existence. Mentally and bodily, he is different to us northern people. His mind runs in an entirely different channel. He exists, he thinks, in a different sphere, and it was this sphere that Islam touched.

He was tempted by earthly spoil, by the love of persecution, and promised licentiousness hereafter, it is often said. Perhaps; but has not the same over and over again tempted Christian Powers?—has not love of persecution found sufficient examples in the history of Christianity to deter us from looking for it abroad? Is not our heaven, painted by St John in the Revelation, tended to increase our desire to share in it by picturing its beauties? The Revelation, it may be answered, is an allegory; yet he who argues thus would have been burned at the stake for his pernicious views not many centuries ago. To those who are capable, though generally unwilling, to understand Christianity, it is a religion at once perfect and superlative. It is an ideal seldom if ever reached. It is a goal to be striven after, with

but little hopes of doing more than one's feeble best
to reach ; and more, far more than all, it is the truth.
But so is Islam to the Mahammedan. It is a goal
which many reach, because its ideals are tangible and
comprehensible. It is a religion founded by a man
of vast intellect to enforce a belief in the existence of
one God, which the intricacies of Christianity had
failed to prove to the Arab races. To them, material-
ists to the very backbone, the Trinity is impossible.
To us it is incomprehensible, but acknowledged.
Christ was the Son of God ! This alone is sufficient
to drive to a distance the Arab, who acknowledges
the Messiah's origin as divine and supernatural, but
to whom the idea of filial relationship with the Deity
is revolting and incredible.

An example of the power that Islam asserted over
the minds of the inhabitants of the Yemen is near at
hand. There were many Christians in that country
at the moment when they received the tidings of the
Prophet's mission. Nejran, a large province, was
governed by a Christian family, and boasted a bishop,
by name Kos, who died during the earlier half of
the seventh century A.D., probably during the lifetime of Mahammed ; yet but a comparatively few
years later we find all traces of Christianity disappeared. Not so in Abyssinia, where it exists
to-day amongst a people given up to one vice at
least, drunkenness, from which were they Moslems
they would be free. Were Europe a Mahammedan

Power, there is no reason to doubt that we should not be in the same state of civilisation as we enjoy to-day. The Turks are an oriental race, and cannot be taken as a fair example; yet they have so far followed upon the lines of Christian Powers that we find them to-day squeezing their people to obtain the means wherewithal to purchase the destructive implements of war, and existing in a very tolerable state of civilisation and drunkenness.

No! the Ethiopian cannot change his skin; and just as Christianity is the religion best suited, apart from its inestimable truth, to Northern people, so is Islam to the Arabs and the children of the south. Each has sorted itself and taken root where best it will flourish. Any attempt to influence one by the introduction of the other must, by the laws of nature which have thus sorted them, be prejudicial to the world at large.

A few words as to the general tenets of the Mahammedan religion.

It must not be forgotten that it was in A.H. 12, a year after the Prophet's death, that the Koran was collected by Zaid, and that therefore there can be little doubt that in its arrangement and sequence it is far from the order in which the words were uttered. The fragments of which it is composed were collected from every source, but although it may be said in its present form to follow no particular chronological order, at the same time there can be little doubt that, apart from this weakness, it contains the words of the Prophet himself. However, in the building up of a new religion, it was impossible to ordain for every class of society likely to embrace it; and on this account the Moslems, especially the Sunnis, hold that, after the sacred book, the "traditions" are next in sanctity. These "traditions" are the teaching, verbal or in example, of the Prophet himself, not absolutely inculcated in the Koran, but handed down upon the authority of "his companions." On these traditions many schools of theology and law have been built up, referring to them in cases in which the Koran does not sufficiently render clear, or perhaps omits altogether some point. Needless to say these "traditions," being almost innumerable and often disputed, have caused more dissension amongst the world of Islam than any passages in the Koran itself.

The central idea of Islam is the unity of God, and the association of any other with the Deity is the one mortal sin.[1] There is no priesthood; the religion is a religion of the people, explained to them by doctors, such as the Sheikh el-Islam, the Moulas, and the Cadis, whose authority is acknowledged, but solely as exponents of religion and law, which it is in no one's power to revise or alter. Idolatry is to be rooted out and trampled under foot. "There is no God but God, and Mahammed is the prophet

[1] Mahomet and Islam. Sir William Muir. 1887.

of God." Soundless, rhythmless, as are the words
to us, their very repetition stirs the Moslem heart;
their very mention is sufficient for an infidel to become a Moslem. They are the only bond that binds
Sunnis and Sheiyas together, the common birthright
of all Islam.

A Yemeni.

The principal and best known of the Mahammedan
tenets, as well as being those on which the religion is
most founded, are the immortality of the soul; the
resurrection of the body; the judgment of good and
evil; heaven and hell; predestination, about which,
however, contradictory remarks are found in the
Koran; the ministry of good angels, and the evil

influence of the bad. To none of these precepts can exception be found, for, after all, they resemble to a great extent our own. But at this point the Koran steps ahead of us by the prohibition of wine, games of chance, usurious dealings, the flesh of swine, or of things strangled or which have died a natural death, all of which are strictly forbidden. How beneficial this has proved and is proving to the Mahammedan races is very clear; and it may be said that it is only when Moslems have come into contact with Jews or Christians that they have broken through these ordinances.

As to other restrictions laid by Mahammed upon his followers, and other privileges allowed to them, a few words must be said. Polygamy is legal, and it is this more than anything, perhaps, that raises indignation amongst Christians. Every Moslem is allowed four wives and as many slaves as he likes. Shocking! yet do we not decorate our church windows with pictures of David and Solomon? do we not read their words in our places of worship? and I doubt if either would have been satisfied with this small allowance. Were not the patriarchs, who after Christ we are taught most to reverence, polygamists? They at least, like the Arabs, have an excuse, which Solomon and David certainly had not—namely, the constant wars in which they were engaged killed off so large a population of the men that the women were greatly in excess. Yet to-day in many Moslem countries it is unusual to find amongst the respectable classes more than one wife. We are by law restricted to one, they are by law and by religion allowed four. After all, they have just as much right to swear that their custom is the best one as we have to put forward our own.

That divorce is lax amongst the Arab races is true ; so are the morals of both men and women. But let us look again at the Kopts in Egypt, or the Christian race of Abyssinians,—are they any better ? Certainly not. Again, in Moslem countries, these laws of divorce are appealed to more by the poorest classes than by the rich. In England the fact that a wretched couple of paupers do not agree has no remedy, until one day the husband jumps on his wife and kills her. In Moslem countries he divorces her, and probably both are married again in the course of a month.

The fact of the case is simply this. To attempt to judge Islam from a Christian standpoint is as ridiculous as to attempt to judge Christianity from a Moslem one. We shudder at the civil codes and conditions of the Mahammedans ; they are horrified at our Trinity, at the decoration of our churches, at lax laws as to purification, at our drunken habits, at the Pope, at our paid clergy, and at a hundred other details. To criticise Islam one must have seen it in its own lands, and that with unprejudiced eyes.

There is but one more question that must be

touched upon here—namely, slavery. Never have there been more exaggerated reports as to slavery in oriental countries than are from time to time cropping up to-day. It must be understood what slavery really is in the East ; it must be remembered that it is not agricultural slavery—that it is entirely domestic slavery. Stories are from time to time appearing of atrocious cruelties to slaves : they are true, no doubt, but they are exceptional—just as, happily, the cruel treatment of children is exceptional in England. It is not after the slaves have passed through the market that they suffer, it is on the long desert-marches in which they are brought from the interior. Another point is scarcely understood in England — namely, that probably ninety-nine hundredths of the slaves in servitude in oriental countries have been born in servitude, and never were brought from the Soudan at all. In this case they have been often reared in the houses of their masters, and as often as not treated as his children.

That slavery is contrary to law and nature all will acknowledge ; that it ought and must be put down is equally true ; but as to the means of doing it ? The slave-trade must be stopped from the interior of Africa, not by the freeing of the slaves already arrived at their journey's end. For instance, the emancipation of slaves in Morocco would mean thousands of men thrown out of doors to gain a livelihood by murder and robbery, or starve ; and thousands of

women driven to be prostitutes.   And this is what
we are attempting to do in the name of progress and
religion !

How vastly Islam was in advance of the pagan religions, which for the most part it replaced in Arabia,

Jew of the Yemen.

need not be mentioned here.   From practising horrible rites of "fetich," from the offering even of human
sacrifices, from dissensions and religious tribal wars,
the mission of Mahammed called the Arabs to some-

thing far higher—far above anything they had known
before. Christianity had failed, in spite of repeated
efforts, to attract them to anything more than the
smallest extent ; Judaism was out of date, and unsuited to the epoch they had reached. They were
ready, were yearning, for a new religion, and Mahammed took the opportunity to found one. In place of
hideous pagan rites, in place of a few converts to an
unappreciated Christianity, in place of Judaic laws of
which the people were weary, he brought amongst
them a new inspiriting religion, lofty in its recognition of monotheism, higher than anything they had
as yet known in its moral code.

But from this simple form of monotheism numerous
branches were destined to sprout; and just as Christianity is split up into innumerable sects, so is Islam
divided into many differences and brotherhoods. It
is with comparatively few, however, of these that we
have to deal in regard to the Yemen,—for although in
early times changes had begun to be apparent in the
course of the religion, it is only comparatively lately
that the enormous quantity of sectarian differences
now existing sprang into life ; and these, with few
exceptions, have but to a very slight extent influenced the political aspect of the country.

The first important dissension in the course of
Islam occurred about the year 37 A.H., when the
theocratic party, recognising that the existence of the
Caliphs was likely to become, and was even at that

time becoming, an excuse for power and a cause of strife, and that the religious influence was lapsing into an autocratic supremacy, stood aside and cried for an oath of allegiance to God alone, and an elected Council of State to regulate affairs. Revolting first against Ali, the nephew and son-in-law of the Prophet, we find them again and again all through the history of Islam bursting forth, egged on by such wild fanaticism as only men of those countries can know. High though, perhaps, the original motives of the Kharejites were, they were too often in after-times fanned by the aspirations of pretenders to power, and it needed all the force of temporal and spiritual rulers to check these outbursts of fanaticism. The Kharejites were again split up into many divisions, all more or less founded upon the idea of treating sin as infidelity, which it would be straying from the objects of this book to specially mention here, except that of the Obadites, who from time to time recur in the history of the Yemen.

Although the Kharejites formed the first absolute split in Islam, there had been gradually growing up what have always formed, and to-day form, the two great divisions of the Mahammedan belief—namely, the sects of the Sunnis and the Sheiyas. To mention some of the standpoints of both. The Sunni tenets are held by Turkey and the greater part of Mahammedan-professing India, while Southern Arabia and Persia and portions of North Africa profess Sheiyism.

The differences of the two, briefly stated, are as follows. While the Sunnis acknowledge the election of the Caliphs from the general professors of Islam, the Sheiyas assert that Ali, the fourth Caliph, was the natural successor of the Prophet, ignoring Abou Bekr, Omar, and Othman. But here again the Sheiya sect becomes split up ; for one division, which continued under the name of Sheiyas, contend that Ali held his right to succeed the Prophet in office in virtue of his personality ; while the other side, the Zaidis, contend that Ali was the legitimate successor and heir of the Prophet, not by reason of his personality, but through his merits. Consequently they assert that the successors in the Caliphate, or Imams, as they were called in the Yemen, must necessarily be of the Prophet's family, but were to be chosen to fill the holy office on account of merit and character, in place of succession by birthright alone, but that in the veins of those elected to the post must flow the Prophet's blood. Amongst those of the former persuasion was the sect of Imamites, and its sub-sects, the Dodekites and Ismailites, the latter of which was founded and flourished in the third century A.H. It was from this branch that the Fatimide dynasty sprang, and their descendants are to be found in the mountains of Lebanon under the name of Druses, who are still awaiting the return of their prophet Hakim. The point on which the Zaidis separated from the sects of the Dodekites and Ismailites is as to the lawful holders of the Imamate or Caliphate after the death of the grandson of Ali.

But the Zaidis were destined also to divide, and at a subsequent period we find the Arab and Persian Zaidis submitting to the allegiance of two separate Imams, one of whom reigned in Arabia and one in Persia.

Even to-day intense hatred exists between the followers of Sunni and Sheiya doctrines. No better example of this is to be found than the fact that when Russia was engaged in a war with Turkey that threatened to be a death-blow to Islam in Europe, not one sword was raised by the Sheiya-professing Mahammedans for her assistance; and Persia and other parts who do not acknowledge the Sultan Abdul Hamid as the rightful Caliph—for the Prophet's blood does not flow in his veins—sat impassively and watched, with but comparatively little interest, the struggle.

The Sunnis derive their name from the Arabic word *sunnat*, a precedent; and their faith is built up, apart from the differences already specified, upon the example established by the Prophet himself, as handed down to them by history and tradition. Their belief can be justly called, perhaps, the orthodox one, for Mahammed himself chose as his successor in office Abou Bekr, who was not of his family. Therefore to them it is no prejudice that the present holder of the Caliphate, or successor in the religious supremacy of Islam, is the Sultan of Turkey, who, it will be seen, fails to be acknowledged by any of the branches of the Sheiya faith on account of his descent.

These few words may prove sufficient to throw as much light as is necessary in the question of the Yemen upon the two great divisions of Islam. It need only be added to how great an extent the Turks, though co-religionists in as far as they profess Mahammedanism, would be separated from the Yemeni people in religious ideas ; and it is this fact, more than even the extortion they practised, that gave rise to the Yemen rebellion.

About 280 A.H. there appeared a new sect in the Yemen, that of the Karmathians, who sprang from the Dodekites and Ismailites, though far exceeding them in fanaticism and excesses. They arose in the Yemen under the leadership of two powerful men, Ali ibn Fadl and Mansur ibn Hasan, of whom the former appears to have been most implicated in promulgating the extraordinary and often revolting tenets of the new belief. Beginning as a hermit, he collected round him a little band of devoted followers, and setting forth, he commenced a series of victories. At length, overpowered with success, he acknowledged himself a prophet, and preached from the pulpit of Janad the rightful use of wine and permission of incest. Continuing his march, his cause grew, and both Dhamar and Sanaa fell before him.

At the latter place his excesses were beyond record-ing.[1] Seventeen years after having gained his enor-mous power, Ibn Fadl died at the hands of an assassin, who, taking advantage of the common Eastern habit of the drawing of blood, secreted poison in his long hair, and after having sucked the lancet to prove it was clean, dried it in his poisoned locks. The historian, El-Janadi, states that there were great rejoicings at his death. The remnants of this sect, inoffensive now and law-abiding, still exist in Bombay.

The next great secession from the direct Islam was that of the Nizarites or Assassins, a name derived from *Hashishiyin*—in other words, the eaters of *hashish*, a narcotic much resorted to in the East. This word was the origin of our present " assassin," but in the East to-day has no deeper meaning than that given above. The brotherhood arose about 400 A.H., a few years after the death of Nizar, son of the Khalifa el-Mus-tansir, whom they asserted had been wrongfully with-held from succeeding his father. Thus they gained their first title, that of " Nizarites." They swore an oath to devote their energies to the propagation of their faith, and many perils they undertook for this purpose, often sacrificing their lives in the fulfilment of their vows. The remains of this once dreaded sect are to-day to be found in Bombay, in Zanzibar, and in the Lebanon.

[1] Al-Baha-'l Janadi, ' Karmathians in Yaman.' Kay's translation, 1892.

The later sect of the Wahabis shows a tendency on the part of orthodox Arabs to the ancient tenets of Kharejite theocracy. With the Sheiyas the contrary is the case, and they incline rather toward transcendental doctrines, bursting out into such mystical rites as those of the sects of Mutazelites and Sufis, or, in the Yemen, in their devotion for a divine Imamate.

How important have been these sects in forming the history, not only of the Yemen but of all Arabia, cannot be exaggerated. Whole dynasties have been built up or overthrown by their fanatical devotees. From the very earliest years of Islam we are constantly coming across the turbulent risings of one or the other ; and while the Sunnis have more or less strictly upheld until to-day their original orthodoxy, with any variation of which they are intolerant, we see the other great division, the Sheiyas, split up again and again into sects and sub-sects, struggling for a theocracy that was impossible, or used by unscrupulous pretenders as a road to power.

Looking at Islam to-day, we find the Sunnis in very much the same religious position as they have always held, even from the very first. Their key-note, so to speak, has been unswerving allegiance to the *sunnat*, or precedent of the Prophet. On the other hand, we find the Sheiyas split up into hundreds of sects and brotherhoods, each following some particular instruction or belief of their several founders, who for the most part have been descendants of the Prophet himself.

One of these sects, now making itself felt in the Yemen, as it is doing all over the Moslem world, is a modern one. I refer to the followers of El-Mehdi Senussi, about which, as one of the coming powers of Islam, a few words may not be out of place. The idea of Sheikh Senussi was to bring Islam back to its original purity—to revive its great social laws, moral and religious, as instituted by the Prophet, and to defend and propagate the same.[1] In this it will be seen that the tenets of Senussism resemble both those of the Sheiyas and the Sunnis—the former in the desire for a theocracy, the latter in the punctilious observance of precedent. Its sole distinctive feature is in its transcendentalism and in the repetition of certain prayers. Like the Wahabis, too, music, dancing, singing, and coffee are forbidden. In fact, the Sheikh Senussi seems to have introduced into his new revival of Islam the doctrines of many of the former sects. The Sheikh himself is dead, being followed in office by his son, who is still living near Siwah, in the desert between Egypt and Tripoli. But what makes this sect so vastly important is its political power, and it may safely be prophesied that the next great revolt of Islam against the Christians in Africa, no matter what form it may take, will owe its origin to this movement. The author, within a

[1] Les Confréries Musulmanes du Hedjaz. A. le Chatelier. Paris, 1887.

few months, heard Senussism preached in Somali-land and in Morocco, in both of which countries, not to speak of the more central Tunis, Tripoli, and the state of Fezzan, it is deeply rooted. If, then, a new movement in Islam is able in the lifetime of two men to gain converts, and many converts, in countries so distantly removed from one another and from the headquarters of its founder, it can clearly be understood the immense power it must hold over the minds of the people ; and one of the greatest drawbacks to European venture in Africa is the undoubted fact that this smouldering fanaticism will one day burst into flame.

CHAPTER V.

THE REBELLION IN THE YEMEN.

IT is seldom that the Sublime Porte is free from trouble regarding one at least of her possessions; and although the Turkish Government has taken, in the case of the rebellion in the Yemen, every means to throw dust in the eyes of Europe, yet sufficient has from time to time leaked out to show how seriously the affair was regarded by the Sultan and his Ministers. From such scraps of information it would be impossible to piece together a history of what has taken place; but the writer, by making a journey of over four hundred miles through the country at the very time of the rebellion, was, as the only European in the interior, with the exception of a few Greek shopkeepers, able to take advantage of his unique opportunity of seeing for himself, and gathering a considerable amount of information on the subject.

But before any account is given of the rebellion, it must be explained of how great a value to the Sultan of Turkey are his possessions in Arabia. It is on

them, and on them alone, that he bases his claim to
the title of Caliph—a title on which his prestige in
the eyes of the Moslem mainly rests. Amongst Mahammedan potentates he is the greatest; for although
many sects of Islam do not hold that one in whose
veins the blood of the Prophet does not flow is able
by divine right to succeed to the Caliphate, the possession of the holy cities of Mecca and Medina cannot
but add to his fame. From all parts of the world
the pilgrims flock yearly to Mecca, there to come
in contact with the Turks as a governing power,
to hear the name of Abdul Hamid blessed daily in
the mosque; and in their eyes, by force of circumstance, the Sultan is inseparably connected with the
Holy Places.

True it is that the Yemen is separated from the
Hejaz, the province in which Mecca and Medina are
situated, by a large tract of country, known as the
Asir. But the tribes inhabiting this district are, and
always have been, largely influenced by the Yemenite
faction, and like them are in their belief of the Sheiya
sect, holding that the claim of the Sultan of Turkey
to the Caliphate is irregular and illegal. This alliance,
not only by blood but by doctrine, which is perhaps
the strongest tie of all amongst the Moslems, caused
the rebellion in the Yemen to be a likely forerunner
to a war in the Asir. The Turkish rule has never
been more than nominal amongst the mountains of
the latter, so that the repudiation by them of the Os-

manli Government, which has taken place, is fraught with no great danger to Turkey, provided the discontent and consequent rebellion remains within bounds, and does not reach the Hejaz. Although largely subsidised by the Turkish Government, there can be little doubt that, did they clearly see their way to success, the members of the Shereefian family of Mecca, direct descendants of the Prophet Mahammed, would attempt to bring back the succession of the Caliphate into their own line, and thus into the strain of the descendants of the Prophet; and to a cause so nearly touching their doctrinal beliefs there is but little doubt the Bedouins of the Hejaz, as well as many of the inhabitants of the cities, would readily lend their aid and assistance.

Therefore it will be seen that to the Turks a successful rebellion in the Yemen meant not only the loss of the southernmost of their Arabian States, but also the probable ensuing loss of the Hejaz, and the fall of the Sultan of Turkey in the eyes of the larger portion of the world of Islam. How many thousands of Mahammedans daily in the mosques call for blessings on the head of Abdul Hamid the Caliph, who would never pray for Abdul Hamid the Sultan! The difference is enormous, though to us somewhat incomprehensible; and it is said, and no doubt rightly so, that his Majesty of Stamboul values far more than his temporal powers the title of "Commander of the faithful." In the one case, as Caliph, he is in the eyes of all Sunnis[1] Sultan of the Moslem world, and as such successor to the Prophet himself. In the other, as a Sultan, he is merely a stranger, an Osmanli, not even of the great Arab race, whose ancestors have by force of arms conquered and left him a kingdom.

From these remarks it will be inferred how vastly important it is to the Sultan and the Porte to retain intact the Turkish possessions in Arabia.

Although it was not until the summer of 1891 that the rebellion in the Yemen took any outward form, the Turks must have been aware, for a long period previous to that time, that their relations with the Arabs were becoming day by day more strained. Yet such is the character of Turkish provincial officials, especially of those so far removed from the seat of the Government as in the Yemen, that they still continued their policy of oppression, trusting to fate that there would be no open hostilities until the jobbery that had put them into power would follow its inevitable course by removing them and reinstating others in their places, on whom would fall the brunt of a rebellion, which they saw might for a time be postponed but impossible to avert. " Make your hay while the sun shines," is the motto of the Turkish official ; and for him, as a rule, the sun shines but for a very short period. It is this extraordinary want of

---

[1] The Sunnis hold that the Caliphate need not necessarily descend in the family of the Prophet.

forethought and co-operation, this shifting of respon-
sibilities upon successors in office, amongst those who
help to rule the destinies of the Turkish provinces,
that is the chief root and origin of all their troubles.
" Let me enrich myself," thinks the official. " In a
month or two I may no longer have the opportunities.
I must make enough in this short period of office to
retire upon. What may follow, what may be the
result of my policy, I care not ; it interests me not
at all."

It was the perpetual practice of these theories that
gradually drove the Arabs into resistance. The rebellion was no sudden affair ; as long ago as several
years back there had commenced on the part of the
Arabs a series of outrages against Turkish officials
that would have rendered apparent to any other nation
but the Turks the danger that was threatening. Cruel
and bloodthirsty as many of these outrages were,
they were the only means in the power of the Arabs
of protesting against the exorbitant taxation and the
oppression that were ruining them. Their appeals to
Sanaa, and even to Constantinople, had resulted in no
amelioration of their condition.

It is necessary, I think, to give but one example
of these outrages. At Dhamar, one of the largest
cities of the Yemen, there lived a certain general, by
name Mahammed Rushti Pasha, between whom and
a neighbouring tribe there had arisen misunderstand-
ing as to the amount of taxation to be levied upon

them. The pasha insisted on the full sum, and a quarrel ensued between the Arab sheikh and himself, the former fleeing from the city swearing revenge. Shortly afterwards Mahammed Rushti being called away to another part of the country, the tribe in question took advantage of his absence to blow up his house and family with gunpowder. His wives, children, and servants died that night, in all some eleven persons. Returning with all speed to Dhamar, the general, with such forces as were at the time in the city, almost exterminated the little tribe who had accomplished so horrible a vengeance. Over the grave of those that died that night Mahammed Rushti raised a mosque and a domed tomb, the interior of which he hung with rich silks. Thither he would repair and sit alone. On the taking of Dhamar by the Arabs in November last, this tomb was looted, and when visited by the writer at the end of January, the city by that time having been reconquered by the Turks, he found the tomb and mosque in ruins, robbed of all its treasures.

That the feeling was so strong as to find vent in such outrages as these—and that mentioned is but one of many—would have made it apparent, one would have thought, that the existing state of affairs could not continue with impunity. But the lot of the Yemeni was to be squeezed to fill the coffers at Constantinople, and to pay for the harems and pleasures of unscrupulous officialdom. Such, then, apart from all religious differences, was the existing state of feeling in the Yemen when in the summer of the year before last the rebellion broke out. Before the conquest of the Yemen by the Turks in 1872 — for although they possessed a firm footing on the coast previous to that period, their power had not made itself felt in the interior—the Yemen was governed by a ruler after their own hearts ; for, being of the Sheiya sect—Zaidis they call themselves—it was necessary to the tenets of their belief that their Sultan should be of direct descent from the Prophet, through Ali ibn Abou Taleb, his nephew and son-in-law. This condition their Imam fulfilled ; for although the Yemen had at different times fallen into foreign hands, still the direct family had never disappeared.

Sanaa, now the capital of Turkish Yemen, was his residence. It is a large city, situated roughly two hundred and forty miles north of Aden, and a hundred and sixty east of Hodaidah. Here the Imam lived the usual secluded and sensual life of an oriental despot, looked upon by the Arabs as a spiritual Sultan, but powerless to hold in check the depredations and robberies of the many tribes under his nominal sway, who, with true oriental zeal, were continually doing their best to exterminate one another. As long as money was forthcoming, the Imam was content to dwell at Sanaa without troubling himself about more external affairs than the management of his own household, and the receiving

of gifts from the Arabs who performed pilgrimages
to his presence. Apparently wanting in education,
except such religious knowledge as is considered
necessary for the welfare of an Oriental of high degree, he possessed no ability to govern, nor does he
appear to have been even renowned as a soldier or
organiser of troops.

Such became at length the state of the country,
that trade almost ceased on account of the attacks
upon the caravans; and the Sanaa merchants—quiet
respectable Arabs—saw nothing but ruin before them,
and considering solely the benefits that would accrue
to themselves by such a step, and ignoring what the
result would be upon the agricultural population,
invited the Turks to take the place. This was accomplished in 1872 by a force from Hodaidah. The
Imam was deposed; but on account of his spiritual
influence over the Arab horde, was permitted to reside
in Sanaa, receiving a pension on the condition that
he would exert his powers in furthering the interests
of the Osmanli Government. This until his death he
fulfilled; on which event the *baraka*, or holy birthright, passed to his relative Ahmed ed-Din, who, like
his predecessor, was by no means dissatisfied to receive
the adoration of the Arabs and the regularly paid
allowance of the Turks.

Such, briefly, was the history of the Turkish occupation of the Yemen and the state of affairs until last
year. The tribes, in the time of the Imam, left undis-

turbed both in their labours in the fields and in their welfare, boasting an independence of centuries, found themselves, on the Turkish occupation, little better than slaves—oppressed, taxed, and retaxed by a people whose extortions ruined them, whose personality they hated, and with whom, although co-religionists, there was no unison in religious views.

But the smouldering discontent was destined to burst into flame, even though the flame might blaze forth but to flicker and die.

On an appeal from the governor of Lohaya, a body of four hundred Turkish troops were despatched last summer to assist in collecting by force the taxes due from the Beni Meruan, a branch of the Asir people, and their southernmost tribe, who inhabit the country lying to the east of Lohaya, a port on the Red Sea coast north of Hodaidah. In command of this force was the very Mahammed Rushti Pasha whose house had been destroyed at Dhamar. The expedition was destined to complete failure, and being surprised by a large body of Arabs, was nearly annihilated before the security of a fort was reached, amongst those who fell being the pasha himself.

In countries like the Yemen news travels with extraordinary rapidity, and the Arabs, hearing an exaggerated report of what had taken place, believed that at last their deliverance had come, for it was rumoured that the great district of the Asir, between the Yemen and the Hejaz, had risen, intent upon exterminating the Turks. Where the news travelled the people rose in arms. Tribal banners long hid away were unfurled, and the cry of " God give victory to the Imam" echoed and re-echoed throughout the mountains and valleys of the Yemen.

Meanwhile the hero of the rebellion, Ahmed ed-Din, was living quietly at Sanaa on the subsidy of the Turkish Government, unconscious of what was taking place, although, doubtless, there was ever present in his mind the possibility of some day regaining for himself and his descendants the throne. He clearly saw that affairs were not ripe for a great rebellion, and almost against his will he was obliged to fly from the capital, and become the head of the rebel movement. Premature as things were, he must in the enthusiasm of his partisans have almost believed in their future success.

It was a new *Jehad*, or holy war ! The Turks were to be exterminated or driven away ; the beloved Ahmed ed-Din—beloved on account of his birth and descent rather than from any knowledge of his per-sonality—was to be reinstated on the throne. One by one the tribes rose, except only the Bedouin inhabitants of the Teháma and the southern deserts, who, possessing nothing but a few flocks and herds, and always wandering, were indifferent to Turkish or Arab rule, and awaited the result before promising allegiance to either side. The same plan was followed by many of the merchants and citizens, whose position and intimacy with the Turkish officials placed them outside the bounds of oppression and taxation, and who in many cases were only too ready to take advantage of their fellow-countrymen's unenviable position, by buying from the Turks the right of collecting the taxes of certain districts; for the privilege of levying dues is a commercial article, sold from time to time by auction, a system that relieves the Government of much anxiety and trouble, but encourages to an almost incredible extent cruelty and oppression.

In what state were the Turks to repress a general rising of this sort? The force in the country was estimated at some sixteen thousand men, although in reality probably far short of that number; for during the two previous years cholera had wrought great havoc amongst the troops. These troops consisted of Turkish regulars, Bashi-bazouks, and a large number of Arab auxiliaries, drawn principally from the Mshareg and Hadramaut, the country to the east of the Yemen, who did not care whom they fought against, or for what reason they were fighting, so long as they were paid, and whose one stimulant to feats of bravery was promised reward. The Turkish troops already in Yemen were in a miserable state. Ill fed, ill clothed, thinned by disease, badly housed, and seldom, if ever, paid, it is no wonder that their spirit was broken in a land where during summer they were liable to a temperature that seldom falls

below a hundred in such shade as their badly built
barracks afforded, and in winter to frosts, and at

Turkish troops on the march.

times snow—to all the vagaries, in fact, of a tropical
climate on the tops of mountains of from seven

thousand to nine thousand feet in altitude. A more pitiful picture than the Turkish soldiers presented when the writer was in Yemen he never saw, and yet they fight like devils rather than men.

A few days after the flight of the Imam, Sanaa, the capital, was besieged by an enormous force of Arabs, as was Amran, another walled city; while those which were not so protected fell, many without even a struggle, into the hands of the Arabs. Menakha, on the road from Hodaidah to Sanaa, offered a little resistance, but in vain. Those of the garrison who were not killed or wounded in the first onslaught of the Arabs were spared on surrender, and taken away prisoners, amongst their number being the Kaimakam or military governor. The same happened at Dhamar and Yerim, on the road from Sanaa to Aden; while in quick succession Ibb, Jibleh, and Taiz, all three large towns situated farther south, proclaimed for Ahmed ed-Din. All Turkish prisoners were spared. Many voluntarily went over to the side of the Arabs; some retired into private life on surrendering their arms. Those of importance were sent to the Imam, where report said they were housed and fed at his expense, doubtless in the hope of persuading them to throw in their lot with his own, and so obtain use of their superior knowledge of warfare. In very exceptional cases do we hear of the cruel treatment of Turks by the Arabs in their days of victory; and even when the tide of affairs was

changed, the writer met amongst the Arabs, in districts where no Turkish troops could enter, deserters
from the Osmanli forces being fed and clothed by the
kindly Arabs ; and in many cases money was supplied
them by their *quondam* enemies to assist them in
reaching Aden, or in escaping by other means from
the hard life of soldiering.

By this time telegrams were pouring into Constantinople from Hodaidah beseeching assistance ;
and the Porte, having at length realised how serious
a turn affairs had taken, exerted all its activity in
forwarding troops to the scene of war. By the time
the new forces had embarked for Hodaidah, the whole
country, with the exception of Sanaa and Amran and
a small city in the Asir, by name Dhofir, had fallen
into the hands of the rebels, the plains and seaboard
towns holding aloof from any participation in the
affair, though probably it was only the presence of
better organised Turkish forces which kept in check
the feeling which no doubt existed almost as strongly
there as anywhere. The Beni Meruan, many of
whose villages lie on the sea-coast, were pitilessly
shelled by a couple of Turkish gunboats.

Ahmed ed-Din remained at Sadah,[1] whither he had
fled from Sanaa ; nor at any part of the revolt did
he take active part in the fighting, a fact that in no
small degree accounts for the subsequent failure of

[1] Sadah is situated about eight days' journey north of Sanaa, on the
borders of the desert.

the rebellion. In all probability he never left Sadah, though in his religious character his movements were always spoken about with much mystery.

Sanaa at the end of October was still in a state of siege, the garrison and townspeople suffering greatly from hunger and disease, though in Amran the state of the inhabitants was still more pitiable.

Badly fed as they were at all times, worse now than ever, one cannot but admire the immense pluck of the handful of Turkish troops who kept at bay for several months an immense horde of Arabs. Not only was their courage exhibited in the dogged resistance within the town, but in their constant and often successful sorties against the enemy.

A short description of the city of Sanaa is necessary in order to explain the positions of besiegers and besieged during the whole of last autumn.

The city, which contains some fifty thousand inhabitants, lies in a wide level valley. It takes the form of a triangle, the eastern point consisting of a large fortress, dominating the town, and built upon the lowest spur of Jibel Negoum, a mountain which rises immediately outside the city walls. The town is divided into three distinct quarters, each walled, and the whole surrounded by one continuous wall. They are respectively the city proper, in which are the Government buildings, the huge bazaars, and the residence of the Arabs and Turks; the Jews' quarter; and Bir el-Azab, where are gardens and villas belonging to the richer Turks and Arabs. The city was once of great wealth and prosperity, and to-day remains one of the most flourishing cities of Arabia. The shops are well supplied with European goods, and a large manufacture of silk, jewellery, and arms is carried on there. The quarter in which the Government buildings are situated presents almost a European appearance, with its large Turkish shops, its *cafés*, and its open places, on one of which, in front of the Governor-General's official residence, a military band discourses anything but sweet music of an afternoon.

But the city, as the writer saw it after its recapture by the Turks, presented a very different spectacle from what it must have done when, surrounded on all sides by a horde of Arabs, a continual shower of bullets was being poured into its streets from the Arab position on Jibel Negoum, which completely dominated the place. Fortunately for those besieged, the rebels possessed no artillery, otherwise their efforts would no doubt have proved successful in gaining an entrance into the town. However, the fire poured into the city was sufficiently harassing to render it expedient to drive the Arabs from their position above the town, and several unsuccessful sorties were made. At length, mustering all the troops at his command, the pasha made a final sortie about the middle of November. Maintaining a steady fire from the fort upon the Arab position, the troops issued from the southern gate, and wheeling to the left after a gallant attack—for the Arabs were in overwhelming numbers —drove the rebels back. They retreated on Dar essalaam, a small village a few miles outside the walls of Sanaa, consisting of perhaps a dozen or so stone houses surrounded by a wall. Bringing up some small field-guns, the artillery opened fire upon the rebels, completely destroying the place and rendering a precipitate retreat of the Arabs necessary, which they are said to have accomplished in the wildest disorder, leaving, as I was informed, several thousand dead upon the field. But the victory was not altogether a blessing, for there being no one to bury the Arab dead, the inhabitants of the city suffered from violent disease, while the stench of the decaying bodies is said to have been terrible. Retiring once more within the precincts of the city, the Arabs again took up their old position; but their defeat seems to have to a great degree crushed their spirits, and the remainder of the siege, severe though the sufferings of the townspeople were, is said to have been less acute than previously. At any rate, the alarm of a successful attack on the part of the rebels seems to have abated.

But relief was at hand. The Turkish reinforcements had landed in Hodaidah under the command of Ahmed Feizi Pasha, formerly Governor of Mecca, and commander of the Seventh Army Corps.

Learning on his arrival at Hodaidah how serious was the state of affairs, he at once took active

measures, and without even waiting for commissariat arrangements to be carried out, marched his
troops *viâ* Bajil to Hojaila, a village at the foot of
the mountains on which the town of Menakha is
situated, and over which the road to Sanaa passes.
Here three days later they were overtaken by the
commissariat camels bringing flour and provisions for
the soldiers. Having rested his men, he commenced
the ascent of the steep road, and here met with the
first show of resistance. But the Turkish soldiers
were fresh and fought well, and the superiority of
arms did its work. With but a short delay to force
the road, Menakha was reached.

There is perhaps in the world no city situated in
the way that Menakha is. At an altitude of seven
thousand six hundred feet above the sea-level, it is
perched on a narrow ridge joining two distinct
mountain-ranges. On either side of the city are
precipices, each of considerably over two thousand
feet in depth. So narrow is the town that there are
places in it where one can stand and gaze down both
these precipices at the same time. To reach it from
the west there is only one path in the steep mountain-
side ; while from the east it can only be approached
by a narrow track cut in the face of a precipice and
winding up it for an ascent of two thousand five
hundred feet. In the hands of well-regulated forces
it would be impregnable ; but the Arab defenders,
learning how easily the new Governor-General and his

troops had forced the road at Hojaila, made no plucky
resistance ; and armed as they were almost entirely
with matchlock and fuse guns—and many only with
spears—they could have made no permanent stand
against the field-guns of the Turks, who are said in
one day to have brought their light artillery from
Hojaila to Menakha, an ascent of nearly six thousand
feet, by a breakneck path. But few shots had been
fired when the Arabs fled, and the Turks once more
took possession of the place. Leaving a sufficient
garrison to protect the town, and to keep open a
line of communication with the coast, Ahmed Feizi
marched on towards Sanaa. About thirty miles from
Menakha, on the road to the capital, is a spot called
Hajarat el-Mehedi, where the track is so narrow and
so bad that even without resistance it would offer no
slight obstacle to the passage of troops. Here the
rebel army under Seyed es-Sheraï, a cousin to Ahmed
ed-Din, took up a position, and a twelve days' delay
and fighting took place before the Turks could force
their way through. But on the twelfth day it was
accomplished, and the rebels dispersed. Halting but
now and again to shell some village, the troops by
hurried marches reached Sanaa, and on their being
sighted by the Arab besiegers on Jibel Negoum, the
Imam's force retired into the mountains to the east,
where no Turkish troops could follow them.

The capital relieved, Ahmed Feizi was not idle.
He arrived in time to save the garrison of Amran,

MENAKHA.

where, as at Sanaa, the Arabs retired on the approach
of the Turkish forces. Returning to Sanaa, he set to
work to reorganise affairs, despatching Ismail Pasha
with a considerable number of troops to recapture
Dhamar and Yerim. Proclaiming military law, which
in this case meant almost no law, throughout the
country, the new Governor-General offered a reward
for the head of every rebel brought to him, and turned
loose upon the Arabs his Turkish troops to loot and
plunder their villages. Marching to the south, Ismail
Pasha halted at Maaber to shell the villages of Jibel
Anis, retook Dhamar without any opposition being
offered, and, leaving a garrison there, proceeded to
Yerim, and thence by Seddah and Sobeh to Kátaba,
where the writer found him encamped with four hundred troops toward the middle of last January. Ibb,
Jibleh, and Taiz returned under Turkish rule without
a struggle.

There is no nation in the world that can put down
a rebellion as the Turks can, but they have a great
objection to any one seeing the process ; and the presence of the writer, turning up suddenly in Sanaa
while Ahmed Feizi Pasha was engaged upon this
task, caused such a shock, that he and his servants
were securely confined in prison as spies in spite of
passports, until, from the unsanitary conditions of
the place and the bad water supplied, he was seized
with a violent attack of fever ; and no doubt thinking that it would be better to get rid of him alive

than have an objectionable corpse on their hands, and probably a good many questions to answer, a guard of soldiers was prepared, and the writer was hurried away to Hodaidah with orders to quit. Yet, in spite of the fact that his relations with Ahmed Feizi Pasha were a little strained, he cannot but testify to his admirable activity and soldier-like bearing — an admiration dimmed only by the cruelty, perhaps almost necessary, of some of his commands. Thus it will be seen, from the day that Ahmed Feizi Pasha took over the governor-generalship of the Yemen, the tide of events had completely changed. A series of Arab victories had ended in a series of Arab defeats. Had Sanaa been taken, the result would doubtless have been different; but in their endeavours to take it they failed. Renowned in history, sacred to them as the former seat of government of their Imams, their want of success in capturing it, together with the action of Ahmed ed-Din, who held aloof from any active part in the warfare, broke their spirits. Had they succeeded in entering Sanaa, had they brought their Imam there in state, there is some possibility that the Turks might have lost the Yemen for ever. They themselves, and Ahmed Feizi Pasha the first of them, told the writer this.

Thus by the end of January the Turks had reconquered all the cities of Yemen with the exception of one, Dhofir, at that time still besieged by the Arabs. Yet in spite of the fact that Turkish rule was again reinstated in the country, in spite of the fact that what with the reinforcements there were altogether some forty thousand troops in the Yemen, the rebellion was by no means stamped out. This is easily understood when the nature of the country is described. Central Yemen consists of a great plateau, upon which are situated the three principal cities, Sanaa, Dhamar, and Yerim. This plateau is surrounded by a system of mountains broken and torn into valleys and cañons, peaks and pinnacles, amongst which it would be impossible for any Turkish force to operate. Many of these mountains reach an altitude of over twelve thousand and thirteen thousand feet, the summits often connected with the valleys beneath by precipices of thousands of feet in depth. The only roads —mere tracks they are—are cut in the face of these walls of rock, and often are not a yard in breadth. Amongst these enormous mountain-ranges — and to the north of Sanaa one can travel for days and weeks amongst them—the spirit of rebellion burns as fiercely to-day as ever. Certainly the towns are now in the possession of the Turks, yet the main roads that connect the towns are unsafe for Turks to pass over, except in considerable numbers together. It was to a large extent from these mountain districts that the revenues of the Government were previously drawn ; for the Arabs of the Yemen, unlike those of the Hejaz and most other Arabian States, are tillers of the soil, living in well-built and permanent villages, one and all roughly fortified, from which they would be able to withstand any band of armed tax-collectors, such as were wont formerly to be sent to levy the dues, as often on behalf of those who had purchased the rights of collecting from the district as on the part of the Government direct. In many of these villages the writer sat, sharing with the Arabs their humble repast, sipping their coffee and smoking their hubble-bubbles, and listening to their strange songs and prayers for the return of the Imam, Ahmed ed-Din, to power.

The rebellion has been outwardly crushed, but the prestige of Turkey in the Yemen has received a severe blow. The exorbitant squeezing will have to be abandoned, with the results that the revenue will probably fall to a tenth of its former sum. Many tribes formerly taxed will maintain an armed independence. The garrisons in the towns must be doubled, and the Yemen as a means of filling the Turkish coffers will be finished. Over the rebellion the Porte has expended a vast sum of money, while any attempt to recoup itself from the scene of action will but bring on a second and probably more disastrous rising.

Little more remains to be told except to consider briefly in what manner a permanent Arab success would have influenced ourselves. It was generally believed amongst the Turks in all quarters that it was British intrigue that stirred up the rebellion in the Yemen, although even the Turks themselves were at a loss to understand what advantages we should reap through such an action. They called attention to the independent States that lie between Aden and the Turkish frontier at Kátaba, the states of Lahej, Dhala, and the lands of the Houshabi, Aloui, and other tribes. Yet Ahmed Feizi Pasha himself informed the writer that, equally with the English, the Turkish Government subsidise their Sultans, Amirs, and Sheikhs; but the object of our subsidising them is misunderstood by the officials of Sanaa and Constantinople. To them it is impossible to consider in the same light as we do the vast importance of trade; and it is merely that the roads which pass through these various States may be kept open and safe for caravans trading with Aden, that we pay large monthly sums to the native rulers. At the same time, it is doubtless an advantage to possess a more or less independent strip of country between our frontier at Aden and that of the Turkish Yemen.

What has been to England the result of the Turkish occupation of the Yemen? It has been a result enormously beneficial. Formerly, in the time of Arab rule, no caravans were able to pass and repass in safety from the interior to Aden. The inability of the Imam to hold the tribes in check rendered the looting of every caravan probable. But since the arrival of the Turks things have altered. By keeping the roads open the Turks have rendered a vast service to England, by, as far as their power went, ensuring safe-conduct to the passage of caravans, while unconsciously their greed in levying enormous export and import dues at Hodaidah and their ports has driven the greater part of the Yemen trade to Aden—a free port. Thus it will be seen how vastly beneficial to England has been the conquest of the Yemen by the Turks; and had the Osmanli Government lost possession of the country, the result could have brought about but one effect—a return to the state of affairs previous to Turkish annexation, and a consequent enormous diminution of the Aden trade both in coffee and exports, and in the European goods and tobaccos from the Persian Gulf, for which the returning caravans create a great demand. Yet the Turks assured the writer that the British Government was supplying arms and assistance to the rebels. In reality the rifles were being smuggled in by private traders from the French port at Obock.

As to what will be the future policy of Turkey in the Yemen it is difficult to surmise. No doubt Abdul Hamid will be guided much by the report of his aide-de-camp Yakoub Bey, who was despatched to Sanaa for the purpose of bringing a full report to the Sultan. Rather than risk a second rebellion, there is little doubt that a conciliatory policy will be attempted; but the Yemen is too far removed from Constantinople to be governed from there, and as soon as affairs have quieted down, the officials will take advantage of their positions to commence once more the oppression of the people and the filling of their pockets. Could they be persuaded that extortion is not the road by which to arrive at a satisfactory system of government, they would find the country daily growing richer, and their relations with the Arabs more peaceable and less strained than at present. But the leopard cannot change his spots ; and it is only probable that as long as Osmanli supremacy exists in the Yemen, officialdom will continue to enrich itself and impoverish the country.

PART II.

A JOURNEY THROUGH THE YEMEN

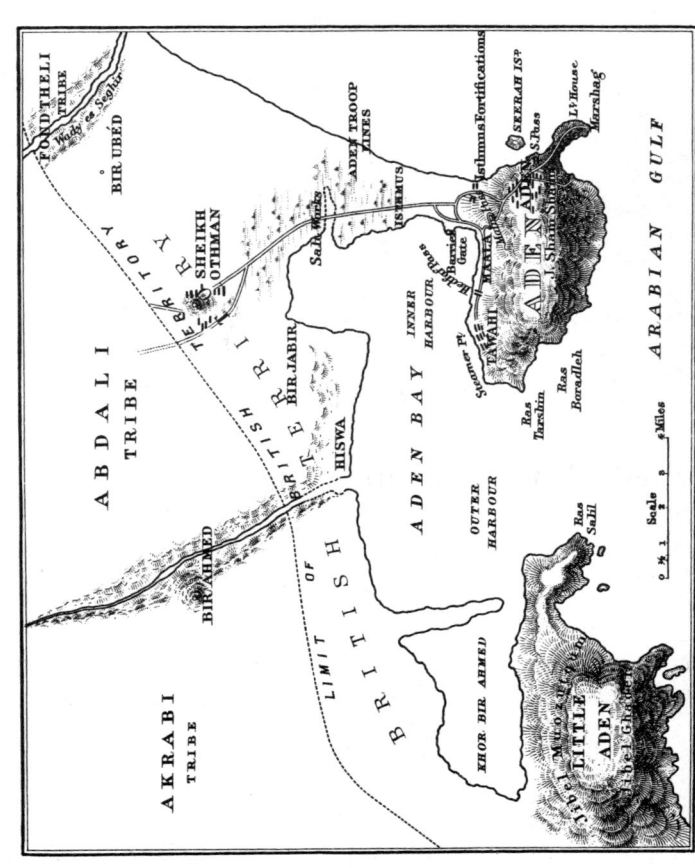

SKETCH MAP OF ADEN AND ITS SURROUNDINGS

To Illustrate Mr. W. B. Harris' "A Journey through the Yemen"

W. & A. K. Johnston Edinburgh & London.

CHAPTER I.

THERE is not a breath of wind to stir the placid surface
of the sea—not a breath to cause a draught upon the
ship and cool us for a second. It is one of those
terrible still tropical days, motionless, silent, oppressive. Nothing to hear but the hissing of the sea as
the vessel's bows plough up the turquoise water, and
the thud, thud of her never-ceasing screw. Even the
Lascars in their white clothes and bare feet, children
of the sun as they are, seem downcast.

We are passing Perim. It lies on the port side, a
dirty blot upon a scene of opalesque transparence, of
shimmering water and palpitating sky.

A youth travelling round the world stretches himself, jots a few lines in his diary, and commences to
tell the old story of the taking of Perim. But he is
soon cried down, and silence reigns again.

On both sides we can see the land,—burning rock
seen through a burning atmosphere. A number
of flying-fish buzz over the surface of the water,

and with a series of little splashes disappear once
again.

.   .   .   .

A few hours later and Aden is in sight, with its
broken and torn peaks and jagged outline. A little
movement is noticeable amongst the passengers, but
it is half-hearted at the best.

Then we enter the grand bay, surrounded by desolate rock and still more desolate desert, and drop
anchor a mile or so off Steamer Point, as the shipping
quarter of Aden is called.

The steamer is quickly surrounded. A few steam-
launches, heavily awninged, screech their whistles ;
while a crowd of small boats manned by coal-black
Somali boys, each striving to be the first upon the
scene, crowd upon us. They are boatmen, divers,
and sellers of curiosities—smart, bright little fellows,
more than half nude, and as black as coal, many with
their hair left long like the cords of a Russian poodle.
Such a screaming and a yelling ! Such a diving after
small coins ! Such a display of leopard-skins, antelope-
horns, especially those of the lovely oryx, and ostrich-
feathers, products of the opposite coast ! A few dull
austere Indians and Cingalese display embroideries
and table-cloths, but the heat seems to depress them,
just as it does the buyers.

It is a wonderful sight to watch the divers, balanced
on the gunwales of the boats, their hands above their
heads, watching eagerly for the tiny splash of a small

TOMB AND MOSQUE OF SHEIKH OTHMAN, NEAR ADEN.

coin, then breaking the water into a series of dancing circles as their dusky bodies disappear into the transparent blue. One can see them too under water, turning like fishes in search of the slowly sinking money. When the excitement had worn off, and those passengers who cared to brave the sun's terrific rays by taking a short run ashore had left, I hailed a boy, who, with the aid of Abdurrahman, my ever-faithful Arab servant from Morocco, stowed my luggage into the boat. Then I said good-bye to the P. and O. steamer, and was rowed ashore.

At some steps leading to a galvanised-iron-roofed landing-place I stepped ashore. What a scene of desolation and dreariness Aden presents to the new-comer! and how soon one gets to like the place in spite of it all! A background of dreary blackish rock, a sandy road, half-a-dozen rickety *gharies* under the shelter of a hideous iron-roofing, with sleepy little ponies and still more sleepy Somali drivers; a white-washed domed saint's tomb, with an apology for a garden on each side, in which a few weary-looking plants were trying to appear green under a thick coating of dust and a sweltering sun; a long crescent of badly built houses, with the exception of the handsome Aden Bank buildings, faced by an expanse of sand and black palings,—and that is Steamer Point, as one first sees it. But as the sun sinks low a figure or two appear, and toward sunset the place wears a gay and flourishing appearance.

Getting my baggage into a hand-cart, I set off for
the hotel, where at least was shade and tolerable coolness, say some 90° Fahrenheit. But in spite of its
dreary aspect, in spite of the dull monotony of its
colouring, one gets quite fond of Aden. The cheery
hospitality of the garrison, the gorgeous early mornings and evenings, the delicious warm January nights,
the club, the verandahs of which are laved by the sea,
the white hulls of the men-of-war in the bay, and the
pleasant evenings spent under their awnings, dispel
all the unfavourable impressions which are at first
so numerous and apparent. In a few days one has
forgotten that the whole place, from the top of Sham-
sham down to the sandy isthmus, is all a volcanic
hideosity; one has forgotten that the whole is so
impregnated with salt as to almost forbid any verdure to grow, and that, should it by chance take root,
the sun is there to kill it. One sees after a time only
the picturesqueness of the place,—the strange torn
mountain-peaks; the gay thronging crowd of many
nationalities all bent on their several businesses,
except the Jews, who seem bent upon everybody
else's; and the Somalis, who are as indifferent to the
general world as they are to the heat, excepting when
a passing steamer lands for an hour or two a flock of
extraordinarily habited travellers—and then the cabs
fly backwards and forwards, the ponies kicking up the
dust, their feet rattling along the hard roads and
making almost as much noise as the cracking of the

jehus' whips; then the Jews, the money-changers, pass and repass, spilling their coins one by one from hand to hand, until the very jingling drives one frantic; and the black urchins, who have learnt English enough to lie with facility, and to beg, worry, and bother until they are paid to go away, appear. Then the curio-seller, be he Greek or Jew or swarthy Indian, creeps out from amongst his moth-eaten lion and leopard skins and his boxes of stale " Turkish delight," and with outstretched hands bids the traveller enter. Then, too, there is the jingling of long tumblers on the wide verandah of the hotel, and a crowd of boats in readiness at the landing-place. Just like a flock of locusts they come and stay their hour or two, and just like a flock of locusts they go, some outward bound, some returning home; and Steamer Point is itself again.

Often as Aden has been described, it is necessary here to make some mention of its various sights and the varied scenes it presents; for, as part and parcel of the Yemen, it cannot be passed over in a book that attempts to deal with that country. If, however, the reader has been there, or has read more pretentious accounts of it, let him skip it over.

Hated, spoken of as typical of the infernal regions, ugly as it is, Aden perhaps can claim an antiquity and an importance throughout all history unparalleled, for its size and its situation, in the annals of the world. When countries, now the centres of vast civilisations, consisted of primeval forests, inhabited by almost primeval man, and filled with wild beasts, Aden was an emporium of trade. With every possible natural disadvantage, except its harbour and its situation, it was inhabited by merchants, who collected and re-shipped by vessel and by caravan the wealth of many lands. Africa, India, the Persian Gulf, poured on to the arid volcanic rock their gold and their purples, their spices and their precious stones.

"Arabia, and all the princes of Kedar, they occupied with thee in lambs, and rams, and goats : in these were they thy merchants. The merchants of Sheba and Raamah, they were thy merchants : they occupied in thy fairs with chief of all spices, and with all precious stones, and gold. Haran, and Canneh, and *Eden*, the merchants of Sheba, Asshur, and Chilmad, were thy merchants."[1] There is no doubt in the minds of competent authorities that the place here referred to as Eden is none other than Aden, while many other of the names mentioned have been identified with ruins and towns of modern Arabia ; but of this more anon.

Ibn Khaldun, in his geographical notes on the Yemen, writing in the eighth century A.H., mentions the extreme antiquity of Aden, speaking of it as a place of importance in the time of the Tubbas, who were the kings descended from Himyar, son of Abd esh-Shems, great-grandson of Kahtan, said to be the

[1] Ezek. xxvii. 21-23.

Joktan of the Jewish Scriptures, the founder of the oldest authentic tribes in the Yemen ; for although they migrated to that country, there are no remains to be traced of the inhabitants who were there before them.

Returning to more historical times, we find that during the reigns of one of the Cæsars, probably Claudius, Aden was destroyed by the Romans,[1] probably in order to divert the trade of India to the ports which Ælius Gallus had founded on the shores of the Red Sea, to which Aden proved, no doubt, a formidable rival. Later we find it conquered by the army of Constantine, and re-named Emporium Romanum.

Returning once more to oriental sources, we find the place split up by the wars and factions which were so constant throughout the Yemen, and Aden several times was besieged and conquered. Most important, perhaps, of these early monarchs was the line of Hamdani princes, who, descended from the Beni Zuray, held it from about 440 A.H. with many ups and downs of fortune, until in A.H. 569 it was conquered by the troops of Turan Shah of the Ayyubite dynasty of Egypt.

In 1487, some three hundred years after the accession of the Ayyubite Sultans over Aden, a period of continued strife, we find the place visited by a Portuguese by name John Pedro de Covilham. This

---

[1] " Arriani periplus maris Erythræi."

expedition was organised to explore that quarter of
the globe after an ambassador had been sent to
Florence by the Christian King of Abyssinia whom
we have learned to know by the name of Prester
John. Covilham eventually ended his days at Shoa,
at the Court of Iskander, or Alexander, the then
reigning prince.

From the next European, however, who visited
Aden we have a more succinct account, though unfortunately his work upon the subject of his travels [1]
is so taken up with personal narrative, and his names
are so unreliable, that it is with some difficulty that
historical events are recognised. I refer to Ludovico
de Barthema, known also as Vertomanus, who travelled in Arabia about the year 1504.

Albuquerque's attack upon Aden forms one of the
most interesting items in its history, and short notice
must be taken of it here. The sovereign of Abyssinia
at this epoch was a Christian, Queen Helena by name,
who, wishing to obtain assistance by which to keep
off the Arab invasions into her own country, sent an
Armenian envoy to the Court of Lisbon. After
wandering about in a somewhat vague way for several
years—he went *viâ* India, where he was detained
twenty-three months—he at length, in 1513, arrived
at Lisbon. He found on his arrival that an expedition was already organised to carry out the proposals

---

[1] Itinerario de Ludovico de Barthema, 1535. Translated by
Richard Eden, 1576.

he was bringing from his queen, and in command of which Alphonso de Albuquerque left India in February of the same year with two thousand five hundred men, two-thirds of them Portuguese, the rest Indians. On Easter eve they arrived at Aden, and at once attacked the place. After a siege of four days further efforts were found to be useless; and bombarding the town, and destroying the native shipping, the Portuguese flotilla sailed for the Red Sea. A second attempt on the part of Albuquerque to take Aden the following spring again failed, owing to the fact that it had meanwhile been refortified.

A few years later, in 1516 A.D., Aden was again besieged, this time by an expedition sent from Egypt under Rais Suleiman; but the city was again found to be impregnable, and the attacking force suffered very considerable loss. However, so weakened had the fortifications been by these repeated attacks, that when Soarez arrived shortly afterwards, the governor surrendered the place into his hands; but on the Portuguese attempting to follow and capture Sulei-man's fleet, the governor made haste to repair the fortifications, and on Soarez's return he found himself baffled, and Aden more firmly in the hands of the Amir Morjaún than ever.

Meanwhile Suleiman had organised an enormous fleet, with part of which he visited Aden. The city was taken by treachery; for the governor, having been enticed on board the ships, was hung, and soldiers landed on beds under the pretence that they were sick men. In 1551 the inhabitants, oppressed by the cruel representatives left by Suleiman, rebelled, and ceded Aden to the Portuguese.

It is not for nearly fifty years later than this date that we find the English in these seas. On the 8th April 1609 a ship belonging to the East India Company, by name the Ascension, visited Aden. Received with every possible courtesy, the captain was, when once safely in the hands of the governor, entrapped and imprisoned, and only allowed to leave Aden after paying heavy fines in goods and money. A year later the Darling and the Peppercorn arrived, under the command of Admiral Sir Henry Middleton. On the Darling proceeding to Mokha, the crew of the Peppercorn were treacherously seized and detained in prison.

The Dutch were the next to appear upon the scene, Van den Broeck arriving with a fleet in 1614, in order to found trading relations between the natives and the Dutch East India Company. Their overtures were exceedingly well received by the officials, but the jealousy of the more influential native merchants prevented their being able to come to any satisfactory arrangement. From this period until the beginning of the present century Aden shared the ups and downs of fate that are so frequent in all oriental places; but as any account of these would prove tedious, they can very well be omitted. In 1802

we find Aden visited by Sir Home Popham, who,
having failed in concluding a treaty with the Imam
of Sanaa, was able to enter upon and carry through
a commercial and amicable treaty with the then
Sultan of Aden. As late as 1833 we find another
example of the treachery of the natives of Aden.
Turkchee Bilmas, as Mahammed Agha was nicknamed,
after his series of extraordinary victories, having demanded and received the surrender of the governor
of Aden, sent thither a mission of forty persons.
They were well received, but during the night more
than half their number were foully murdered, the
rest escaping in miserable plight.

In 1835 steamers of the Indian Government having harboured in Aden, made use of it as a coaling-
station ; but it was, on account of the difficulty of
obtaining labour, changed for Makulla, a port to the
east on the Hadramaut coast. After, in 1837, being
sacked by the Foudtheli tribe, the attention of the
Indian Government was called to Aden by the fact
that a ship flying British colours, the Deria Dowlat,
being wrecked near that port, the vessel was looted,
and the passengers, some of whom were native
ladies of rank, insultingly treated. Captain Haines,
in command of the war-sloop Coote, arrived in
December, and laid a claim before the Sultan
for twelve thousand dollars compensation. A plot
being in the air to obtain possession of the person
and papers of Captain Haines, he sailed for India,

returning in October 1838 to enforce the carrying out of the cession of Aden in return for an annual payment to the Sultan of nearly nine thousand dollars a-year. Having been insultingly treated, Captain Haines commenced to blockade the port, until, in January 1839, H.M.S. Volage and H.M.S. Cruizer arrived upon the scene. A message to surrender being left unanswered, the town was bombarded and taken, the Sultan and his family escaping to Lahej, a city some thirty miles in the interior. The capture of Aden is curious as being the first addition to the Empire made during the reign of Queen Victoria.

It is wonderful to notice how soon it became apparent to the natives that they had nothing to fear from the British occupation ; but, in spite of this feeling of satisfaction in the eyes of the lower-class natives and the merchants, the chiefs of the Abdali tribe, in spite of solemn bonds to the contrary, attempted to retake the place. In this they failed, and, exasperated at their want of success, commenced a series of depredations upon the caravans and local property of Arabs residing in Aden. After a severe struggle in 1841, in which two Arab forts on the mainland were destroyed by the British troops, affairs remained in a more peaceful condition until, in 1846, Seyed Ismail, a fanatical Shereef, preached a holy war and the retaking of Aden from the infidels. Augmented by many local tribes, three separate attempts were made upon Aden, each of which was successfully repulsed. Like all such failures in the East, the Seyed was stamped as an impostor, and, his army having dissolved, he was killed by a Bedouin in 1848. In 1850 the crew of a man-of-war's boat landing on the north side of the bay was attacked, and some of the number were wounded, one man being killed. A still more melancholy affair happened in February 1851, when a shooting-party was attacked at the village of Wáhat, of whom Captain Milne was killed and several others badly wounded. A series of like depredations and outrages continued to take place, until in 1858 an attack was made upon the Arabs and the battle of Sheikh Othman fought, which ended in the blowing up of the fort and the village, and the opening of negotiations for a friendly understanding between the British Government and the Abdali Sultan.

From this time on affairs became more quiet; but on the Turks conquering the interior of the Yemen in 1872—they had held a firm footing on the Red Sea coast before this period—it was found necessary to demand the withdrawal of the Osmanli forces from the tribe lands surrounding Aden. At this epoch, too, Little Aden, a sister peninsula which forms the western shore of the Aden bay, was purchased, and in 1883 British territory was extended across the isthmus, by which arrangement the entire shores of the harbour fell under the jurisdiction of the British Government. Included in this deed of pur-

chase is the village of Sheikh Othman, now a flourishing little township, with a police station and a clock
tower dominating its principal square. Bungalows
have been built there and gardens laid out, and
Sheikh Othman to-day presents quite a prosperous
appearance, though the less said about its inhabitants,
for the most part Arab dancing-girls, the better.

Thus, then, the extent of territory in the possession
of the British Government in the vicinity of Aden
may be described as follows : Aden on the east,
Little Aden on the west, and an intermediate strip
along the north shore of the bay; the total area
forming some seventy square miles. Of these, Aden
alone is fortified.

The peninsula is situated one hundred and twenty
miles from the Straits of Bab el-Mandeb, in latitude
12° 47′ N., and longitude 45° E. It is five miles in
length and three in breadth, and consists of hills of
bare grey-black rock, the highest of which, Jibel Sham-
sham, reaches an altitude of nearly eighteen hundred
feet above the sea-level. The volcanic origin of the
place is clearly demonstrated by the fact that there
exists a large crater, which, owing to the broken
spurs of rock by which it is surrounded, renders
a greater portion of the peninsula uninhabitable.
However, in such parts as are suitable for building
the most has been made, and an extraordinary
number of people find room to exist upon the barren
rock, which of itself produces none of the necessities

of life. Including the population of Sheikh Othman,
the census return in 1891 was over thirty - eight
thousand, whereas at the time of the British conquest
in 1839 the population numbered only some six
thousand.

The greater portion of the population consists of
Arabs and Somalis. The Arabs are for the most
part labourers, ship-coalers, and some shopkeepers
and traders. The Somalis prefer the lighter trade
of cab-driving, the rowing of small boats, and such
work. They seem perfectly incapable of stationary
labour, and unable to conquer their nomad traits.
Almost every nationality is found in Aden : besides
the Europeans there are Hindus, Parsees, Turks,
Egyptian Arabs, Persians, Chinese, Seedy boys,
Abyssinians, Jews, and many natives of India of
different types and classes. Principal amongst the
British Indian subjects are the Parsees, who act as
agents and shopkeepers, in which professions they
equal the meanness—or shall I call it business talent
—of the Jews. One sees them everywhere with their
long white flimsy garments and curious head-gear
resembling a coal-scuttle. They have brought to
Aden a spark of the ever-living fire of Bombay, and
have established themselves there with their temples
and womenfolk, and are annexing a very considerable
proportion of the trade.

The peninsula of Aden boasts two towns and an
important village. The former are Aden proper,

situated on the level bottom of the crater, and
Tawahi, at Steamer Point, which contains some
seven hundred houses, inhabited for the most part
by those who gain a livelihood dependent upon the
shipping. The large town of Aden proper contains
some eighteen thousand inhabitants. The principal
village is Maala, where the native craft, strange
dhows and *bugalas*, anchor ; and here nearly all the
native trade is shipped or landed, as the case may be.

Before entering upon any description of Aden as it
appears to the traveller of to-day, it may be as well to
finish such statistics as are necessary here. First, as
to the anchorage that Aden affords to shipping. The
bay, which attains its greatest length almost due
east and west, consists of two distinct portions, the
inner and the outer harbour. The former, almost
landlocked, extends to a length of some five miles,
while the latter is the large portion lying between
Little Aden and Aden. The depth varies from three
to five fathoms in the western bay and at the
entrance, while a couple of miles outside ten and
twelve fathoms can be found. A small island in the
inner harbour, opposite Tawahi, serves the purpose of
a quarantine station. Very considerable improvements have lately been carried out, and the depth of
certain anchorage in the inner bay successfully increased by aid of a large dredger—a veritable eyesore
amongst the strange and picturesque native craft
with which at certain times the bay is crowded. The

larger steamers, such as the P. and O. and the Messa-
geries Maritimes, lie at some distance from the shore,
tôward the mouth of the harbour; but the British
India, Austrian Lloyd's, and several other important
lines, bring their ships in close under Steamer Point.
This, however, is due to the fact that they usually
remain a longer time there, and that it affords them
greater and cheaper facilities for coaling.

It is, of course, as a coaling-station that Aden is
most renowned. In 1891 some 165,000 tons were
imported, which, together with the other trade of the
colony, brings the value of imports and exports up
to a sum of over five millions sterling per annum.
What result the opening of the coaling-station on the
island of Perim may have on the coal trade of Aden
remains yet to be seen, but it seems improbable that,
as was said at the time, it will ever become a more
important place than the other.

Apart from the commerce in coal, there is by no
means an unimportant trade carried on with the neighbouring coasts of Arabia, the Persian Gulf, the Red
Sea, and the African coast. This is principally in the
hands of native merchants, and a very considerable
quantity of the cargo is transported in native sailing
craft. The chief articles are hides, coffee, feathers,
gums, dyes, spices and perfumes, silk, and mother-of-
pearl shells and ivory.

The coffee trade which now finds its outlet at Aden
was formerly almost entirely in the hands of the

JTY-K

Mokha and Hodaidah merchants; but the former
town is now deserted, and the heavy dues of the
Turkish authorities at the latter have diverted a large
part of the coffee to Aden, a free port, although a
considerable amount is still shipped from Hodaidah
to Aden by sea. The coffee which reaches Aden
direct is brought down by caravan from the highlands of the interior and sold to the Aden merchants.
A very considerable quantity is also brought across
from the African coast, shipped almost entirely from
Zeilah, one of the Somali ports, to which spot it is
brought on camels from the highlands of Harrar and
the Galla country, all of which is practically suitable
to the growth of the coffee tree, which necessitates a
high altitude above the level of the sea. The ostrich-
feathers are the produce of Somali and the Donakil
country. Mother-of-pearl shells are brought from the
Persian Gulf and the Red Sea fisheries, and ivory
from Somali-land and Abyssinia. The food for the
garrison is imported from the African coast and from
Arabia. Sheep and goats are weekly shipped in large
quantities from Berbera, Bulhar, and Zeilah; while
oxen, vegetables, fodder, and fuel are brought in by
camel-caravan from Lahej and the surrounding country.

What, however, astonishes one about Aden is the
fact that it has no local industries. All skilled labour
has to be imported from China or India; while even
such simple trades as mat-making, boat-building, and
suchlike are almost neglected.

The climate of Aden is by no means so bad as it is generally described to be, and I believe that statistical returns give a very fair average of health there. The temperature for the whole year averages about 85° Fahr. in the shade, the extremes being 72° and 102°. During my visit the thermometer only once rose above 90°, and then only for a short period, and once fell as low as 74°. The sky during the winter months is unclouded, and the climate may be said to be delightful, though great care must be taken not to get chilled at sundown. Early in June the south - west monsoon breaks. Damp and unpleasant as this ocean wind may seem, it is the sole cause that renders Aden inhabitable for Europeans during the summer. The changes of the monsoon, May and September, are the worst periods in the year, the thermometer often varying only between 100° in the day and 90° at night! The rainfall of Aden is very changeable, in some years rising to eight inches, in others being only one-fourth of an inch; but it is sufficient to keep alive a few plants, that do their little best to break the monotony of the dull rocks. After a shower the valleys sometimes wear quite a green appearance, but as a rule this does not last long, for the sun and dust soon dry them up again. However, it is said that there are no less than one hundred and thirty species, of over forty different orders, the most common being *Euphorbiaceæ*, the *Acacia eburnea, Caparidiciæ,* and the lovely *Adenum obesum*.[1] A few wild dogs, jackals, and foxes can be found in the rocky valleys ; and birds are common — kites, hawks, flycatchers, and wagtails being permanent residents, while many species pay the place an occasional visit.[1]

Having thus briefly run through the statistics of Aden to such an extent as I deem necessary for a work of this kind, I will continue with the personal narrative of my journey, and, having exhausted my books of reference, describe Aden as it appeared to me.

I have said elsewhere that the terrible feeling of oppression soon wears off, and that, after only a few days' residence in the place, one has forgotten how truly desolate and dreary are the great brown peaks that rear their heads so far above one on all sides. I never was in a place that so shocks one at first, and yet which one so quickly comes to like. It took only a day or two to shake off the feeling of the hideous barrenness of the place ; and having made a few friends, I soon began to perceive how charming life can be made with all the disadvantages of such surroundings and climate as Aden possesses.

The club, the very verandahs of which are laved by the sea-waves, is one of the best of its kind in the East ; and many a pleasant evening I spent there, listening now and again to a military band which once a-week discourses sweet music in its precincts.

[1] Three Hours in Aden. Bombay, 1891.

Pleasantest amongst many pleasant recollections of Aden is the kindness I was shown by all with whom I came in contact—kindness that extended not only to entertaining, but in rendering me great service in arranging my journey into the interior of the Yemen. I cannot here attempt to thank all those who took pity on a stranger, but I must not pass on without saying how grateful I am to General Jopp, H.M. Political Resident, and to Colonel Stace, C.B., Assistant-Resident, for their many kindnesses.

As soon as I had settled in at my hotel and rested a day to study my whereabouts, I set to work to see the sights of the place. Fortunately they are not very many, though some of them, such as the street scenes in the bazaars, one can never tire of looking at. Our hotel, too, was a "sight." It was full of curiosities, from the exceedingly stout and none too clean Greek who kept the place, to the dirtiest of dirty kitchens I ever saw. The centre courtyard, surrounded by a rickety balcony, had once been used as a *café-chantant,* and the stage and framework still remained, festooned with cobwebs. Below, the Greek kept a curiosity-shop, which seemed principally to contain moth-eaten skins of what once may have been wild beasts, and rusty Somali spears. His "Turkish delight" was good. I found he sold it to my servant at exactly half the price he charged me, so I made Abdurrahman buy it in future, and between us and Saïd, my Yemen man, we did a large business with

him. However, on the whole, the place was inhabitable, and in a climate like Aden one lives mostly out
of doors on the verandahs.

My first stroll to see the sights was confined to the
little town of Tawahi, in which the hotel was situated,
and which is generally known under the more general
designation of Steamer Point. There is little to see
in this quarter, though a crowd of natives lying out
on their long wood-and-string beds in front of the
tiny *cafés*, smoking the murmuring hubble-bubble,
is always a picturesque sight. But it is only in
the back streets that one finds this, the front of the
town being faced with what is called Prince of Wales
Crescent—in other words, a semicircle of ill-built
stucco houses, with the exception of the handsome
offices of Messrs Luke, Thomas, & Co., to whose
representative, Mr Vidal, I am under many obliga-
tions for kindness. Facing these hideosities of houses
is an open sandy space, in which a few young palm-
trees, caged and coddled, were trying to grow. A
row of black palings divides this sandy space from
the beach. A hideous cab-stand of galvanised iron
roofing does not add to the picturesqueness of the
scene ; nor, for the matter of that, does the thin filmy
coal-dust that so often floats upon the breeze, to dirty
one's white clothes and render life gritty and unbearable. Yet in spite of this depressing view—in spite
of the bare rocks that rise above the town—all my
recollections of Tawahi are pleasant.

Having explored this little township, which can be done comfortably in half an hour, I entered upon a longer undertaking,—I chartered a rickety conveyance and drove to Aden proper. The town lies in the centre of the crater of an extinct volcano, and one cannot help thinking how unpleasant it would be for the inhabitants did the eruption that must once have taken place recommence.

Driving from Steamer Point to Aden, a distance of some four or five miles, is by no means an exciting process, although one's nerves are kept in constant tension by the extraordinary evolutions of the cab, and the thought that at any moment it may fall to pieces—ditto the pony, which a Somali jehu on the box causes by aid of his whip to keep up to a gallop. Through the pass of Hedfaf, along the flat that leads to the village of Maala—its harbour crowded with native craft, while Arab sailors sit mending the sails on the beach—away up the winding road to the Main Pass, a zigzag cutting between high walls of rock, then down again, until, issuing from the tunnel-like pass, one sees the town of Aden before one's eyes—a great white block, broken up by the streets that run at right angles to one another, and disfigured by hideous barracks and Government offices. The plain in which the town lies, being in reality the floor of the crater, is almost a circle, from which torn and ragged spurs of rock rise on all sides, except where through a gap one can catch a glimpse of the sea and Seerah island,

until they join in the peaks of Sham-sham and its
neighbours. There is but little to attract the eye

Main Pass, Aden.

about the desolate prospect, except the relief afforded
by the clean white town. Away on one of the hill-tops

stands a tower. Like the Towers of Silence at Bombay, it serves as the scene of the strange funeral rites of the Parsees; and here the birds of prey congregate to devour the corpse, too impure to defile fire or earth or water.

But the sight of all Aden is the tanks. I remember long before I visited Aden listening one evening during a long sea-voyage to an old ship's-carpenter discoursing on the Bible. "The Garden of Eden!" he said; "why, of course it's true! It's Aden to-day, and there's the tanks to prove it. I seed 'em with my own eyes." However, in spite of the dear old man's religious beliefs being strengthened by having seen the famous Aden tanks, I fear they can claim no such antiquity as that with which he connected them. In all probability these great reservoirs were built at the time of the second Persian invasion, in the seventh century A.D. In this case the tanks at Aden are much later in date than many of those existing in Southern Arabia, of which the most important was, without doubt, the great dam of Mareb, or Sheba as we know it. Although I was not fortunate enough in my travels in the Yemen to be able to reach the ruins of this extraordinary work, I think that a few words upon the subject may not be out of place here.

The dam of Mareb was built probably some 1700 years B.C. by Lokman the Adite, though some authorities attribute its construction to Abd esh-shems, father of Himyar, founder of the Himyaric dynasty, and

great-grandson of Kahtan—Joktan of the Hebrew
Scriptures. Monsieur d'Arnaud, who visited Saba in
1843, describes the ruins of the dam. He says that
it consisted of an enormous wall, two miles long and
one hundred and seventy-five paces wide, connecting
two hills. Dikes allowed the water to escape for
the irrigation of the plain below. These openings
are at different levels, so as to render practicable
a supply of water at whatever height the contents
of the reservoir might stand. The destruction of
this great work took place probably about a hundred years after the birth of Christ; but although
the catastrophe is referred to in the Koran, no certain
date can be affixed to its occurrence. The fact that it
stood the enormous pressure of water which must
have constantly been present for some seventeen
hundred years, testifies to the immensity and solidity of its construction.

The tanks at Aden cannot, of course, compare with
the dam of Mareb, yet they are in their way colossal
undertakings, and the labour and time expended in
their construction must have been enormous. They
number about fifty altogether, and if in working
order, would be capable of holding upwards of thirty
million gallons. We know that at the time of the
invasion of Raïs Suleiman in 1538, the inhabitants
of Aden were entirely dependent upon these great
cisterns for their water-supply. On Captain Haines
visiting Aden in 1835, he found several of the tanks

in use, but many were filled up with the *debris* that the torrents had washed from the mountains above.

In 1856 the restoration of the tanks was commenced, and now thirteen are in working order, capable of holding nearly eight million gallons of water. Their site is well chosen. They lie above the town, immediately under the high rocks that form the foot of Jibel Sham-sham, and in such a position that all the drainage of the rain-water is accumulated into channels, and poured into the succession of cisterns that lie one above another.

The tanks are formed in various ways: some are cut into the solid bed of the rock, which is covered with a hard polished cement; others are dams built across the ravine; while a third variety of shape is formed by angles in the precipices being made use of, two of the walls of the cistern perhaps being the natural stone, and the others formed of masonry. The upper tanks are the first filled, the lower for the most part being supplied from the overflow of those above. In spite of the enormous space to contain the water and the slight rainfall of Aden, a series of heavy showers will not only fill the tanks, but cause an overflow stream of such bulk that very considerable damage has at times been caused by it, as it poured along its channel through the town to the sea.

It was upon these tanks and a few poor wells that Aden at one time depended entirely for water, until in fact, in the fifteenth century, when Abdul Wahab constructed the aqueduct that brought water from Bir Ahmed into the town.

Beyond these tanks there is but little to see of the long-past glories of old Aden; nor have the Arabs displayed in their modern buildings, with the exception of one decorative mosque, any attempt at architectural beauty. Mons. de Merveille, who visited Aden in 1708, has left a description of the ruins of wonderful marble baths that he saw at that time; but no remains of these are known to exist to-day, nor is there any trace of the mosque built by Yasir or the pulpit of the Day Imran. In fact, beyond the tanks, its historical traditions, and the strange peoples who flock its streets, Aden can claim but little to interest the traveller.

What a sight the bazaars of Aden present of an evening! Often and often I would drive out just to spend the last hour or two of daylight in idly sauntering through its streets. What strange peoples are to be seen there! Indians gorgeous in scarlet and gold and tinsel; Somalis in their plain white *tobes*, their hair left long and hanging like the cords of a Russian poodle on either side of their heads, and often their raven locks are dyed a strange brick-dust red colour by a clay they smear over them; Arabs, too, with long black silky curls bursting from under their small turbans, nude fellows, except for their loin-cloth of native-dyed indigo cotton, the colour of which clings to their copper skins with strange effect; creeping, crawling

Jews; niggers from Zanzibar; Persians and Arabs from Bagdad; Parsees and Greeks.

Then is the time, when the heat of the day is over, to seek some *café* at the corner of a street, and watch the people pass. Here at a table four Somali warriors, glorious in their very blackness, are playing dominoes with the manners of *bourgeois* on the boulevards; there a group of Arabs are chatting over a hubble-bubble pipe, the mouthpiece of which they pass one to another, over cups of the husks of the coffee-berry, their favourite beverage.

Great strings of camels pass and repass in the street. Rickety cabs rattle along, the drivers calling to the crowd to make way; and throughout the whole permeates Tommy Atkins, sublime in his self-consciousness, and a very good fellow withal. Ay, the bazaars of an evening are a sight to be seen,—a collection of strange peoples, only to be equalled perhaps on the bridge between Stamboul and Galata at Constantinople.

There remains but one more sight to see in Aden, the tunnel that connects the town with the isthmus, and which passes under the Munsoorie hills. This excavation is three hundred and fifty yards in length, and is lit throughout with artificial lights. It is sufficiently high and wide to allow of carriage and caravan traffic. A second tunnel connects two separate portions of the isthmus lines.

Immense improvements have lately been carried

out in the fortifications of Aden, and during the time of the writer's visit several new forts were being erected. There is no doubt that the strategic position of the peninsula justifies a large expenditure upon its defences. The immense value it would prove in time of war as a coaling-station cannot be overrated. At the present period its garrison consists of the Aden troop of cavalry, three batteries of the Royal Artillery, one regiment of British infantry, one regiment of native infantry, and one company of sappers; while in the bay lies a gunboat and a transport steamer of the Indian marine. The troops are spread over the peninsula, the cavalry having lines on the isthmus itself. Altogether, when the new fortifications are completed, Aden may be said to be, both as regards its defensive powers and in its commercial character, one of the most successful spots in the world.

CHAPTER II.

ADEN TO LAHEJ.

WITH the kind aid of friends at Aden, my preparations were easily made for my journey into the
Yemen—far more easily, in fact, than I had been led
to suppose would have been the case. Everywhere
in the bazaar were rumours of the rebellion still
raging in the interior—vague rumours, the truth of
which it was almost impossible to gather ; while, more
dispiriting still, there was the fact that for several
months no caravans had arrived from any distance
in the interior, while those which came from Lahej
and the surrounding country brought tidings, by no
means reassuring, of the impassable state of the
roads in the interior, and the constant depredations
of the turbulent tribes, who were taking advantage of
the serious political troubles to enrich themselves by
robbery and plunder. Added to this, I was warned
by several European merchants and traders that even
in times of peace it was an almost impossible task to
enter the Yemen from Aden. One and all advised

my proceeding to Hodaidah, and from there attempting the road to Sanaa. In spite of this, I decided otherwise. My reasons were these. Hodaidah being the nearest port to the capital, and the principal seaport of the Yemen, it would be only natural to find there great activity on the part of the Turkish officials, —an activity that would not only prevent my being allowed to pass along the well - watched road, but would also probably put the Turks upon the lookout in other quarters. It may seem strange to the reader that any great difficulties should be put in my way; but so serious had been the rebellion, and to such an extent had false reports been spread from Constantinople concerning it, that the officials were determined if possible not to allow the truth of what really had been and was taking place to leak out. There were at this time, with the exception of a few traders at Hodaidah, absolutely no Europeans in the Yemen; for one scarcely counts the Greek shopkeepers to be found in all the large towns as any but natives, to so great an extent do they assimilate themselves to the customs and manners of the country. I knew, then, that did I attempt to reach Sanaa from Hodaidah, and should I fail, as most probably would be the case, my chance of proceeding into the country from any other quarter would be practically at an end. It was for this reason that I decided to make Aden my starting-point; and should I be unfortunate in my journey thence, to fall back

as a last hope upon Hodaidah. This, happily, I was
not obliged to do; for my plans, as will be seen,
were successful.

But there were several other matters to be thought
over besides this. Granting that I could reach the
capital of the Yemen from Aden, how could I best do
so with tolerable safety? Here my experiences in
Morocco stood me in good stead. My first idea had
been to purchase my camels, but on second thoughts
I decided not to do so. Not only would my camels
tempt the tribes through whose lands I would have
to pass to robbery, but even the native Arabs I
might hire as guides to go with me might not prove
indisposed to relieve me of two or three valuable
beasts of burden. It would be safer far, I argued,
to hire my beasts, as in that case it would be to the
advantage of my men to see that not only I myself
but also my baggage-animals would arrive at their
destination in safety. How, then, to find the right
men and animals without spreading the fact all over
the bazaars that a mad Englishman wanted to go to
Sanaa, in spite of dangers and the rebellion? I had
recourse to Messrs Cowasjee, Dinshaw, & Co., a great
house of Parsee merchants, and through them was
put into communication with an Arab trader. This
gentleman I called upon, and found exceedingly
pleasant; and more than that, I found that he understood perfectly my North-African Arabic, and that
his educated Yemen dialect was comprehensible to

myself. I unfolded to him, over coffee, my plans,
with which he seemed not a little amused. He told
me in return to leave everything to him, and to appear
again at his house the following afternoon. This I
did, and after coffee and preliminary remarks he
introduced to me a strange character, an Arab of
the mountains of Yemen, a man of something under
forty years of age, framed like an Apollo, lithe and
beautiful. I must give a few words of description of
this strange creature. Tall, lithe, and exquisitely
built, his skin of dull copper hue showed off the
perfect moulding of his limbs. Over his shoulders
on either side hung loose black wavy curls, standing
out like the wigs of the old Egyptians. Except for a
loin-cloth of native indigo workmanship, and a small
blue turban, almost lost in the spreading masses of
raven hair that burst from beneath its folds, he was
naked. Here and there his flesh had taken the dye
from his blue raiment, giving it a strange blue tint.
Tucked into his girdle was a dagger—*jambiya*—of
exquisite Yemen silver-work; while round his left
arm hung a long circular silver box containing some
charm. In features he was extraordinarily handsome. The brow was high, the eyebrows arched, the
eyes almond-shaped and brilliant, his nose aquiline
and thin. Added to this a fine firm mouth, the
upper lip closely shaven, while on the point of his
chin he wore a small pointed beard about an inch in
length. A strange contrast he was to my Arab host,

an elderly highly respectable-looking merchant, with
eyelids darkened with antimony — *kohl* the Arabs
call it—and his grey beard dyed a shade between
saffron and salmon-pink. An enormous turban was
balanced on his closely shaven head, and he was
habited in robes of yellow and green.

Coffee being brought for our half-nude guest, we
began to talk matters over, with the result that for
an absurdly small sum my new-found friend undertook to deliver me safely in Sanaa. At all my questions about the road he laughed. Somehow he had
such an air of sincerity about him that I trusted him
from the very first, nor was I wrong. "You have
nothing to do or say," he said, smiling ; "only bring
your baggage here the day you want to start, and I will
see to the rest." In half an hour it was all arranged.
Three camels were to take me and my servants, and,
after a certain distance, when, in fact, we entered the
highlands, they would be changed for mules. As to
guides and men, I had nothing to do with them.
There would be always enough animals to carry my
scanty baggage, my servants Abdurrahman and Saïd,
and myself. "When will you be ready ? " asked the
Arab, rising to leave. "To-morrow," I replied, expecting to be met with excuses for so hurried a
departure. But no ; and half an hour later I was
rattling back to Steamer Point in the wheeziest old
ghary that ever existed, with a fat pony galloping
ahead and an excited Somali jehu on the box.

It did not take long to make my preparations, and these over, I turned into bed in a fever of delight at the idea of getting away. At dawn I was up. I knew it was hopeless to attempt an early start, so, having seen all my baggage put in order—it consisted of only a sack of clothing and a mattress and blanket, a couple of saucepans, a kettle, and a few stores mixed up with the clothes—I turned in again.

About nine I dressed; and as there were no signs of anything or anybody, I sat down impatiently to wait until something should happen. At length Abdurrahman, my faithful Moor, who had come with me from Morocco especially to make this journey, appeared. His only fault is that, when he is particularly wanted, he is sure to have found some place as difficult to discover as the North Pole in which to oversleep himself. He was followed an hour or so later by Saïd, clad in new raiment, gay as the sunshine, and not the least ashamed of himself for being so terribly unpunctual. However, one could not be angry with this butterfly, who, from his mass of wavy black hair to the soles of his leather sandals, was a picture of dandyism. Often and often in the marches before me Saïd's bright cheery manner and ingenuous narration of his conquests amongst the female sex kept us, tired and weary as we were, in shouts of laughter. He was as good as mortal man could be when once we had torn him away from the fascinations of Aden, his earthly paradise.

At length, collecting the men and the baggage into a couple of gharies, we set out for Aden proper, the old fat Greek who kept the hotel waving his hand to me, and wishing me all good-fortune as we drove away.

At the other end, of course, all the worry commenced again. However, there was nothing to do but to bear it patiently. First, no signs of men or camels. At length, after much searching, we captured the beautiful Arab of the previous afternoon; and, never letting him out of our sight, we at length ran our camels to earth in a back-yard. Leaving Abdurrahman to watch the luggage and the camels, Saïd and I sauntered out to do our last shopping. The heat was terrific, but even my impatience did not ruffle Saïd's equanimity. He seemed to have a smile and a few words to say to every one he met, and, added to this, he insisted on bargaining for a considerable period of time over every item of our purchasing; and if at length he could not beat the shopman sufficiently low down, he would saunter off to another shop, and commence the whole business over again. It was exasperating!

At last everything was completed, said Saïd, and we turned back once more in the direction of our camel-yard. Abdurrahman, wearied with waiting, had gone off to a *café* to have a cup of coffee with the camel-men! I sent Saïd to find them. In about an hour Abdurrahman and the men returned, not having seen Saïd, who presently came smiling in, gay as a

singing-bird, with the excuse that he had forgotten
to say good-bye to one of his lady-loves, whose beauty
he began to sing in flowery praises until I peremp-
torily silenced him.

Then they loaded the camels. I sat by and
watched, wondering what we could have forgotten.
Saïd presently was struck with a bright idea, and
before I could seize him had fled to buy a jar of ghee,
or rancid butter, for our cooking on the road. Pursuit
was hopeless, but at last I could wait no longer.
Fortune favoured me, and I found him. He had, so
far, forgotten all about the ghee, and was testing the
smoking capabilities of a quantity of hubble-bubble
pipes, one of which I purchased, and which I found
to be a veritable passport on my journey. Then off
he went to buy the ghee, the pipe under his arm ; but
I accompanied him, and brought him safely back
again.

With a sigh of delight I watched the camels laden
with my baggage saunter off with slouching gait out
of the yard and along the yellow dusty road, followed
by the men. Half an hour later we drove out
through the Main Pass gate of Aden, down the
steep winding hill, and along the isthmus, to join
our baggage-animals at the village of Sheikh Othman, on the mainland.

It was almost sunset, and grand and beautiful the
jagged outline of Aden looked as we left it behind.
The bay, placid as glass, reflected the great rock, and

the ships that lay so peacefully upon its motionless
waters. The sky, a mass of primrose yellow, still
trembled with the heat of the afternoon sun. Far
away beyond the crowded masts of the native craft,
Little Aden, rival of its sister rock, rose a pale
mauve against the sky. Then the sun set, and our
cab came to a standstill with a jerk that threatened
to break it to atoms ; while our Somali driver, good
Moslem that he was, alighted to pray. The air was
fresh and cool, and we descended for a few seconds
to stretch our limbs. One could not help thinking
of the strange mixture of the past and the present.
This grand lithe figure rising and falling in prayer,
now upright with outstretched hands, now prostrate
with his forehead on the ground, seemed like some
memory of the long dead glories of Islam, whereas
he was in reality only a cab-driver.

On again, on over the level plain where many
an army has met and fought over the possession
of the barren rock we were leaving behind us, until
in the fading of the after-glow we drew up in the
quiet square of Sheikh Othman.

I was intensely happy. A feeling of exhilaration
at the journey before me ran through my being—
and we were really started ! I could not let the
Somali driver go back, so I paid him for his stabling
for the night, and dragged him off to the little *café*
where my camels and men were resting ; and here
we, Arabs and Moor, Somali and Englishman, calling

" Bismillah "[1] together, sat down to our humble repast of fowl and coffee.

But I could not sit still. I longed for the rising
of the moon to start again, and under the guidance
of my great Arab friend, set out to wander through
the half-deserted streets. From time to time one
could catch a glimpse into the *cafés* of which Sheikh
Othman principally consists, filled with dusky Arabs
and laughing women, many dancing in the circles of
their admirers, for the little town is given over to
pleasure. And as an echo to the music, one heard
the soft gurgle of the hubble-bubble pipes, the grey
fumes of which filled the air of the houses with hazy
indistinctness. On we walked between the high
walls of gardens, out on to the desert, to where,
in its little grove of palm-trees, stands the tomb
of the patron saint, Sheikh Othman, with its domes
and its mosque and strange tower of sun-dried bricks.
This tomb it is that gives the name to the little
town.

The moon was rising, so we hurried back to the
café, and after a final smoke and a cup of the
steaming coffee, we loaded our camels, and bidding
farewell to our Somali guest, prepared to start.
Then I found that my Yemen Apollo was not
coming with us. I was sorry at this, but it could
not be helped : as long as the men who were to
accompany me were *his* men, I had nought to

[1] " In the name of God "—the Arab grace before eating.

fear.   So I bade him adieu, and mounting my camel,
was lifted into the air, and set out.   Abdurrahman
and Saïd followed my example, and, accompanied
by three strange dusky men, we wended our way
through the quiet squares and streets out into the
desert beyond.

Twice had the village and fort of Sheikh Othman
been destroyed by British troops before, in order to
extend our frontier in that direction.   The place,
and a little of the surrounding country, including Bir
Ahmed, were purchased by the British Government
from Sultan Ali of Lahej.   So diplomatically are
affairs to-day managed in Aden, that not only does
Sheikh Othman enjoy immunity from plunder and
robbery, but the whole caravan-roads passing over
the wide strip of country in the Abdali, Aloui, and
Dhala country are in a condition of complete tranquillity, and almost absolutely safe for native caravans.

Out into the desert, with slow patient gait, passed
our camels.   What a wonderful night it was !   I had
seen the desert before in other lands, but never to
compare to this.   In Egypt the nights are cold ; here
a soft balmy breeze bore on its wings the scent
of the mimosa bushes, which dotted the sandy surface.   A heavy dew was falling, and seemed to
awake every drop of fragrance of the little yellow
fluffy buds.   Above us a sapphire sky, brilliant with
stars and moonlight.   Around us miles upon miles
of sandy plain, shimmering silver.   Beyond the hum-

ming of the insects there was not a sound except the
thud-thud of our camels' soft feet upon the softer
sand.   So still, so tranquil it all seemed, that one
scarcely dared to breathe.   One felt that one was
passing through some strange dreamland, whose
earth was silver sprinkled with sapphires, whose
heavens were sapphires dotted with diamonds.

Those who have not known the nights of the
desert can never realise them.   It passes the pen
of man to describe.   It is like the periods in fever
when the fever leaves one, for it is these nights that
nature has given us in compensation for the burning,
scorching days.   It was but the first of my night-
marches—there were many more to come; yet I
never tired of them.   The rhythmic gait of the
camel, the gliding along under the myriads of stars,
never wearied me.   One could not weary of anything
so surpassingly beautiful.

At a spot, irrecognisable in the desert, our men
shouted to the camels to lie down, and we dismounted.
Saïd spread my carpet, while the Bedouins collected
the dry mimosa twigs, and by the light of the little
fire they lit I could see my camels regaling themselves with evident relish on the dry bushes, the
thorns of which were an inch or two in length.   Then
commenced the drinking of coffee, and the gurgle
of the hubble-bubble, until, calling to the grunting
animals again, we loaded our camels and set out.

As early dawn began to tint the eastern sky we

PALACE OF THE SULTAN OF LAHEJ.

entered the oasis in which Howta, the capital of the
Sultan of Lahej, is situated. The aspect of the
country completely changed. In place of the pale
yellow sand, dotted with stunted bushes, there were
wide fields of durra, or millet, growing in all the
luxury of a damp tropical soil. The fields are divided
from one another by hedges of rank vegetation, and
little channels, here above the level of the surrounding land, here running in and out amongst the durra
stalks, supplied unlimited water to the crops. From
amidst the tangled mass of dazzling green rise palm-
trees, many of them hung with trailing creepers.

Here and there grazed the pretty humped cattle of
Southern Arabia, tended by nude boys and girls,
who shyly watched the Christian passing by on the
back of his camel. And then the town—the great
mud-built city of Howta, full of wild-looking Arabs,
and dogs, and fever, the palace of the Sultan dominating the whole, and having the appearance that
at any moment it might slide down, and crush the
houses and huts and hovels around it.

Under the guidance of my Bedouins we put up at
a small native *café*, preferring to be at our ease rather
than to have to enjoy the hospitality of the Sultan,
to whom, thanks to Colonel Stace, the Political Resident at Aden, I bore letters of recommendation. We
easily made an arrangement to reserve the entire
accommodation of the *café* to our personal use, and
spreading the carpet and mattress, I settled in for an

hour's rest. The place in which we had taken up our quarters consisted of a yard enclosed in a high hedge of impenetrable thorns, forming a zareba. At one end was a large mud-brick room, thatched with rough matting, as was also a verandah in front of it. Besides this, the guest-chamber, there were one or two poor huts of mats in which quite a number of families seemed to exist. What with goats, and dogs, and fowls, and children, and fleas, the place was lively. A funny group we must have made, my men and I; but I had discarded my hat for a *tar-boosh*, or fez cap, as less likely to attract attention in travelling. It is curious the part the hat plays between Moslems and Christians. Apparently to them it is the outward and visible sign of the infidel, for as soon as one has changed it for their own more simple head-gear their fanaticism diminishes to an incredible extent. Of all European clothing, the hat forms the greatest barrier to confidential intercourse between Arab and Christian, and one of the names in common use in North Africa for Europeans is "the fathers of hats."

We had not been very long ensconced in our new quarters when a gaudy creature came to call. Apparently, from the number of weapons he bore, he was a sort of armorial clothes-peg. In fact, his whole costume consisted more of swords and daggers than it did of clothing, while a long spear added to the general effect. His wavy hair hung on either side of his face in flowing curls, and his arms were encircled above the elbow with silver chains, bearing charms and boxes containing mystic writings. He shook hands as though he had known me all his life, and sat down with a crash of his weapons that reminded one of the fall of a coal - scuttle. Coffee was soon prepared, and the hubble-bubble, murmuring away in a corner in the possession of Saïd, who had already changed his clothes and brushed out his curly locks, was handed from mouth to mouth. After a while my guest announced that he had been sent by his lord and master, the Sultan, to wish me welcome, and invited me to proceed at once to the palace.

Before, however, I tell of my interview with Sultan Ali Mhasen, some little account of Lahej and its rulers is necessary.

The tribe of Abdali, the inhabitants of Lahej, share with the Subaiha, Foudtheli, and Houshabi, the possession of the south-west coast of Arabia, from the Straits of Bab el-Mandeb, the gate of tears, to nearly one hundred miles east of Aden, and reaching inland an average distance of, roughly, some fifty miles. Of these, the Subaiha are the most warlike, being of a more distinctly wandering nature than the others; while, on the contrary, the Abdali tribe to whom Aden once belonged, whose capital is to - day Howta, are the richest and most peaceful, their habitations being fixed abodes,

except in the case of such as are shepherds, and are
thus necessitated to change their pasturage. As I
have already said, the town of Howta lies in a
great oasis, supplied with water from rivers flowing
from the highlands farther inland. This oasis is
richly cultivated, the principal products being durra
—*jowaree* the natives call it—cotton, and sesamum,
and more especially vegetables and fodder for the
Aden market. Besides palms, there are several
other varieties, one a luxuriant shade-giving tree,
called by the natives *b'dam*, of which a fine specimen can be seen close to the precincts of the
Sultan's palace. The soil produces no less than
three crops in the year, the climate being almost
equable.

The town of Howta is situated some twenty-seven
miles north-west of Aden, and extends over a large
area. There is no possibility of obtaining any
certain estimate of the number of its population,
which probably reaches as many as ten or fifteen
thousand, what with Arabs, Jews, a few natives of
India, and a considerable number of Somalis. The
extreme heat and dampness of the climate render
the place too feverish to allow of Europeans residing there with any safety, and even a sojourn of
a few days is generally sufficient to bring on an
attack of malaria. The water, too, is very bad, and
officers going to shoot there from Aden are warned
to carefully avoid it.

Although the present state of the territory of the Sultan of Lahej is one of tolerable peace and security, throughout all the history of Southern Arabia one finds it appearing and reappearing as the scene of battles and plots and assassinations. After the terrible massacre of its inhabitants by Ali ibn Mehdi in the twelfth century, it was several times taken and retaken, and the atrocious acts of cruelty of one, at least, of its conquerors, are recorded by historians. Omitting the many consequent attacks and wars which took place within its territory, we find it for five months of the year 1753 held by the rebel Abd er-Rabi, during which period Aden existed in a state of blockade. However, it was before this period that the present reigning family had obtained possession of the throne, their founder and first Sultan, ruling over Aden as well as the surrounding country, being Foudthel ibn Ali ibn Foudthel ibn Sáleh ibn Salem el-Abdali, who in A.D. 1728 threw off his allegiance to the Imam of Sanaa, and declared himself an independent ruler. Again, in 1771 Lahej was besieged, this time by the Azaiba tribe, who succeeded, however, in holding it only for the period of two days. Notwithstanding, in a history otherwise consisting almost entirely of massacres, wars, and murders, we have here and there a glimpse of a happier state of affairs, such as the sumptuous entertaining by the then Sultan of Aden and Lahej of the British troops

after the evacuation of Perim in 1799. Mr Salt,
in his work entitled 'A Voyage to Abyssinia,' and
published in London in 1814, gives a most charming
account of the then Sultan Ahmed, and Abou Bekr,
his representative in Aden. Wellsted also refers to
this Sultan as a remarkable instance of an Arab
chief whose great desire seemed to be to further
trade and receive foreign Mahammedan merchants
as residents into his country. His friendship toward
the British is attested in many works and accounts
of his estimable policy and sagacity. He died in
1827.

I have already described elsewhere the shipwreck
of the Deria Dowlat in 1836, which ended in the
taking of Aden in 1839 by the British troops. In
1849 a treaty was engaged upon between the Sultan
of Lahej and the British Government (as to trade,
&c.), and with several ratifications and alterations the
treaty still exists. The Sultan receives a monthly
stipend from the British, or rather the Indian, Government, for protecting the trade-routes which pass
through his country, and also certain other payments
in return for the ceding of Sheikh Othman and other
spots nearer Aden. In all, the Sultan draws a very
considerable sum from the Aden treasury *per mensem.*

Having said all that is necessary, perhaps, in a work
which has as little pretensions to being a history as
this has, on the general history of Lahej, I will resume
the narrative of my story at the spot where, under the

guidance of the gorgeous and muchly-armed soldier, I was escorted to the palace.

This building is a huge block of houses, built entirely of sun-dried mud-bricks, but plastered and decorated to such an extent as to give it the appearance of being of much greater solidity than a large hole here and there in the wall points out to be really the case. The principal building is covered with domes and cupolas, with the effect of a conglomeration of a cheap Italian villa and a stucco Constantinople mosque. However, from a distance the place has a very imposing look, and so large is it that on clear days it is visible from Aden. It is not until one approaches it closely that one discovers the incompetency with which it is built; for pretentious as it is, there are places where quite large portions of the mud-brick walls have come away, and at one spot one obtained an excellent view of the interior of a room on the first floor through one of these enormous gaps.

Passing through a large courtyard, we entered by a small door, and after ascending a rough staircase, and wandering along intricate passages, found ourselves in the presence of Ali Mhasen el-Abdali, Sultan of Lahej. The room in which the Sultan was seated was a large square chamber. A heavy beam of carved teak-wood ran down the centre of the ceiling, supported on pillars of the same material. The floor was richly carpeted in oriental rugs, and silk divans were arranged along the walls. Light was admitted by

large windows, over the lower portion of which was
trellis-work. At one corner of the room sat a group
of men, some five or six in all ; while on a table close
by were three handsome silver hubble-bubble pipes
from Hyderabad, tended and kept alight by a half-
nude Arab in a blue loin-cloth.

As I entered and kicked off my slippers—for having so far resorted to oriental ways as to adopt the
tarboosh, or fez, I held also to their custom of not
walking on their carpets in boots—one of the group
rose to meet me. He was a stout elderly man, with
a kindly pleasing expression, dark in colour ; and
although not strictly handsome, he possessed a
manner, common to most Orientals of position, that
could not fail to charm. Grasping me by the hand,
he led me to the divan, where I seated myself beside
him, and, salutations over, proffered me the amber
mouthpiece of his pipe and a bunch of *kat*, a shrub to
which the Yemenis are much addicted. This plant is
known to us as the *Catha edulis*. It resembles
rather a young arbutus in the form and shape of its
leaves. The leaves are eaten green, growing on the
stalk, and are said to cause a delightful state of wake-
fulness. The taste is bitter and by no means pleasant,
though one easily accustoms one's self to eating it.
An amusing remark was made by my Moorish servant
in the presence of the Sultan which tickled the old
gentleman exceedingly. He held out to Abdurrahman
a bunch of *kat*, which he politely refused. When

MY RECEPTION BY THE SULTAN OF LAHEJ.

asked by the Sultan why, he naively replied, "That is what the goats eat in my country," thinking it to be the common arbutus of Morocco. In Yemen it is considered a necessary luxury; and as it only grows in certain parts of the country, where it is carefully cultivated, and has to be transported often a long distance, it fetches a high price. That we ate with the Sultan of Lahej had been brought some forty miles or more that very morning, for it must be eaten fresh.

Sitting next to the Sultan was a Shereef, a descendant of the Prophet in other words, a tall handsome young man, clean shaven, and richly dressed. A gold dagger of great antiquity that he wore in his belt, and which he kindly showed to me, was as perfect a thing of its kind as it has ever been my lot to set eyes upon. The Sultan himself was robed in a long loose outer garment of dull olive-green, displaying a *kuftan* beneath of yellow-and-white striped silk, fastened at the waist by a coloured sash. On his head he wore a large yellow silk turban, surrounded by a twisted cord of black camel's hair and gold thread.

The hubble-bubble was a sore trial. I was gradually, under the guidance of Saïd, learning to inhale it; but to have constantly to fill my lungs with the strong smoke was by no means a pleasant task to a novice like myself. The inhaling, even through water, of the tobacco used in these pipes is by no means a thing

one can easily accustom one's self to, and for a long
time a whiff too many will bring on giddiness.   However, so attentive was the Sultan in handing me the
amber mouthpiece that I stuck bravely to the task,
although by the time I left I felt a sensation of in-
cipient *mal de mer* in a rocking-chair or the car of a
balloon.   As much of the smoke seems to go to the
brain as does into the lungs.   What with the pipe
and the *kat*, and the declining of Arabic irregular
verbs in a dialect I scarcely knew, I was not sorry
when, after an hour or so of conversation and agony,
I was allowed to leave.   Nevertheless, I had enjoyed
my visit to the Sultan Ali, whom I found to be
a pleasant - spoken kindly old gentleman, extremely
fond of showing off various treasures he possesses,
amongst which is a unique sword of Bagdad work, said
to be eight hundred years old.   Through the blade
is bored a hole, which the Sultan explained to me
was the mark that it had taken over a hundred lives.
From the condition of the steel it might have been
made yesterday, and would be quite capable of taking
a hundred more.   During my visit I had been watched
with great interest by two of the Sultan's children, a
little boy and girl, who, contrary to Arab customs,
were present all the time.   They were pretty dark-
skinned little things—the boy nude except for his
loin-cloth of striped silk, the girl dressed in a mauve
garment embroidered in gold.

Leaving to go, the soldiers who had brought me

into the Sultan's presence again escorted me to my
café, on the way to which we visited the palace stables.
There were a great many horses in the ill-paved yards
which serve as the royal stabling. Mats and thatch,
and in places rough brick roofs, keep off the heat of
the sun from the horses, some of which were very fine.
One white mare from Nejed was especially lovely,
though from the nature and heat of the country she
looked terribly out of condition. The pedigrees of the
Nejed horses are most carefully kept by their breeders,
and all over Arabia they are estimated as the very
finest to be procured.

The Sultan of Lahej has his own coinage, a small
copper piece of minute value, bearing the inscription
" Ali Mhasen el Abdali," and on the reverse " Struck
in Howta," which, by the way, is anything but true,
as they are made in Bombay, by contract.

Returning through the courtyards of the great mud
palace, I left the royal precincts, and, seeking once
more the quiet shade of the café, spent the heat of
the day in sleep, waiting for the cool of the afternoon
before sauntering forth to see the sights of the town
of Howta.

CHAPTER III.

LAHEJ TO KHOREIBA.

WHEN I awoke the heat of the day was over, so, under the guidance of Saïd and one of my camel-men, I sauntered out to see the town of Howta. The place presents, on the whole, an appearance rather of dirt and squalor than of what one expects the capital of an Arab Sultan to be like. The streets are narrow, and built without any idea of regularity, turning and twisting as they do in every direction; nor are the houses even built in any attempt at being in line. Here one juts out into the narrow byway, there another stands back off the street behind a thick hedge of bristling thorns. Nearly all the houses are surrounded by these zarebas or yards, into which the cattle are driven of a night. Strange mangy dogs bark at one as one passes along, and their bark is echoed from within by the yelps of puppies. There is, in fact, but little to see in Howta. Perhaps the sights best worth noticing are in the market, where under the shade of an enormous *b'dam* tree sit women selling bread, while the surrounding strip of sand is crowded by Arabs with long spears and their camels. Here also are exposed for sale vegetables, camel and horse fodder, and many other market products, which are sent on to Aden. Not far from this market are the bazaars, narrow covered-in streets with rough little mud-brick shops on either side, filled with cotton goods, for the most part of European manufacture ; a few gaudy muslins from India, however, giving a brilliant hue to some of these dusky little box-like shops. A whole bazaar is put aside for the workers in metals. It forms a thatched square, divided up by low walls, some three feet in height, like sheep-pens, in which the various metal-workers sit, each with his forge. The scene is a most picturesque one. The sunlight falling in through holes in the ill-thatched roofing strikes upon the burnished metal until the daggers and spear-heads sparkle and glisten like diamonds. The air is hazy with the fumes of the forges, and rings with the never-ceasing fall of the hammer upon the metals. And what workers! Great lithe men, grand in the exposure of their bare limbs ; their raven locks loosely falling upon their shoulders, and waving backwards and forwards with the motion of the workmen's bodies. The workmanship of Howta is rough. In spear-heads they excel ; but they fail in the silver-work of their dagger-sheaths to attain the results reached by the silversmiths of the larger towns inland.

Returning to the *café* where I had put up, I found
the camels ready to start, so mounting once more, we
set out. Leaving the town behind us, the way took
us for the first few miles through rich cultivated land,
watered by a careful system of irrigation, and gorgeous in its verdure. Emerging from the fields, we
struck into wilder country, torn up into great ravines
by the Wadi Lahej—a river that, in the dry season,
is but a tiny stream, but after rains a series of vast
torrents, its many channels becoming filled with the
huge mass of water, often carrying away much of the
cultivated land, and doing no little damage. Sometimes the trunks of big trees from the far interior
are carried over the desert—where at ordinary times
the sand absorbs the water to such an extent that it
never reaches the sea—and cast into the bay at Aden.
From this it can be judged how severe are the rainfalls when such comparatively rare occurrences do
take place.

The river which I mention here under the name of
the Wadi Lahej is also known by the name of the
Mobarat. It has two channels to the sea, but, as
already stated, is at most seasons exhausted by the
desert sands of the low-lying coast country. The
principal channel is the Wadi el-Kebir, or great river,
which flows out near Hashma, a small village in the
Bay of Aden, the other being the Wadi es-Seghir, or
small river, which empties itself into the Ghubbat
Seilan, a bay to the north-east of Aden, and formed

by the peninsula itself and by Ras Seilan, a point some thirty miles along the coast.

Wild and depressing the scene was. Ahead of us, almost as far as the eye could reach, stretched the desert, unbroken by even a single bush, and gradually sloping up to broken rocky peaks, which glowed a dull leaden crimson under the rays of the setting sun. We were leaving the oasis behind now, and no longer the peasants returning from the fields stood to gaze on us as we passed by; no longer their wild songs rang in our ears—songs sung by the sons of the desert and echoed by its daughters, as, hoe in hand, or leading the flocks and herds, they wandered back to the town. Now it was only occasionally that a warrior with spear passed us, on foot or on camel-back. Then night fell,—night such as we had experienced on the previous march, and which I have so dismally failed to describe,—night which fails all description. But we went on, the camels patiently plodding their way. It was eleven o'clock before we halted and spread our carpet under a clump of thorny trees, close to the river-bed, which we had been following since our departure from Howta. Here we rested for a few hours, our fire twinkling and flickering and bursting into little flames as we threw the thorny twigs upon it, for the night was chilly and a heavy dew falling.

There is no water, the Arabs say, more poisonous than this stream of Lahej, and we had been carefully

M

warned against drinking it; but in spite of this my servants regaled themselves plenteously from its feverish stream. There is no fallacy greater than to suppose the average Arab can go long without water. In cases of hereditary necessity perhaps they do, but in all my experience of foreign lands I have seen no thirstier race than the Arabs. They are for ever drinking. All my journey through the Yemen, my men were constantly alighting from their animals to drink. In the mountains, where the water as a rule was good, this led to no bad results; but their constant habit of drinking from slimy pools and nasty streams brought on attacks of fever in the cases of both Saïd and Abdurrahman. No more unpleasant position can be imagined than that of a traveller with two fever-stricken servants, both shouting that they were going to die, and refusing to take quinine because it tasted so nasty. The drinking of this water of Lahej brought on fever in both these men. I provided them with unlimited coffee, which, with boiling the water, does away with a great part of the risk; but, rather than have the trouble of making it, they preferred to drink the poisonous liquid. However, they suffered for their perversity.

It was dawn when we started again, pale - grey dawn, which struck cold and chilly. An hour or two of desert, unbroken in its monotony; but away ahead of us we could see the outpost fort of the Sultan of the Houshabi tribe, whose territory we

were soon to enter, and a few miles nearer, half
hidden in thick thorn-trees, the frontier castle of the
Sultan of Lahej.

We had hoped to make a good march, but fate
was against us, for after a few hours on the road a
gentle wind rose up. At first it was cool and refreshing, but as the heat of the day increased it became laden with fine grains of sand, and by no means
so pleasant. At length it became unbearable, the
stinging sensation as the sand struck one's hands
and face being most painful. Calling a halt, we
crawled under some thick bushes, the men hurriedly
arranging a strip of canvas so as to obtain the most
protection from its scanty folds. We were only just
in time, for a few seconds after, having crawled
under its shade, the wind increased in strength and
became a veritable gale. The sand, which up till
now had been but thin, commenced whirling up in
clouds until the air became darkened with it. Hud-
dling together, we tied our turbans over our mouths
and waited for a cessation. It required three of us
to hold on to the slender covering of canvas—a mere
strip that I used to put between the carpet and the
ground—to prevent its being carried away. The
desert wind was intense in its heat, and the burning,
gritty grains of sand found their way under one's
clothing and into one's ears and eyes until life became unendurable. I had seen a sandstorm or two
before in my life, but none like this. The poor

grumbling camels lay down and wagged their necks slowly from side to side, while the Arabs cursed. A sandstorm is lovely in a picture, and is exciting to read about, but personally to experience it is quite another thing, and for the three or four hours that we lay panting for breath under those thorny mimosa-trees we suffered exceedingly. So strong was the sand-laden wind that it was impossible for the men to go even as far as the river to get water, and our throats were parched with thirst. In spite of the suffering, however, one could not help noticing the extraordinary atmospheric effect. The sky took a brick-dust red hue, and seemed literally to glow, the fierce sun burning scarlet and fiery through it all, though at times even the sun was scarcely visible. Happily it was the only sandstorm we experienced on the whole journey, and I hope I may never see a second such as it was.

Almost as suddenly as the gale had come on it died down again, and during the afternoon we were able once more to push on upon our journey. Reaching El-Amat, a fort of the Sultan of the Houshabi tribe, I delivered the letter of recommendation I bore from the Political Resident at Aden, and, refusing the Sheikh's kind invitation to alight, pushed on. This fort, like that of the Sultan of Lahej which we had passed shortly before, is a large, square, mud building, two storeys in height. Useful as it may be in times of war as a defence against Arabs armed only with matchlock-guns and spears, it would not stand a couple of shot from any field-gun, unless the structure is so soft that the ball would go right through it, as is not improbable. Near this spot we came across a herd of gazelle, but they were gone and out of sight long before we came within range.

The tribe in whose country we now were is the Houshabi. They have always been on the best of terms with the British, and on the murder of Captain Milne in 1851, elsewhere referred to, they refused to harbour the assassin, a fanatical Shereef. By their position they have an advantage over the Abdali tribe, of which Lahej is the capital, as the river of the latter is supplied with water from the ravines and mountains of the interior of the Houshabi territory, and they have on several occasions in times of war been known to divert its course. However, happily, the relations of the two tribes are for the most part friendly, so that it is not often that they have recourse to such extreme measures.

On again over the desert, which, as we approached the rocky hills, showed more signs of vegetation and life. Here and there were Arabs tending flocks and herds and cattle, though what there was for them to graze upon beyond the thorny bushes it was difficult to say. At length we left the sandy plain and entered a deep narrow gorge at the foot of Jibel Menif, a high barren mountain. Here the scene entirely changed. Instead of over the open expanse of desert,

JTY-N

our way now led us between walls of rock, the path
often a mere track in the river - bed, in which at
places water was running, and at others had sunk for
a time below the surface.

Afternoon was well on, and the change from the
sunlight outside to the cool depths of the gorge was
a pleasant one, but the scene looked sepulchral and
gloomy. The rocks with which the river-bed was
strewn and the cliffs on either hand were of a curious
black colour ; nor did the scanty vegetation, consisting
principally of what the Arabs call *athl,* a thorny
mimosa, do much by their verdure to enliven the
scene, for in spite of their proximity to a stream
which made some pretence at running water, they
looked parched and withered and dry.

The gloomy effect increased as the evening came
on. Although the sky above us was still streaked
with the radiance of the setting sun, we in the gorge
caught only its barest reflection, and a deep purple
gloom seemed to settle over everything. At one spot
by a deep pool in the rock a caravan was settling in
for the night. The wild cries and singing of the Arabs,
and the groaning of the camels as they were being
unladen, added much to the weird effect of their
already lit camp-fires, by the light of which we could
catch glimpses of the wild fellows as they hurried to
and fro, spears in hand, preparing for the night.
However, we did not stop, but with an exchange of

" Salaam âlikoum," [1] passed on into the night. The darkness was complete, but the uneven state of the ground and the constant ups-and-downs in the path clearly demonstrated that we had left the river-bed, and were crossing country at right angles apparently to the streams and nullahs, judging by the constant ascents and descents.

A few hours later we caught glimpses of fires in the jungle, and one of the Bedouins creeping on ahead and exchanging a few remarks with the camel-men who were spending the night there, he called to me to proceed, and glad I was to cry to my camel to lie down, and a few minutes later to stretch myself on my carpet before a fire, in the camp of an Arab caravan, at a spot called Zaida. The villages in this part of the Yemen are few and far between, and what there are belong almost entirely to wandering tribes of Bedouins, who are here to-day and who knows where to-morrow ; so that the caravans passing up and down the rough track that leads into the interior have to camp where best they can, regardless of the whereabouts of humankind, being dependent upon their own resources for food and fodder.

We spent the whole of the next day at this spot, for the reason, our men said, of resting the camels ; but I rather think they had fallen in with fellow-tribesmen and friends amongst the caravan-men with

---

[1] The salutation of Moslems all the world over.

whom we were sharing camp. However, I was not sorry; for, anxious as I was to push on into the interior, the rest was by no means unpleasant, and I found plenty to amuse and interest in the people by whom I was surrounded. Fortunately, too, there were Bedouin shepherds in the neighbourhood, and fresh food was procurable, while a few thorn-trees gave a little shade from the sun's fierce rays. Amongst the caravan-men was a Turkish soldier, fleeing from the starvation and cruelty and misery then existing amongst the Osmanli troops engaged in crushing the rebellion in the Yemen. His neck and wrists and ankles were deeply wounded by the fetters he had been made to wear, for once before he had deserted but been recaptured. A very considerable number of these deserters from time to time reach Aden, whence, after they have made a little money— for they are always ready to work—they embark once more for their native lands, often some hill-tribe of Asia Minor. In no way was the hospitable character of the Arabs better shown than by their kindness to these Turkish runaways. As long as they were soldiers in the service of the Osmanli Government they were looked upon as lawful game by the Arabs, and any who bore a weapon was liable to be shot at any time; but as soon as they threw down their arms and sought the protection of the Arabs and their aid in assisting them to escape, they became their brother-men, their co-religionists, and the poor half-

starved fellows were fed by their *quondam* enemies,
and often given money to help them on their road
to places where their recapture would be improbable.
I saw many instances of this during the time I was
in the country, and quite a number of the Turkish
deserters spoke to me with tears of gratitude of the
kindness they had received from the Arabs. Happily
there were less melancholy sights to see and less
doleful stories to listen to during the day we lay
under the shade of the thorn-trees. A number of
young Arabs, youths learning the art of becoming
caravan-men, had brought with them their pets, for
the most part apes and monkeys, with which the
valleys of the Yemen abound, and great fun it was
watching them playing and jumping on the backs
of the camels. They were very tame, and confined
by no chains, being quite loose to go and wander
where they pleased, but never leaving their friends
the camels, which munched their fodder regardless
of the antics being carried on upon their backs. It
was difficult to say which were the most active, the
monkeys or their masters.

But still more amusing were the strolling musicians, dancers, and players on pipes and drums, who,
finding a little piece of level sand, exhibited their
strange dances before me. There were three of these
mummers amongst the Arabs. Standing in line,
they struck up their music, one beating a rough
drum, one playing on a double pipe, the other sing-

ing. As they sang they stepped slowly backwards
and forwards, at periods turning and twisting round.
Strange nude creatures they were, with long silky
hair and silver daggers, and the eye never tired of
watching their graceful movements.

Saïd and Abdurrahman took advantage of our
delay to cook bread. However, owing to the fact
that we had no baking-powder nor anything to take
its place, and that it had to be cooked in Arab
fashion by rolling the dough round a heated stone,
it was not altogether a great success. Hunger,
nevertheless, rendered it palatable. As for butter,
we had not yet broached the pot of ghee that
Saïd had purchased before we left Aden. It was
rancid then, and the few days of hot sun on the
back of a camel had not added to its charm,
though it had added very considerably to its flavour.
When we opened the clay with which the jar was
sealed the whole valley became full of its odours.
One could have run a drag with only a crust and
three drops of it. Once having opened the jar, the
Arabs went for it wholesale. It served them for
two purposes—for fodder, and as pomade for their
raven locks. The manner in which they applied it
did not make its consumption more appetising, for
they dipped their long fingers into the jar and then
ran them through their hair until the effect was
gorgeously shiny—at a distance. At close quarters
the odour rather negatived the picturesqueness. Of

course I could have brought stores from Aden ; but to have attempted to enter Yemen with anything like a caravan would have been impossible, as the suspicions of the Turks on the frontier would have been excited. I had decided to take as little as possible, so as to be able to pass as a poor Greek trader ; nor had I laid my plans unsuccessfully, for the scarcity of stores was well compensated by the facilities I gained on account of having so small a quantity of baggage.

Later in the afternoon we made a start. The road was dreary and desolate, continually ascending and descending, and strewn with black stones and rocks that rendered our progress very slow. Almost the only level piece we crossed was a great circle of rocky ground enclosed on all sides by hills, the whole bearing the appearance of having been the crater of a volcano ; and as all the surrounding mountains show signs of volcanic action, this hypothesis is not at all improbable. Late at night we reached the village of El-Melh, where were a few miserable Bedouin huts ; but on the inhabitants assuring us that they possessed neither water nor provisions to spare, and evidently looking upon us with some suspicion, we proceeded on our way. The track was rough, and one had to clutch on to the ropes that held our scanty baggage to the camel's backs to prevent being hurled bodily off down the steep sides of some nullah. At long length, camp-fires ahead told of some caravan biv-

ouacking there, a sure sign of water, and our camels
hurried forward, and without even a call to make
them lie down, wearily deposited us amongst a group
of Arabs seated round a few blazing fires. Their
spears, stuck in the ground before them, flashed and
flashed again in the dancing firelight; but the appearance of fierceness was belied by their kindly welcome,
and an invitation to dip my fingers with them in the
steaming pots of food. Watering the camels and
giving them fodder, we returned once more to the
fires, and spent the night in songs and story-telling.

Before daylight we were on our road again, following
for a little way the course of the river Sailet el-Melh.
The country here had become more mountainous, one
flat-topped peak being particularly noticeable. The
natives call it Dhu-biyat, but I can find no mention
of this name elsewhere. On the summit is a tomb,
that of a certain Seyed Hasan, about whom there
seemed to be traditions of his having possessed remarkable powers, but as to whose history apparent
ignorance prevailed, nor can I find any records of
any powerful Imam having been buried on this
spot. It is probable that he was merely some local
Seyed or Shereef, and that his repute has not reached
the centres of Arabian civilisation. The summit of
this mountain is said to be quite flat and rich in
pasture, and Bedouins of the Houshabi tribe have
built a village there, and graze their flocks and herds.
Near this spot the valley opens out, and one enters

the Beled Alajioud, a level plain of green fields, with
a river flowing through its centre. Here one leaves
the wandering Bedouin tribes and enters a land of
fixed abodes, for houses well built of rough stone
stand about the valley; and at one spot is a village
perched on a slight eminence, and crowned with a
square tower. This turned out to be the border
village of the Aloui tribe, to the representative of
whom—a village Sheikh—I presented my credentials.
There was the usual group of men and women and
children and dogs, the usual exchange of compliments
and banter; and although at first they had appeared
a little high-handed, we parted the best of friends.

The country hereabouts shows signs of cultivation,
large fields being green with the durra. As the sun
was very hot, we halted in the middle of the wide
bed of the Khoreiba river, and settled ourselves down
under a clump of oleander-bushes. The scenery was
prettier here than any we had seen, as there were more
trees to vary the dull monotony of the reddish-black
rock and the yellow land. We had been seated about
an hour when there came skimming along the river-
bed, mounted on a beautiful camel, a veritable Apollo
of an Arab, a specimen of the finest type of the
Yemen race, whom perhaps it is scarcely justifiable
to call Arabs at all, so much has their blood become
mixed since the days of Kahtan, the founder of the
Yemenite tribes, and Adnan, that of the Arab. However, the term Arab can be generally used, as there

are scarcely any discernible differences, except in traditions, between the Arab and the Yemen blood. Noticing us, the man alighted from his camel and crawled into the shade in which we were sitting. After coffee, wishing to give the new-comer an example of the powers of the Christian tribes—as he called them—I unpacked an electric machine I had with me in my sack of bedding, and administered a gentle shock to the beautiful Arab. He never lost his presence of mind,—he merely smiled, rose and girded up his loins, mounted his camel, and sped as fast as the slight little desert dromedary could carry him down the river-bed.

The camels of the southern district of the Yemen are famous for their breed and fleetness. They are slightly built, with fine legs, the very opposite to the heavy slow-paced camels of North Africa. Many are especially kept and trained for riding purposes, and their fleetness is extraordinary. However, this breed seems not to exist any farther in the interior than about eighty miles, as where the country becomes mountainous we find a heavy, shaggy, black camel, the very opposite to his brother of the Tehâma, as the plains which divide the highlands of the Yemen from the sea are called.

While we were still laughing over the flight of the Arab on coming in contact with civilisation in the guise of a small electric machine, two Englishmen appeared in view, riding horses, and guarded by a

considerable number of Indian troopers and a few of
the Aden corps, and followed by a large train of
baggage-animals.   I had been told before leaving
Aden that I might meet a surveying-party under
Captains Domville and Wahab, who had been told off
by the Indian Government to organise a survey of
the tribe-lands lying between the Turkish frontier
and Aden.   Although they had been successful up to
this point, they began here to meet with difficulties
on the part of the natives, which at length, after I
had passed on into Turkish Yemen, became so demon-
strative that guns were once or twice resorted to by
the natives, and the scheme had to be abandoned
before it was completely carried out.   I spent the
afternoon with them, and very pleasant it was.   I
was able also to obtain from them the correction of
my aneroid barometer, for so far I had not resorted to
boiling-point tubes, keeping what few instruments I
had with me as much as possible in the dark, so as to
excite as little suspicion as possible.

After dinner in the luxurious camp of Captains
Wahab and Domville, I sauntered back to find my
men already preparing to load the camels, and soon
after midnight we made a start.   It was a bright,
clear, moonlight night, but chill and cold, a sure sign
that we were ascending to the highlands, which an
altitude of nearly two thousand feet on my barometer
showed to be the case.   The Arabs shivered and
chattered as we pushed along through the valley.

Presently the road ascended on the left side of the stream, and we crossed a plateau at an elevation of a few hundred feet above the river. The cold as dawn appeared became almost intense, and I was glad to alight from my camel and run races with my men, getting often a long way ahead of the caravan. Then we would sit down and light a little fire of mimosa-twigs, over which we would huddle together to keep warm until the camels caught us up again.

Dawn changed to sunset, and the world became alive again. The scenery had altered. We had once more entered the valley of the Khoreiba river, and still the great, bare, rocky mountains rose on either side; but the valley itself was green and fresh, and the banks of the stream, which appeared in places tumbling and dancing over the rocks, again to disappear below the surface, were covered with thick jungle of dense tropical vegetation, the trees hung with garlands of creepers. Birds chirruped and hopped from bough to bough; great painted butterflies sailed by, rivalling the sunrise sky in gorgeousness; and monkeys and apes chattered and grunted on the steep mountain-sides. After the journey of desert and rock, the change was a delightful one. Spying a few female camels grazing in the jungle, we surmised that there must be a Bedouin encampment near, so, alighting from my lofty perch, I set out with a couple of the men to find them—no difficult task, as we came across them within the first half-hour. They had pitched their little mat huts in a natural clearing in

A Valley in Yemen.

the thick vegetation, where they sat idly about, the
women carrying firewood and milking the cows, the

men, each armed with his dagger and spear, smoking long wooden-stemmed pipes with clay bowls.

They received us kindly, and we had soon joined their little circle, and were chatting away as if we had known each other for years. Great laughter was caused by a very elderly female, with buttered hair —rancid butter, if you please—and greasy saffron-dyed cheeks, kissing me. The joke I could not for a time understand; but it finally turned out that the fact that I was clean shaven and in breeches led her to suppose that I was of the female gender, as in the Yemen the men wear loin-cloths and allow their beards to grow on the points of the chin, while the women decorate their lower limbs in tight-fitting trousers. The old hag, on being pointed out her mistake, laughed as much as any; and while I was engaged in scraping the saffron and butter off my blushing cheeks, went off to fetch us a big bowl of fresh goat's milk.

Shouts from our camel-men in the river warned us that we must not remain any longer, so pushing our way through the thick brushwood, we resought the river-bed and mounted once again.

At nine o'clock, the sun being very hot, we unloaded under the shade of some big umbrageous trees, and settled in for the heat of the day. At our feet ran the river, dancing and rippling over its pebbly bed, for all the world like some Highland trout-stream, except for the fact that above and

around it twined masses of flowering creepers and
strange aloes, while a palm-tree here and there
raised its feathery head above the dense undergrowth. Away on the opposite side of the river,

Castle of Amir of Dhala.

about half a mile distant, and perched on the summit of a high rock, loomed the frontier fort of the
Amir of Dhala, a square tower surrounded by some
lower buildings. The place looked a regular acropolis,
and seemed impregnable. On a gorgeous Sheikh ar-

riving, I presented the last of the letters which I had brought from Aden, for the Dhala territory was the farthest in touch with the British authorities, and beyond lay Turkish Yemen. Evidently he considered the epistle satisfactory, although he was unable to read it, and he spent the day with us there. A right good fellow he was; but his reports of the turbulent state of the tribes beyond, and of the murder and plunder with which the mountaineers were daily amusing themselves, were anything but reassuring. He informed me that the name of our halting-place was Mjisbeyeh, of which I found the altitude to be two thousand five hundred feet above the sea-level.

Off again in the afternoon, passing the picturesque village of Thoba, above which to the left we caught another glimpse of Jibel Dhubiyat, with its white-domed tomb. The fact that we had now entered the land of fixed abodes became every hour more apparent. At places were signs of skilful irrigation, while ever and anon villages of stone houses piled on to the summits of rocks peeped from amongst the green fields and the mimosa-trees. One of these, by name Aredoah, was particularly picturesque, although the surrounding country was more barren than it had been. The scenery, too, became very fine. The black volcanic rocky hills had given place to mountains of limestone, which towered above the surrounding

KHOREIBA.

country. Principal amongst these were Jibál Ahurram and Ashari.

At one spot a charming scene met our eyes. Under the shade of a great creeper-clad rock sat an old schoolmaster, book and rod in hand, while at his feet squatted a number of small boys, into whose heads he was apparently beating verses from the Koran. A regular stampede occurred at our approach, and the young *tholba*[1] rushed alongside our animals clamouring for alms. I got one or two to show me the books from which they were studying, and found them to be excellently printed copies of the Koran from Beyrout.

As evening came on we kept passing the flocks and herds, lowing as they came in from pasture, driven by, or more often following, some child, who, with wide-open eyes, would stand still and cease the music of its cane pipe to watch our little cavalcade go by. Not a breath of wind was stirring, and the smoke from the evening fires of the little stone houses curled up and up, all mauve and purple, into the cloudless sky. In groups the men sat about, under the shade of the trees, idly listening to the hum of the insects and the song of many a tiny stream. The whole scene was one of perfect peace.

---

[1] *Tholba,* the plural of *thaleb,* a name generally applied to those who have studied the Koran—members of the priesthood.

The track then entered a narrow gorge between high precipices of rock, from which echoed and re-echoed the cries of the apes and monkeys. We were entering the country known as Beled Ashari, under the rule of the Amir of Dhala,—quiet, peaceable folk, shepherds and tenders of flocks.

As we proceeded, the gorge narrowed until the scenery in the dusky evening light became almost oppressive. Just before darkness set in we arrived at our halting-place, at Khoreiba, below the village of the Amir of Bishi, where, under the shelter of a great *b'dam* tree, we settled in for the night. The village is built of stone, and situated on the left bank of the river, the collection of stone houses being overlooked by a strange pile of natural rock crowned with a still stranger tower, a position that completely commands the valley. The altitude of this spot I made to be four thousand feet above the sea-level. The spot was a charming one, with the green valley below us, and above the perpendicular precipices, too steep almost for any scrub to hang to. Here and there along the river-bed were shade-giving trees, which stood out black against the fields of young corn, as yet only a few inches in height.

The success of my journey depended on the next day or two. We were fast nearing the Turkish frontier. Should I be allowed to pass? To have to turn back would mean the most bitter disappointment. Each day's march was interesting me more and more in the country I was passing through, and very keen I was to carry my journey to a successful issue, and to reach Sanaa, the capital; especially keen, perhaps, as, with but one exception, every one at Aden had prophesied failure, and told me I was insane to venture into the Yemen at the time of the rebellion, when even in days of peace it was rash and unsafe.

CHAPTER IV.

ACROSS THE TURKISH FRONTIER.

WE had left the Amir of Bishi's village some way behind when the sun rose the following morning. The track continues along the river-bed until the valley terminates in a steep ascent. However, the old - world Arabs have built a paved way up the slope, which renders its surmounting much easier than it otherwise would be,—not that it is by any means a simple process as it is. Scrambling up on foot, we reached the summit some time before the camels, and were able to rest for a time and watch the poor grunting brutes toiling in and out the intricate turns in the path ; for it is a mere track winding through great piles of overturned rock, and along the edges of steep inclines. I found the ascent from the valley of Khoreiba to the summit to be over six hundred and fifty feet, giving us an altitude of nearly five thousand feet above the sea-level. The view looking back was a very lovely one. Below us lay the valley of Khoreiba, shut in with its precipitous walls of rock, under which, amongst green fields and shady trees, flowed the river, a streak of silver thread. Away beyond at the farther end of the valley one caught glimpses of the peaks of other mountains, rearing their fantastic heads into the clear morning sky.

When the camels caught us up we filled up our water-bottles at a spring of clear water and set off again. These water - bottles—*zemzemiya* they call them in the Yemen, and in Morocco *guerba* (plural *guerab*)—are a regular institution of Arab travel, nor would it be possible to proceed without them. They are made of leather, those in Arabia being cut into shape, while those of Morocco are the whole skins.

Now and then we would catch a glimpse of a herd of apes scampering away up the steep rocks with resounding grunts; but more often we could only hear their cries, for their colour does much to conceal them from view amongst the limestone rocks.

So cool and pleasant was the air at the elevation we had reached, that instead of remounting our camels, who, poor beasts, were tired with the rocky ascent, we strode out on foot. Leaving the village of Dar en-Nekil on our right, we passed through a gorge of low walls of rock, and then descended to the level of the plateau, which here extends for a considerable distance, broken now and again

by rocky peaks and hills. This plateau, one with
that on which Dhala is situated, may be said to
circle round Jibel Jahaf, a limestone mountain
situated just above the large village of Jelileh,
where, although not within their frontier as delimi-
tated, there is a small Turkish fort. The plain is
well cultivated, and ploughing was in active progress at the time of my visit, besides being dotted
with trees; but from the fact that the young corn
had not yet commenced to push, the country looked
somewhat barren and dreary.

Across the plateau all passage seems to be blocked
by an immense range of mountains, one continued
precipice without any apparent break. The range
bears two names,—the eastern part Jibel Mrais, and
the western Jibel Haddha. A few miles over the
plain brought us to a steep ascent leading to the
village of Jelileh. Although the absolute frontier
of the Turks is at Kátaba, a town a few hours'
distance to the north-west, they have erected here
a fort, and over a round tower perched on a hillock
floated the red flag with its star and crescent.

One of my camel-men was a native of this village,
and it was to please the good fellow that I decided
to spend a night there, as otherwise I should have
been tempted to push on and try to cross the
frontier that day. Wishing to avoid as much attention as possible on the part of the inhabitants,
I did not spend any time in the village street, but

alighted from my camel at the door of the yard of
my man's house, and at once entered his abode. As
a typical Yemen house of the poorer class, some
description may not be out of place. Like all the
dwellings in the highlands of the Yemen, it was
built of solid squared stone, and consisted of two
large towers, some thirty feet square at the base and
twenty at the summit. The lower floor contained
an arched stable, the roofing supported on pillars
of stone. To the next storey an outside stairway
led one. This floor contained a passage and two
decent-sized rooms, the walls plastered on the inside
and the ceiling made of wood. The floors, like the
walls, were coated in cement. The staircase continuing led one on to the flat terraced roof, round
which ran a stone wall some three feet high. The
whole showed a great amount of labour and no
little skill in its construction. The second tower
was larger, but being put aside for the women,
I did not of course see the interior of it. It
contained, however, four storeys. Into one of
these rooms in the men's tower I was shown by
my host, who, no sooner was this accomplished, was
flying all over the place stirring up his womenfolk with entreaties and curses to prepare a meal
befitting such a guest. Meanwhile from my window
I could obtain a very good view of the surrounding country, ay, and more, of my host's wives and
daughters. How ugly they were ! What little

attraction nature might have given them was completely concealed under their artificial adornments. Their hair, plastered with butter over their foreheads in straight fringes, literally dripped with grease, while their copper skins were thick with paint the colour of red-lead, arranged in a triangle on either cheek, as well defined as is that of the clown in our Christmas pantomimes. Their loose

A Girl of the Yemen.

upper garment was more attractive, being of dark-blue linen embroidered round the neck, sleeves, and edge in coloured silks ; but to do away with any grace which this simple and classical garment might give them, they encased their legs in ill-fitting indigo trousers, with embroidery round the ankles. However, my host was evidently very proud of his ladies ; for no sooner did he catch a glimpse of them peeping over the parapet of their apartments, or straining their heads out of the little windows, than he would shout vociferously to them to retreat, which they would do, again to reappear and continue their criticisms of the newly arrived stranger. Meanwhile the male relations of my camel-man had appeared, to join me in the feast which was being prepared,—men and youths and boys, nearly a score in all, who quite filled up the two rooms and passage of our apartments, while nearly every one brought his long straight pipe or his hubble-bubble, and there was a murmur and gurgling of water as we inhaled the cool smoke. Besides the guests who arrived to call we had other visitors, those tamest of wild beasts—the fleas. It is strange that while many an author has told of the friendly fellowship of the dog and the horse toward mankind, the intense love of companionship of the flea toward the human being has been neglected. There is no need to tame him artificially : the moment he is old enough to swallow food he becomes the friend of man—nay, more, he will never willingly part company with him, especially in Arabia. His only equal is the mosquito, and for affection he almost beats the flea. As I write these lines one has been settling on my hand, and on my refusing to notice him he called attention to his presence by a gentle nip— result, a large white lump ; and when I tried playfully to catch him, he flew away : they always do.

On my next day's march depended the success of my journey. Once across the Turkish frontier, I felt that unless any unforeseen event occurred I should reach my goal. But I knew how strict the orders were to allow no stranger to enter Turkish Yemen, lest news of the rebellion, which had for some months been disturbing the country, should leak out. However, I felt that I was attacking the least probable frontier of the country, and one where they would scarcely be expecting a stranger to attempt to enter.

A ride of only a few hours brought us the following day from Jelileh to the *jimerouk* or custom-house of Kátaba, situated on the south side of the Wadi Esh-Shari, and about three miles distant from the town, which lies to the north, off the caravan-road. The ride was a short but a hot one, and except that all the plain was under plough, the country seemed dry and desolate. Away to the right could be seen the large village of Thoba, a collection of towers on a rocky hill, from which stand up prominently the white domes of a mosque and tomb, forming quite a landmark on a scene otherwise a monotone in yellow.

The buildings of the frontier custom-house consist of a low block, forming a fort and a large enclosure for the camels and mules of the caravan-owners, the whole covering a large extent of ground. The lower rooms of the main building are used as stores for the goods in transit, while the portion of the upper storey not inhabited by the officials is divided up into small rooms for the use of people passing and repassing, being let out on hire at so much per night. The whole place wore a depressing and a depressed look. For three months no caravans had passed over the roads, and trade was dull. The goods on their way up from Aden to Sanaa lay strewn about the place, as there were no means for their further transit.

Three months before, the last caravan to go through had been looted, and a ransom of three hundred and sixty dollars had to be paid before the merchants had been released by the mountaineers.

It seemed strange to think that on that yellow building depended the success of my journey, and it was with anxious thoughts that I passed through its open gateway, by the side of which, in the depth of a cave-like chamber, an old Arab was brewing coffee. Dismounting in the yard, I sought a shady corner to sit down in while my men went and routed out the authorities. A few minutes later they appeared, and such a group they formed! First came an exceedingly dirty Turk in a filthy shirt and a well-worn pair of military trousers; following him appeared a gorgeous creature arrayed in purple and fine raiment, no less a person than the Sheikh Besaisi, well known for his influence amongst the Arab tribes, and by happy fortune a kinsman of the most disreputable and savage of my camel-men. His clothes, too, need description. On his bullet-shaped head he wore an immense yellow-and-crimson turban, wound round with a camel-hair and gold cord; flowing robes of dark-blue silk were fastened at the waist with a yellow sash, in which was stuck one of the most beautiful daggers I have ever seen. This *jambiya* was of exquisite silver-work inlaid with gold Byzantine coins of the reign of Constantine. A few rough turquoises in the sheath gave a tint of colour to one of the most beautiful weapons I ever saw. I longed to make a bid for it; but I knew that should I ever mention so large a sum as its value, my chance of getting on would be so much the more diminished, for it was certain that I should be gently squeezed before being allowed to proceed, and that did I let out that I had any considerable sum of money with me, it would make the squeezing a more serious process, and perhaps prevent my getting on at all, and certainly announce to the world in general that I was worth robbing. Following the Besaisi crept a wizened man of perhaps some thirty-five years of age, dressed in the costume of the people of Mecca. These three were the officials of the *jimerouk*, though they resembled rather three characters of opera-bouffe.

Salutations over, I was asked to ascend, and a few minutes later found myself seated with my hosts in a small, stuffy, and very dirty room. They were too polite to ask straight out who I was, so I began to open the attack myself. I had been to Turkey; the man who had not seen Stamboul had never lived! Glorious Stamboul! All the world over it was a pleasure to meet the Turk; he was always a gentleman, always kind and polite; and how inexpressibly glad I was to meet the Turk before me he might imagine, after I had been travelling all the way from Aden with only camel-men and a couple of uneducated servants; and would he accept a box of cigarettes and an amber cigarette-holder, which I had brought from

my little shop in Port Said with me,—where, by
the by, my wife and children were starving—(signs
of tears)—owing to this accursed rebellion; three
months the coffee I had bought in Sanaa had been
lying there, and for the dear wife and little ones'
sakes—(tears)—I was imperilling my life in these
strange lands to get my coffee down : meanwhile my
brother, a Greek like myself, was looking after the
shop; and how delightful the Turks always were,
&c., &c.   So much for number one, my friend in
the dirty shirt; now for number two.

Was this, then, the Sheikh Besaisi ?   No ; it could
not be that my infidel eyes were blessed with the
sight of his honourable corpulency.   His fame was
all over the world.   Port Said rang with his name.
His honour, his boundless wealth—(exorbitant old
tax-gatherer !)—his immense charities, were famous
throughout all countries : indeed this was a blessed
day for me.   (Box of cigarettes and amber mouthpiece)—number two dead.

Whence came he, number three ?   No ; it could not
be that his family was from Fez.   Mulai Idris, their
patron saint, might he protect me !   Had I known
that I was destined to meet a Fez Moor here, I should
have hurried up from Aden.   Fez, every street of it,
I knew, from the tomb of Sidi Ali bou Rhaleb to the
Dar al Makhzen : and here was Abdurrahman, a
Tangier Moor.   How good the Deity had been in
joining us together in the bonds of friendship !—

cigarettes and amber mouthpiece ; general embracings
and *tableau !* *Exeunt* officials.   Screams of laughter
from Saïd, which I had to choke by sitting on him
on the top of my mattress, lest he should be heard—
and then coffee.

No Englishman crossed the frontier into Turkish
Yemen in January of 1892.   No ; the only stranger
was a penurious Greek shopkeeper of Port Said, who
rode his baggage-camel.   He was attempting to reach
Sanaa to obtain some loads of coffee he had bought ;
and so great was his love for his wife and children
that he was running the risk of being murdered and
plundered in order to obtain money to buy them
food, and to save them from an untimely death from
starvation.   I think they believed my story : if they
didn't at first, a few dollars wisely expended proved
to them that it was true, and after two days of
artificial tears and real dollars permission was given
me to proceed.   But the squeezing was not quite
at an end, and my rifle was taken from me, on account of no arms being allowed to enter the Yemen
during the rebellion.   For this I demanded and obtained a receipt, and eventually, after eight months'
delay, the rifle.[1]   However, I would willingly have
sacrificed anything I had at the time, so long as I was
allowed to proceed.   It was an anxious two days, for
until within an hour or two before my leaving the

[1] This rifle was returned to me on the eve of my departure from Tangier for the Atlas Mountains in October 1892.

jimerouk I had not received any answer to my petition
to be allowed to proceed.

At length they told me I might go on. Meanwhile
Saïd had been at work. Our camels were tired, and
he had arranged that only one should proceed, a couple
of mules being supplied in the place of the other two.
This my men agreed to, as they preferred to hire
mules on, rather than have their camels attempt the
next few days' journey, one of the greatest difficulty,
and which necessitated as silent and as quick marches
as possible, as the country was in a most disturbed
condition. Happily the contract which I had made
at Aden stipulated that in country in which camels
travelled with difficulty mules were to be supplied,
and I had no trouble in having this carried out,
although, unfortunately, only two mules were forthcoming. The simplicity with which my animals were
changed for me seemed extraordinary ; but the fact is
that these caravan-roads are worked by " companies,"
relays of animals being kept at various spots along
the road for transporting goods from district to district or town to town.

No doubt the manner in which the country is split
up into tribal districts makes this necessary, while
again the natural features of the Yemen are such as
to render it almost impossible to take the same
animals for any great distance. For instance, the
fleet camels of the Abdali of Foudtheli districts would
be useless in the precipices and ascents of the country

between Kátaba and Yerim; while the mountain-mules suffer exceedingly in desert-travelling, their feet sinking deep into the soft hot sand.

As soon as permission was granted me to proceed I was off. I did not wish to give the people in charge of the frontier any chance of changing their minds, so at mid-day, when they had all retired for their siesta, we sallied forth from the gate and entered Turkish Yemen.

I had told more untruths in the last forty-eight hours than I liked to think about; but, curious to say, my delight at having crept through was far more keen than any remorse I felt for my wickedness. The road does not enter the town of Kátaba, for which I was by no means sorry; for under the walls of the little place we could see a large Turkish camp pitched, that of the division of the army under Ismail Pasha, which had come on here after the retaking of Dhamar and Yerim, two of the larger cities of the central Yemen. Giving them a wide range, we soon were out of sight of the camp, and after crossing the Wadi Esh-Shari, we entered wild broken country, the foot-hills of the great range of mountains that appeared to block our way ahead. A sad incident happened before leaving the *jimerouk*. A poor Turk, whom I had noticed slouching about the place in rags, came to me just as I was leaving. Kissing my hand, he besought my protection in Turkish, which an Arab in the Osmanli service

translated to me. His story was a pitiable one.
He had been enrolled in the conscription from some

Village of Aredoah.

village near Smyrna, and sent with his brother to
fight in the Yemen. At length, after much fighting

and many privations, he reached Kátaba, where the roll of the surviving troops was called. His name was not on the list, and it was found to have been a mistake that he ever left his native country. Ismail Pasha, then at Kátaba, commanded him to be stripped of his uniform and turned loose, on the ground that he was not a soldier of the Sultan's at all. This was done, and the poor fellow wandered away, a stranger in a strange land, until the Sheikh Besaisi took pity on him, and fed him and clothed him (!) at the custom-house. He spoke no Arabic, and the Arab interpreting for him was the only one who spoke a word of his native tongue. He prayed me to take him on with me. This unfortunately was impossible. The presence of a Turk with me would render me very liable to danger from the Arabs; but I advised him to try and reach Aden, where, being as strong and good-looking a young fellow as ever lived, I felt sure he would get work, and in time find his way back. Beyond giving him the wherewithal to find his way to Aden, I was unable in any way to assist him.

Rough as the country we were passing through was, it presented here and there little patches and valleys rich in cultivation. In many places the scenery resembled a lovely garden. The lawns were barley, scarcely three inches high, while trees stood here and there about the fields. Little streams and pools of water added an effect of coolness, while the rocky hills were clothed in plants and flowers, noticeable amongst them being a scarlet-flowering aloe and a variety of the euphorbia. Great ant-heaps, some six and eight feet in height, stood like sugar-loaves amongst the rich vegetation. After a glorious sunset, night came quickly upon us, and the scenery was lost in the darkness.

On we plodded in the dark, our little mules carefully picking their way over the rough boulders and stones with which our path, now a river-bed, was strewn. The people of the surrounding tribes had taken advantage of the rebellion to throw off any form of government, and it was therefore necessary to proceed at night. Once or twice we could catch glimpses of their village-fires glowing far up on the steep mountain-sides, and now and again even catch the yelping of their dogs, whose quick ears had heard the footfall of our animals on the hard stones; but the villagers took no notice more than to shout to one another, their voices sounding far away and sepulchral in the thick darkness. The river-bed over which we were travelling commenced shortly to ascend, and the path was by no means an easy one to get along in safety.

"We must wait here for the men," said an old Arab, an acquisition from the Besaisi. What men he meant I did not know, but as he seemed to be the recognised head of our caravan I refrained from asking. We dismounted and lit a fire in a hole in

the rock, round which we clustered to warm ourselves at its welcome heat : not that it was allowed
to blaze, for the Arab, fearful lest its glare should
attract notice, kept damping the wood sufficiently
to keep the blaze low without putting it out
altogether.

For a time we waited, but there being no traces
of " the men," we left the burning embers as a sign
that we had passed on, and continued our journey.

It was a picturesque scene this little halt of ours,
with the dark figures of the half-nude Arabs, each
one armed with a spear, bending over the glowing
fire, and one that will not easily be forgotten. It
was difficult to say which sparkled the most, their
polished spear-heads or their glossy locks. Every
now and again a bright flame would leap into the air
in spite of our precautions, showing us that the cliff
above was hung in clusters of feathery creepers, while
strange aloes and cacti appeared in the crevices.

Rougher and steeper grew the road as we proceeded.
At length in the middle of a rocky ascent a shout from
behind, answered by one of the men, announced the
arrival of the long-expected party, who had seen our
signal and were following us ; and a few minutes later,
in the starlight, for the moon had not yet risen, we
could discern dark shadows hurrying along after us
on the track. A wild crew they were too, six or
seven of them armed with matchlock - guns and
spears. Of all the antiquated weapons I have come

across upon my travels, these guns of the Yemen are
the most curious.   The stocks are straight, and end in
a lump like a croquet-ball, which forms the shoulder-
piece ; the barrels are long, and nearly always rusty.
A hole in the barrel communicates with a pan on the
outside, into which a little loose powder is dropped.
The trigger possesses no spring except a weak re-
bounding arrangement.   The nipple is formed like a
fork, into which slides the fuse, made of aloe-fibre
and slow burning.   When the trigger is pulled the
" match " descends into the loose powder, and the gun
may go off or no.   The chances are about equal, I
should think.

For an hour more we crept along the dark road.
Thorny mimosas tore our clothes and baggage and the
poor mules' legs, and at places threatened to bar our
passage altogether.   Then we left the path, and descending by a steep rocky slope, we entered a deep
nullah, half a mile or so along which a halt was
called, and my guides informed me that this was to
be our night's resting-place.   Fastening the strip of
canvas sheeting, or rather such as remained of it after
the sandstorm, over the boughs of a thorn-tree, as
protection from the heavy dew, we lit a fire and set
to work to cook our supper of tough old goat and
rancid butter.

This bivouac in the ravine below the large village
of Azab was the last night spent out in the open ; for
although we continued for the next few days to take

advantage of the darkness to push through the most difficult country, we were able to rest in the *cafés* of villages, and after Yerim, in the regular caravanserais, some of which had pretensions even to being clean and comfortable.

Next morning I was able to see more of my surroundings. We had spent the night in the rocky course of a stream, in some of the pools of which was water. Opposite us the hills rose almost precipitously, strewn with boulders, and here and there tangled in clumps of mimosa-trees and other thorny brushwood. Away up the nullah stood Azab, a village perched on the very summit of a high hill, a confusion of walls and towers.

We spent the day quietly under the little shade the scanty trees gave. A couple of the men went to the village to buy provisions, and returned with a bowl of rancid butter, bread of a thin consistency that would have served any purpose other than edible, from boot-soles to wrapping up parcels in, and a goat whose age was unfathomable. However, one cannot be too particular when travelling in such countries as the Yemen.

At sunset our mules were packed, and we set off once more, creeping out of the nullah so as not to be seen from the village above, the inhabitants of which would be only too likely to take advantage of our position to go shares in my belongings—probably forgetting to give me my portion, unless they did so

VIEW OF AZAB.

with one of their curved daggers. The last glow of daylight still hovered in the sky; the last rays of the setting sun still tinged with pink and purple and gold the huge jagged peaks of the mountains before us. Very grand it is, this range of limestone, torn into all manner of fantastic shapes, the peaks here resembling some bewitched feudal castle, there the tapering spire of a cathedral.

The track was as rough as usual, and constant short ascents and descents rendered our progress very slow. When darkness was complete, except for the glimmer of the stars, our men called a halt, and ranging themselves in line upon the soft white sand of a stream-bed, cried "Allah Akbar," and rose and fell with monotonous motion in prayer. Wild shadows they appeared in their nudeness and shaggy locks,—wild shadows that some fevered brain might imagine; but the odour of the rancid butter and oil on their hair proved their reality. No decent ghost would smell as they did.

Enjoining silence on every one, the men lit the fuses of their guns, and a couple going ahead to keep a sharp look-out, we pushed on. Like the glow of cigarette-ends, I could follow the spark of their guns as they crept along.

The valley becomes more distinct as one proceeds, the mountains closing in on either side, leaving but little level ground beyond the absolute course of the stream, and that was uneven enough. Hanging over

the river-banks were trees and thick undergrowth,
but the darkness prevented one seeing anything but
their outline. At length our path seemed abruptly
to end. Here a halt was called and we dismounted.
From this point commenced an ascent I shall never
forget. A winding path, a mere track in the face of
the precipices, climbs the mountain - side until an
elevation of over eight thousand feet above the sea-
level is reached. The night was as yet moonless, and
one could scarcely see a step in front of one, and it
was bitterly cold. Lightening the animals as much
as possible by dividing the baggage amongst the
men, every one taking his share, except Abdurrahman, who carried my shot-gun, we commenced the
ascent. Any moment man or beast might have made
a false step and alighted somewhere in the valley
beneath. Not only was the ascent trying, but it
must be also remembered that we were now in rebel
country, and that our discovery would mean certain
death, to myself if not to all of us. The very tribe
whose lands we were entering, the Kabyla el-Owd,[1]
had only a few months before thrown off the Turkish
yoke, and celebrated their day of independence by
cutting up their Sheikh into small pieces and distrib-
uting him over the country, as a warning to others.
Our party, including our new retinue supplied by
El-Besaisi, numbered in all some ten persons ; but
with the exception of my shot-gun and revolver we

[1] *Kabyla*=a tribe.

had no weapons worth considering as such, unless it
came to hand-to-hand fighting, when ten-foot-spears
may be useful. However, our numbers made any
attack from a small party improbable. Up and up
we toiled, often on all-fours. We had not ascended
many hundreds of feet before we found that our remaining camel was perfectly incapable of surmounting
the difficulties of the road, while his constant mum-
blings and gruntings threatened every moment to
bring the natives upon us, and already we could hear
their dogs barking in the villages below. Once or
twice, too, men called to one another, and lights could
be seen moving about. Then we would lie still and
hold our animals so as to ensure silence. At length
it was decided to send the camel back, and two of the
men undertook the job, trusting to be out of danger's
way before daylight. This made extra weights for
the men and mules, but they cheerily lifted their
burdens and our scramble recommenced.

I began to think the ascent would never end.
Steeper and steeper it became, until, two hours after
commencing, and having climbed over two thousand
feet in that time, we reached the summit, where on a
ledge of rock some humane person has built a well to
rejoice the heart of man and beast with its cool waters.
Here we rested for ten minutes, but more time we
could not spare, tired as we were, for a long march
had yet to be covered before dawn. Passing through
a gorge at the height of eight thousand one hundred

feet above the sea-level, we began once more to descend ; and scrambling down through thick undergrowth and over loose rolling stones, we reached the level of a valley, along which our road now lay, and through which flows the Wadi el-Banna, a large stream which reaches the sea, when flooded, at Ras Seilan, some thirty miles north-east of Aden. How the apes chattered and roared as we disturbed their night's rest ; and every now and then we could hear the stones rattling under their feet as they scampered away. Collecting our little band together, and examining our weapons, we continued our march in silence through the strongholds of the Kabyla el-Owd.

CHAPTER V.

SOBEH TO YERIM.

WITH this descent to the level of the valley commenced the most dangerous and difficult part of the
whole journey. The surrounding country was thickly
inhabited, and dotted with villages, capture by any
one of which meant the destruction of our caravan, if
not of ourselves. A long march yet lay before us
until a place of tolerable safety could be reached, and
there remained only a few hours more of night. It
would mean a fast and difficult walk at any time, but
now especially so in the midst of so many dangers.
The road had not been traversed even by Arab traders
or members of strange tribes for more than three
months. For this period the district had remained
closed, and I could not help feeling, as once more our
head-man enjoined the strictest silence, that I was
rather foolhardy in attempting to be the first to open
it again.

Leaving the track, we struck into the thick brush-

wood in order to avoid as much as possible approaching the villages. One, however, we were obliged, by
nature of the country, to pass much nearer than was
pleasant. This was Sobeh, the principal stronghold of
the Owd tribe. How silently we crept on ! But sure-
footed as were our little mules, they could not help
now and again making a false step, and rattling the
stones with which our path was strewn. When this
happened we would all stand still for a second, holding our breath to listen. Once a dog barked, others
took it up, and presently it seemed as though a
hundred yelping curs, intent on our discovery, were
doing their utmost to give warning of our proximity.
Happily they did not leave the village, but, after the
custom of Arab dogs, barked from the shelter of
their masters' homes. Nevertheless, the noise was
loud enough to wake a man, who shouted to another,
and a conversation took place. Seizing me by the
wrist, my men dragged me into a thick cluster of
bamboos, whence we could see a light, evidently
a lantern, flickering in the village only a few hundred yards away. It was an anxious moment; but
at length the dogs ceased their barking, and the
light disappeared. Waiting to make sure that all
was quiet, we stole on again, thankful at our narrow
escape.

Then the moon rose, but the cold was too intense,
and I was too tired to admire the lovely mist-swathed
valley and the broken mountain-peaks. Once or

twice more we awoke the dogs, and once again, too, a man shouted to know who was passing; but we did not hide this time, as dawn was approaching, and my men whispered to me that even as it was it would be a mere chance if the sun did not rise to find us still in the enemy's country.

At length it came, cold steely-grey dawn; then the sky flushed crimson and pink, and we put on our final spurt, driving the mules before us with sharp cuts from bits of rope, and hurrying as fast as our feet would carry us. The sun was nearly up when one of the men pointed out to me, a long way ahead, a solitary tower standing on the edge of a precipice overlooking the river. "Once there," he whispered, "we are safe; they are friends of ours." At length we almost ran. The sun would be up in a quarter of an hour, and the cold grey mist which at present helped to conceal us would rise.

A little before the great gold orb appeared over the mountains to the east, we forded the icy-cold river and scrambled up to our looked-for goal, Beit en-Nedish.

This village, standing on the very edge of high precipices, presents a most picturesque appearance. In the centre rises a high tower, the largest of these solidly built Arab *burj* we had as yet come across, it being six storeys in height, as far as one could judge from the windows. The summit seemed to be unfinished, and only half roofed in. Around it stood a

few low stone houses with flat roofs, while a little
farther from the
precipice was a
mosque, and a larger
part of the village.
A graveyard sur-
rounded the whole
on the mountain-
side. Near the tower

Beit en-Nedish.

were a few shady trees, adding not a little to the
picturesqueness of this strange spot.

A yelping and barking of dogs welcomed us, but we paid no heed to them, but straightway lit a fire by which to thaw our chilled limbs ; and setting some coffee in a rough earthen pot to brew, I rolled myself up in my carpet, and was soon fast asleep. When I awoke a warm sun was streaming down upon us. A crowd of laughing, chattering Arabs had gathered round us, and were seated in a semicircle anxiously waiting for me to awake. When I did so I was stiff and sore, and without more ado, pulling out some clean clothes from my sack of baggage, ran down to the river and bathed in the cool fresh stream, after which I joined the circle, whose centre of interest was myself—a thing the like of which they had never seen before. Meanwhile breakfast was ready, and inviting a few of the throng to join us, we said " Bismillah "—" In the name of God " —and dipped our fingers into the rough earthen pan.

What a glorious morning it was, and how fresh and lovely everything looked ! The dew still sparkled on the green trees and grass, the mist still hovered in the valley beneath, and the hot sun was tempered with a gentle breeze. It was like a spring day in England. How cheery we were, too, after our night's dangers and fatigues, all laughing and joking in the exhilaration of high spirits ! But our hopes for a day's rest were soon dashed to the ground, for my men received timely warning that it would be safer for us to proceed, and a few hours later saw us on the way again.

We had entered Arabia Felix ! On all sides of us were tiny streams, splashing and tumbling through fern-covered banks over pebbles and stones. One does not realise what music there is in the sound of running water until one has travelled, as the writer has once or twice in his life, over deserts where the muddy pools are two and three days apart. But the deserts and rocky valleys were all forgotten now —they seemed merely the imaginings of the past. Everywhere were green fields in which the young barley showed promise of rich crops, everywhere great shady trees and jungle covered the slopes. The sun was hot, but at that great altitude the freshness of the air compensated for it. My men went merrily on, singing and laughing, and now and again running races and brandishing their spears —and yet we had rested only two or three hours after our march of nearly twelve hours, during which we had covered some thirty miles of road, and what a road !

Here we came in contact for the first time with the mountaineers, a much finer people than those of the plains. They are, as a rule, taller and better built, their limbs being freer in action and their legs more gracefully formed, no doubt owing much to the fact that they are great walkers. Like the people of the plains, the men wear their hair long, shaving their

MAN AND WOMAN OF THE HIGHLANDS OF THE YEMEN.

upper lip but allowing a small beard to grow on the points of their chins. As well as the dark-blue loin-cloth, stuck full of daggers, they wear a thick sheep-skin coat, the wool on the inside, the rough skin being coarsely embroidered in black thread. This forms a very necessary precaution against the cold, to which these high altitudes expose them. The women, like their sisters of the plains, wear dark-blue skirts, embroidered round the neck and sleeves and on the breasts in coloured silks, and now and again in gold or silver thread. Their heads they cover with dark-blue hoods, often richly but coarsely embroidered. While the men are often almost divine-ly handsome, the women are just the contrary, being generally thickly built. No doubt the hideous tight blue trousers and the oil and paint on their faces tends not a little to disfigure them. In the cold early mornings the oil on their hair hangs in little solid drops on the points of their fringes; but as the heat of the day increases it trickles down their faces, washing away the red-lead-coloured powder, with which they so thickly smear their faces, in long streaks.

From Beit en-Nedish we proceeded on a three hours' ride, and crossing the river at a ford that might have been in the upper waters of the Tay, we ascended the opposite bank to Beit Saïd, a large and prosperous-looking village, situated on the west bank of the river amidst groves of shady trees.

Before reaching this spot two large villages have to be passed, one on each side of the river. They are respectively on the left bank Nadir, above which the Turks had built a fort, and on the right bank Ghadan—both large and flourishing villages, well and handsomely built of stone. The fort was now in possession of the Arabs, as, in spite of its commanding position, the Turks had found it untenable, and deserted it on the breaking out of the rebellion. With the exception of Ismail Pasha's camp and the custom-house at Kátaba, this was the first sign we had as yet seen of the occupation of the Yemen by the Turks.

The land, carefully terraced to allow of more cultivation, presented from a distance an appearance of a great flight of steps, so evenly was this immense work carried out. Although at this spot the terracing was comparatively simple compared with many other places, owing to the slope being gentler, it showed signs of an enormously laborious task. But, compared to places that we afterwards saw in the Yemen it was *nil*. At one spot I counted one hundred and thirty-seven of these terraces on the side of a mountain, one above another, and each and every one, as far as one could judge, higher than it was wide ; that is to say, the stone wall supporting the small strip of cultivated land was perhaps nine feet in height, while the supported strip was only six ! This is particularly noticeable in the coffee-growing districts. However, as it was in this valley of the Wadi el-Banna that we first came across this process of cultivating the soil, although it was well known to me in the Atlas Mountains, Madeira, and many parts of Europe, it struck one as showing not only a propensity for hard work not usually found amongst Arab peoples, but also no little amount of skill and engineering.

In other parts of the Mahammedan world the Arabs are exceedingly fond of making and planting gardens, and even trying experiments in cultivation ; but whether failure or success awaits their efforts, they allow the whole concern to fall into disrepair, and the fields and gardens to become thick with weeds. It is not usually so much a want of experimenting as a want of continuing that is the ruin of so many Arab peoples. I have known Moors plant gardens which gave promise not only of beautiful surroundings but of considerable profit ; I have known them plant them with all manner of fruit-trees, and build aqueducts to bring the water from some distant spring, a work of by no means little expenditure, and a few months later I have seen the place deserted, goats feeding on the young orange and almond trees, and the place run to wreck and ruin. But not so in these valleys of the Yemen. Here the supporting wall of every terrace was in excellent repair, here every little artificial channel and aqueduct brimmed over with water, and the whole surroundings wore not only the appearance of great laborious skill, but of the idea being present that the people were aware of the necessity of maintaining the results of their labours in a state of repair.

It was a trait of character I had never before met with in the Arab people, and I was immensely struck with it. In the Atlas Mountains, five hundred miles in the interior of Morocco, I have seen on a small scale the same industrious attention; but in that case the people are Berbers, untainted with Arab blood. In the country of the Gallas surrounding the city of Harrar one finds much the same; but again, however nearly the Somalis may be related to the people of the Yemen, the Gallas are no doubt a perfectly distinct race. It may be argued that the necessities of life and the nature of the country would render existence impossible were the people not obliged to terrace and cultivate their lands in this manner; but I have passed in many parts of the world where the same argument would apply, and found an entirely different state of things existing. I rather believe this attention to cultivation, and especially the growing of coffee, &c., to be due to the existence of true Yemeni blood in the veins of the people, apart from their mixed Arab pedigrees. There is little doubt that this system of fixed abodes and attention to agriculture could not have been introduced in the Arab invasions of the Yemen, but was existent there long before the time of

MOSQUE AT BEIT SAID.

the introduction of Islam. All the historical records point to this effect, and it was probably owing as much to this as to the natural wealth and beauty of the country that the province obtained the name of Arabia Felix.

We found the village of Beit Saïd to be by far the most flourishing we had as yet entered. A large open space divided a pretty little white mosque, half covered by trees, from the rest of the village. The houses were well built of stone, one especially fine, being of two storeys in height, with arched doorways and heavy wooden doors. This we found to be the caravanserai and house of a cousin of the Sheikh Besaisi of Kátaba, to whom my men were well known, and who quickly made us welcome in an upper chamber of the house, to which an outside stone stairway led. The room was small but cool, and we quickly unpacked our baggage and stored it away, settling in for a much-needed rest.

A crowd watched our operations,—a gathering of men, women, children, and dogs, who, open-mouthed and open-eyed, watched the strange little caravan arrive, whispering their criticisms to one another. However, they were quite polite, the presence of El-Besaisi no doubt keeping them at a distance ; for, like his cousin at Kátaba, he was no small personage here.

We found the people of Beit Saïd extremely pleasant ; in fact, the callers almost crowded us out of our

room, they were so many, a constant crowd watching
with the greatest interest the strange visitor. The
rest was a welcome one, and we hoped not only to
spend the day here, but to obtain, for the first time
for many days, a night's repose; but fate was against
us. Having turned in about eight P.M. in a portion
of the big store, where, except for the rats, I felt I
should be quieter than in the guest-room, I was soon
asleep, weary with all the anxiety and travel which
we had accomplished.

I had been asleep only an hour or two when I felt
myself quietly shaken. I asked who was there. A
voice whispered in my ear, "Hush! do not speak."
I struck a light, and as a wild long-haired creature
leant over me to blow it out, I had just time to see
that the man was a stranger. "Get up," said the
voice again; "you are in danger. Not a word, mind.
Give me your bedding and carpet." In the dark I
hurried into my clothes, while the unknown seized
my carpet and such baggage as I possessed, and left.
I waited for a few moments, when he returned.
"Your mules are already being laden," he continued;
then seizing me by the hand, added, "Follow me." I
followed him out into the quiet moonlit streets, and
keeping under the shadows of the houses, left the
village. Here I was surprised to find my mules
already laden. No one was stirring, and in the
bright moonlight we passed silently away from the
place without disturbing a soul. Our road was a

difficult and a steep one : at many places the track, under two feet wide, was cut into the side of a precipice, far down which we could see the white mists hovering over the damp valley.

The reason of our flight I was at a loss to understand, yet never for a moment did I doubt that there was a reason. I somehow, without knowing why, trusted the man who had warned me. He was a stranger, and as far as I could remember, as I watched him leading our little caravan over the awful road, I had never seen him before. Once in my life already I had been saved by a stranger, who had risked his own to save mine—an Arab too, but in a land far away from the Yemen. I need not tell the story here : sufficient that I arrived at his house weary, by night, my bare feet bleeding with the stones and thorns, pursued by men who had vowed to take my life ; and that he, good noble fellow, found me and took me in, bathed my blood-stained ankles, and tore up his own clothes to bind them in, and, after keeping me in hiding for two days, escorted me in safety out of the country. He died a few months later, foully murdered in a blood-feud. Perhaps it was the recollection of this that imbued me with so much confidence and trust in my new-found friend. That I was not wrong the sequel will show.

Sometimes a stone loosened by our animals' hoofs would fall, and, bounding from rock to rock, disappear into the darkness. At each of these occurrences our

guide would utter a guttural sound of disapproval.
Once or twice I ventured to ask him the reason of
our sudden flight, but was always met with a sharp
" Silence ! " in reply.   On and on, until some three
hours after leaving Beit Saïd our path commenced to
descend, and, slipping and sliding down slopes of sand
and stones, we entered the large village of Seddah,
now wrapt in sleep; then on through the village of
Mundah, and out into the open country again.   The
dogs barked a little, and one or two men, armed with
spears, accosted us, but, after a few words whispered
with our men, we passed on again.   It is at Seddah
that the valley turns to the west, and here the Wadi
Thuba flows into the Wadi Banna.   This latter river
has a direction almost north and south, and although
the Banna is the main stream, the other continues
the general direction of the valley.

An hour later, leaving the valley and mounting a
steep ascent, we crossed an elevated plateau, finally
arriving at the village of Ṣôk el-Thuluth.   I had been
given no idea of whither we were going or where our
new guide considered it safe for us to rest ; and when,
on nearing the village, he told me that I might stay
there as long as I liked, it was a most pleasant surprise.   The streets of the little place were deserted
except by the dogs; but after knocking long and
loudly at a door, we succeeded in awakening a
woman, who turned out to be the proprietress of the
small *café* and caravanserai of the place.   She was

a good kindly soul, and did not grumble at being
turned up at one A.M. on a cold morning. Admitting
us into a cave-like room with a stone arched ceiling,
reeking with the pungent odours of strong tobacco
and coffee—not to mention the odours of its Arab
occupants, who lay sleeping about the floor rolled up
in their dirty sheepskin coats — she lit a fire, put
water on to boil, and then commenced by violently
kicking the Arabs in order to awake them, calling
to them to turn out and make room for a more
honoured guest. I persuaded her to leave them in
peace,—more out of regard, it must be said, for my
own slumbers than for theirs ; and calling to Saïd
and Abdurrahman to make up my bed on the roof,
was soon asleep.

When I awoke it was dawn. What a sight met my
eyes ! Never had I before, and I think never since,
seen such a view as lay before me. Sôk el-Thuluth,
or " Tuesday market," as its name implies, is situated
above the junctions of the Wadi Banna and Wadi
Thuba, on a spur of the mountains of the main
valley. Below me lay the great valley up the straight
course of which we had been travelling for the last
two nights. Over its green fields floated a transparent hazy mist, through which I would watch the
river sparkling and flashing like a silver serpent, as it
passed on its way to the desert and the sea. Along
its banks the dark-foliaged trees stood out clear and
defined. On either side of this silver streak lay ter-

raced fields, rising step by step from the water's
edge to where the mountain-slopes became too steep
for cultivation. Here they were covered with thick
jungle undergrowth, while above rose precipice upon
precipice, crowned, thousands of feet in the pink
morning sky, by broken crags and pinnacles of rock,
touched with snow. At my very feet, for I was on
the house-top, the villagers, rejoicing in the glorious
morning, were passing out to their labours, and the
flocks and herds bleated as they sought their pasturage. Women carrying beakers wended their way to
the spring; while the men, spears in hand, their long
glossy locks tumbling in unrestrained glory over the
shoulders, added a fierce element to a scene of the
most perfect peace and beauty. It was worth all the
desert travel and all the dangers of our night marches
to see what I saw then. This was Arabia Felix!
As I gazed the mists rose, every detail in the valley
became distinct : little villages far below, crowning the
rocky mounds on which the Arabs of the Yemen so
love to build, stood out from the green fields all grey
and severe, each a fortress in itself, with its battle-
ments and towers. Around the pink-and-gold crags
hovered little fleecy clouds, attracted by the small
patches of snow — now hiding, now disclosing the
grandeur of the mountain pinnacles.

All our dangers were over; from here our road was
safe. We were soon to enter the great plateau of the
central Yemen, now safely once more in the hands

of the Turks, though woe betide the Osmanli soldier who found himself alone and without protection. As I looked upon that glorious valley, more glorious than ever now that the sun had risen, I could not realise how exciting a time we had experienced in passing through it, so lovely, so quiet, so peaceful it seemed.

Calling to Saïd, I told him to send me the man who had led us to Sôk el-Thuluth the night before.

He had gone!

Never a word of thanks, never a reward! He had left me sleeping, and gone back to his own affairs and to his own life. Like the character in some play that appears but once, so had this Arab come and gone. My men had tried to stop him, had tried to keep him until I awoke, promising him a reward, but he had laughed and shaken his raven curls, and, spear in hand, girded up his loins and vanished. Strange good fellow! he saved my life, and never even gave me the opportunity of thanking him!

We had left one of our men the night before behind us at Beit Saïd. He had gone off in the evening to supper in the house of a friend, where he had slept, unaware of our flight. In the early morning he had found us gone, and followed us, not by the roundabout mountain-track we had come by, but by the main road.

He solved the mystery of our flight, for but a few miles from Beit Saïd he found the road held by some forty men, armed to the teeth, whose object was my plunder. How little the poor fellows would have got! A few dollars and a little shabby clothing, an old carpet and a mattress, and that was about all. But they had imagined that I was a trader taking up great sums of money, and had resolved my death—for life is cheap out there—and the plundering of my goods. I asked our man what they had said to him. He replied that they had asked after me, and that finding I had been warned and escaped them, they went off laughing and swearing, apparently rather amused at the whole episode.

Our rest had done us all good, and we set out with light hearts, knowing that no probable dangers lay ahead.

The path leads one along the east side of the valley, at a great height above the river, often, like that we had traversed the night before, only a footway cut in the edge of the precipices. Here for the first time we came across the coffee-plant, growing amidst tumbling waterfalls on terraces built up against the steep mountain-side. Everywhere was water, here in artificial channels, there in tiny streamlets. Wild flowers abounded, and in places the walls of rock were green and white with jasmine. A thousand feet below us were the villages, on to the roofs of the houses of which we looked from above. It seemed but a step from us to them. At one spot my men pointed out where a short time before a camel and its load had fallen from an overhanging rock. It never touched the precipice, they said, until it fell upon a ledge they pointed out to me hundreds of feet below, and thence it bounded into the valley.

Rich in the extreme is this part of the country, owing to its everlasting supply of water, and many are the tales the Arabs of the plains tell of it. Beled el-Hawad they call it, of which Howra is the chief village,—a place like a feudal castle built on a pile of rocks.

After a time the road turns to the right, and, following the course of a small stream, ascends a valley. To the left of this valley, on the very summit of a high mountain, is the village of Ofar, to reach which necessitates a climb of a thousand feet or more from the road. At several places one passes drinking-fountains, erected, like the great tanks we were afterwards to meet with in the plateau, for the refreshment of man and beast. They are simple affairs, but excellently built. In form they are usually square, and domed, some six feet each way perhaps. A trough on the outside supplies the water for the animals, while a hole in the wall, large enough for one to insert one's head through, is for human beings. Within the water rises to the level of this hole, being carried off by an overflow pipe into the trough below, so that the clear liquid just reaches the level of one's lips, while the roof above keeps it fresh and cool. These fountains, common all over the Yemen, have been

usually erected by private philanthropists for the
benefit of their fellow-men.   Unlike the custom in
England, no flowery inscription tells the world the
name or the generosity of the builder—they are the
memorials of anonymous benefactors.   Here, too, we
came into contact for the first time with the mountain
camel—a very different beast from that of the Tehāma
and desert, being a rough-haired, heavily-boned creature, usually black in colour and the picture of ugli-
ness.   Those of Lahej and the surrounding country,
renowned throughout Arabia, are light in colour and
remarkably finely built, and often exceedingly pretty.
To those who think that the camel is essentially a creature of the desert, and incapable of traversing with
ease stony or rocky country, the fact that we were
passing caravans of camels nearly eight thousand feet
above the sea-level, and on the worst possible roads,
must seem strange.   It is well known, of course, that
the camel of Central Asia traverses mountainous
country, but I doubt if many are aware that it forms
also the beast of burden in the extreme highlands of
the Yemen, travelling over roads which one would
have thought impassable almost for a mule.   Yet so
it is.

At length the end of the little valley was reached
at an altitude of only a little under nine thousand
feet above the sea-level.   A slippery rocky path winds
up the last few hundred yards of the ascent, which is
extremely difficult to surmount, both for man and

beast, for the constant traffic of centuries has polished the surface until it shines like glass.

Here the beauty ends, for one has reached the plateau of central Yemen—a vast plain lying at an average altitude of about eight thousand feet above the sea, broken only by hideous ledges of black volcanic rock, which crop up here and there from its level surface. It was too early yet in the year for the young grain to show; and the scene that met our eyes, as we rested ourselves and our mules after

Inscribed stone at Munkat, near Yerim.

the steep climb, was a dreary one—miles of yellow level plain, and black jagged rocks. A short but steep descent brings one to the level of the plateau, over which, with but little exception, the road passes from this spot as far as Sanaa, the capital.

The natives have made use of the ledges of rock, which appear in every direction, as sites for their villages, many of which are perched on the extreme summits, while others lie on the slopes. At one of these—by name Munkat—we stopped for a little

while, to see the place and some curious Himyaric
remains still existing therein.

This is, I think, the first mention I have made of
the strange people, descendants of Himyar, who formerly inhabited the Yemen ; but rather than enter into any account of them and of other historical matters
at this point, I have reserved these questions for
separate chapters, as I have also done in the case
of the geography, trade, and general description of
the Yemen. It has been my wish, as far as possible,
to separate the account of my journey from other
and more important matter, so that each may be
taken separately. In all matters historical and geographical, I have consulted, as far as has been in my
power, the best authorities upon the subject; but in
the account of my own travels I have thought it expedient, instead of breaking the narrative with incur-
sions into more serious subjects, to omit, except in
cases in which it may illustrate and explain more fully
than would otherwise be the case, nearly all reference
to historical or political affairs.

Munkat is a walled village containing a considerable number of houses, one of which, a kind of fort, is
curiously perched on an enormous boulder, and a pretty
white mosque, surrounded by tanks of good water.
Built into the wall of the mosque are stones inscribed
in Himyaric characters, and some also in Kufic.
Copies of the former were, I believe, taken some
years ago by Dr Glaser. In another part of the

village is a white marble column, some eight or ten feet in height, of Himyaric origin, which is said by the villagers to have appeared suddenly at this spot. The ignorance of the natives in this part of the country is astonishing; for out of many stones they showed me, some were in Arabic and some in the Himyaric character, but the inhabitants were uncertain as to which was which. They seemed, however, to reverence these remains to some extent, as they had carefully built them into the walls. At one spot, over a doorway and in a prominent position, they had carefully placed a marble stone containing the first chapter of the Koran — "Bismillah Alrahman Alrahim," &c.—upside down. When I told them of their mistake, it was quite sad to hear their excuses. "We are only poor people," they said, "and we are terribly taxed. We have to till the soil to feed ourselves and the Osmanli Pashas, and there is no time to learn to read or write." In many parts of the country to such an extent do they have "to feed the Osmanli Pashas," that they scarcely get ought to eat themselves. It is the old tale of cruelty and oppression, of extortion and corruption.

The regard shown by the poor villagers of Munkat for these inscribed stones is not by any means uncommon, a great reverence for writing being innate in all Arab peoples. I once had an Arab servant, himself perfectly illiterate, who treasured a torn manuscript copy of the 'Arabian Nights.' Its contents he

did not know, nor had he ever taken the trouble to
find out : that it was a *book* was sufficient for him,
and he carried it about as a sort of talisman. In
spite of its good luck, it did not keep him out of
prison, when one day he helped himself to things that
weren't his.

One of the most beautiful sights to be seen upon
the plateau of the Yemen are the lizards—little creatures of gorgeous metallic blue, now pale turquoise,
now transparent sapphire, as the sunlight dances on
their backs. In no other part of the world have I
come across such gorgeously coloured reptiles, although
I have seen the same lizard, but less brilliant in hue,
in the mountains of the Zarahoun, to the north of
the road between Fez and Mequinez, in Morocco.

An hour or two more of winding path and we were
in sight of Yerim, one of the principal towns of the
Yemen, which but a short time before had been taken
by the Arabs in the rebellion, and retaken by the very
Ismail Pasha whose camp we had seen at Kátaba.

CHAPTER VI.

THE immediate approach to Yerim is over a level plain a mile or two in width, across which, immediately in front of one, lies the town—a poor enough looking place, lying half on the level ground and half on the steep slope of a mountain, Jibel Samára. This flat ground is dotted in places with tanks, and here the townspeople congregate to do their washing, and many a pretty group we passed of men, women, and children engaged in that wholesome pursuit. Eastern washing processes are too well known to need any description here : suffice it to say that it is generally performed by men, whose one desire seems to be, by stamping on the clothes and beating them with large stones, to see how many fragments they can tear them into. They are generally successful in sending the things back in shreds. It must be an invigorating profession ; for the fact that one places the clothes upon a rock, and then proceeds to dance first on one leg and then on the other with all the energy and

strength one possesses, at the same time issuing a
series of low cries, must tend to strengthen not only
the limbs but the lungs also !

We did not stay, however, to watch the washers,
but hurried on into the town ; for although I had
some days before successfully crossed the frontier of
Turkish Yemen at the *jimerouk* near Kátaba, this
was the first time I was to find myself in a Turkish
garrisoned town.

As soon as we had approached the place Turkish
soldiers became apparent, and a miserable crew they
were. A few were sauntering about near the gate,
laughing and talking to others who leaned over the
parapet of the old tower that forms one corner of the
fortified entrance to the place. Passing through the
gateway without any particular notice being taken of
us, we proceeded by narrow streets to an open square,
which serves as a market, and entered the huge doorway of a large caravanserai or khan. This place,
typical of the country, calls for some description.
The building was evidently an old one, the material
used being stone on the lower storeys, and above sun-
dried bricks. An archway led one into a large covered
space, some ten or fifteen yards in width, and perhaps
thirty in length. There was no light admitted except
from the great doorway and a curious barred window
above it. This portion of the khan was of great
height, the roof of the building forming the only
obstacle between it and the sky. This roof was

UPPER FLOOR OF A KHAN AT YERIM.

supported by large arches on buttresses running out from the wall on either side. A series of brick fire-places for charcoal ran along one side of the building, divided from one another by low brick seats, where the Arabs could sit and brew their own *keshour*, or drink of coffee-husks. Farther in the space served as a stable, and there were quite a number of camels, mules, and donkeys within its precincts. The opposite side to that on which the stoves were was taken up by a staircase leading to a long gallery. Here the better class of people, such as merchants and native sheikhs, congregated. The buttresses supporting the roof divided the gallery into compart-ments, and it seemed to be the custom for a party to engage one for themselves, where they would spread their carpets and smoke their hubble-bubbles, calling to the khan servants below for their coffee and food, and charcoal for their pipes. One end of this gal-lery, on the left of the staircase, formed a little room, which I was able to procure for my use. The fact that it was built immediately above the kitchen, and that the thickest of wood fumes crept up between the ill-laid boards, did not add to my comfort. The ceiling and walls of the whole building were black with the smoke of ages, but the scene was a most picturesque one, and I sat at the doorway of my little chamber and sketched the place.

However, I was not to be left very long in peace, for an impudent young Turk came and began to

search my luggage, and to speak in such an imperti-
nent manner that he had to be ejected. I knew that,
whatever orders he might have had, he would have
received none that would allow of his conducting
himself in this way—for the Turk, be he what he may,
seldom if ever fails to be polite. There is an innate
manner in him that is always charming, in spite of
the many other drawbacks to his character.

I called on the Kaimakam a little later and told
him what had happened, saying that I was quite
prepared to have my luggage searched, but asking
that I might be treated with a certain amount of
decent respect. The Turk of whom I complained
was sent for, and such wrath did the Kaimakam show
with him that the young man, a junior clerk in one
of the Government offices, had to ask me to beg the
Governor to forgive him, which I readily did. I
found my host as pleasant and gentlemanly as any
Turk I met in the country, and he insisted on my
spending an hour with him and his brother officers.
I showed him my passport, for here there was no
longer any need to pretend that I was a Greek trader,
and he seemed much impressed with the number
of seals and stamps with which it was covered. Of
what value the wording and decoration of this British
passport was at Sanaa will be told anon. But more
astonished still was his Excellency at the fact that I
had pushed through the Owd tribe and arrived from
Kátaba—for, as he said, the road had been impass-

able for many months, and he laughed heartily at an Englishman having been the first to open it again. Yerim, he said, was the dullest of dull places, and he longed for the society and gaieties of his native town —some out-of-the-way spot in Asia Minor, the name of which I had never even heard.

Returning from his residence to the khan, he followed me half an hour later and returned my call, accompanied by a couple of his officers. However, the fact that one could scarcely see across the room for smoke did not tend to detain him long, and I was soon left to my own devices.

As soon as it was cool enough, under the guidance of Saïd, who knew the place well, I sauntered out and strolled through the bazaars; but although I wore on my head a Turkish fez, all sorts of rumours had been spread about concerning me, and I was the whole time the centre of a large crowd, who, though they pressed me rather hard, were polite but dirty, so that I found it advisable after a short time to beat a retreat.

Yerim apparently has no great pretensions to antiquity, although there formerly stood on the same spot, or somewhere in the immediate neighbourhood, a city of the name of Dhu-Ruayn. The ancient capital of this district is Zafar, the ruins of which, lying some miles to the south-east, are still visible on the summit of a circular hill.

There is but little to see in Yerim. The town is

essentially a poor one, and although built partly on the slope of a mountain where stone is procurable, the houses are almost entirely composed of sun-dried bricks. Dirt and squalor abound on every side, and the streets of narrow bazaars show no signs of any great commerce or trade. What little importance the place can lay claim to is owing to the fact that it lies on the main road from Sanaa to Aden, and is a garrisoned city. Like Dhamar, it fell into the hands of the Arabs during the rebellion at the end of 1891, but was retaken by Ismail Pasha, whom we had seen a month or two after its recapture, encamped at Kátaba. The Arabs, however, seem to have gone to no excesses ; and beyond taking prisoner the Kaimakam, who was still at this time in the hands of the Imam at Sadah, and his officers, behaved with great leniency toward the Turks, many of whom threw in their lot with the Arab cause.

During the evening I received many callers, who came probably from curiosity rather than from any other reason. Amongst them were several of the "Ashraf," of the family of Ahmed ed-Din, the leader of the rebellion, who had seen all through that their cousins' cause was a hopeless one, and had remained neutral during the war. I found them exceedingly pleasant, and they conversed for a long time about their country. One was especially a fine man, young and exceedingly handsome. As is the custom amongst the nobility, these guests all had closely-

shaven heads. One or two of them were richly
dressed in silk robes, and wore daggers of exquisite
silver and gold work. It was late before I got rid of
the last of them, and was able to seek a few hours'
rest before starting again.

At dawn we were off, our caravan augmented by a
couple of Arab soldiers in the service of the Turks,
who, by the by, would have proved of little advantage in an attack, as they were armed solely with
spears; but in all probability they were sent to
watch my movements. The Turks employ a very
considerable number of these soldiers in their service, many being of the class of "Akhdam," probably descendants of the Abyssinians who invaded
the Yemen in A.D. 525; while others come from
Yaffa and Hadramaut, and are ready to fight against
any one so long as pay and booty are to be
obtained.

We left Yerim by a gate to the north of the city,
near which is a picturesque stone mosque, with a
white dome, which I had failed to notice the previous day.

Emerging through the gateway, the track proceeds
for a time along a straight level road, lying below
the slopes of Jibel Samára, on which a few Arabs,
mounted on ponies, were galloping to and fro, with
the evident purpose of thrilling me with their eques-
trian powers. They were good riders certainly, and
very picturesque they looked with their long black

hair waving behind them, and the rising sun sparkling on their polished spear-heads.

The level surface of the plateau over which we
were passing made one forget the great altitude we
had reached ; and such is the appearance of the surrounding country, that one could scarcely realise that
one was not on some low level plain, but at an elevation of over eight thousand feet above the sea-level.

At one spot, however, this is forcibly brought to
one's mind, for the road passes close to the edge of
a deep narrow gorge through which flows the river
Kha.   This valley presents a most extraordinary
appearance as seen from above, for it is nothing more
or less than a huge slice cut out of the plateau.   We
passed it at its apex, and could see down nearly its
whole course.   The distance from side to side at
the upper part is extraordinarily small, the sides of
the valley being formed of perpendicular precipices.
Far, far down below us, some thousands of feet at
the nearest part, were the coffee-groves and villages,
dotted here and there along the broken rocks that
fringed the edge of the river, which we could follow
with our eyes, a thread of silver, till it was lost in
the hazy mists that lay across the valley many miles
away.   Beyond this again rose the torn fantastic
peaks to which we were now becoming so accustomed.
It was a wonderful sight, and we reined in our mules
and stood, Arabs and European alike, gazing at it
with wondering eyes.   The Wadi Kha, unlike so

many of these Yemen rivers, eventually reaches the
sea.   It flows into the Wadi Zebeed, and continuing
its course through the city of that name, and across
the Tehámá, reaches the Red Sea at Ras Zebeed,
opposite the island of Jibel Zukur.   Just as suddenly
as we had come in sight of this strange gorge, just so
suddenly did we lose it again, and only a few minutes
after having left its brink the surrounding scenery
assumed its former appearance, that of a dusty rocky
plain.

Close to this spot is a mark in a rock which is
supposed to be the footprint of Ali, the son-in-law
and one of the successors in the Caliphate of the
Prophet Mahammed, or of his horse, there seems to
be no certainty which.   The imprint itself is vague
enough to be anything, but too large to be either
of those mentioned.

Below the village of Digishúb we stopped to refresh
ourselves and take breakfast.   A few rough stone
huts have been erected by the roadside, near which
some kind philanthropist has built a series of small
tanks, supplied with delicious cold water by a spring.
In one of these tanks live an enormous quantity of
fish.   The water is very shallow, and the pond small,
and were it not that the passers-by feed them on
crumbs, there would be but little chance of their
being able to exist in such a small space.   Unlike
fish in the springs of Morocco, they are not held in
any way sacred, and the Jews often catch and cook

them, though the Arabs say that they themselves
never touch them.

The funniest old specimen of age, rags, and dirt
made our coffee for us—as dishevelled an old witch as
ever man set eyes upon.   She is reported, in spite of
her filthy condition, to be of great wealth—for the
country, of course—and is apparently a well-known
character upon the road.   Quite a number of caravan-
men, who happened to be resting there, kept up a
continual volley of chaff, which reached its climax
when, on hearing of her reported riches, I offered to
become a Moslem, and lead her a blushing bride to
the altar.   She took it all in very good part, and
laughed as much as her begrimed parchment-like
skin would allow, but I feared now and again it
would crack.

On the road between Digishúb and the city of
Dhamar are three sets of old Himyaric tanks, cut in
the solid rock, as are, with the exception of a few
where the nature of the country allows of some small
gully being made use of, all the tanks of this period.
Although resembling somewhat the tanks of Aden,
there are here none of the natural advantages to be
found at that place ; for there the crater pours its
water by aqueducts and natural channels into the
tanks, which are built tier above tier in the wall of
rock and between precipices.   These between Digishúb
and Dhamar, however, lie in the level plain, and are
excavated.   They are dependent entirely upon the

rainfall for supply, and, as far as has been found possible, the water has been drained toward them ; but this, owing to the dead level of the country, is to a very slight extent practicable. These tanks are circular in form, and of considerable size and depth. At one spot a flight of steps descends to the water's edge, while a smaller tank above the steps can be filled from buckets, &c., for the animals to drink from. The entire tanks are lined with intensely hard cement, which takes a peculiar polish, and on one were visible rough designs of men on horseback, and gazelle, scratched into the plaster evidently at the time it was originally applied. The extraordinarily perfect condition in which these tanks are to-day, steps and all, speaks to the excellence of the workmanship of those who excavated and built them ; and the caravans are still mainly dependent upon these extremely antique reservoirs for water for the men and their beasts of burden.

Again, the plateau is broken by valleys to the west, but in no way to compare with that through which the Wadi Kha flows. There a slight descent takes one from the boulder-strewn undulating hills to the flat ground again, broken here and there by rocky barren crags which stand out against the dull yellow earth. On one of these is situated Dhamar el-Gar, a village of some size ; and on approaching this spot we caught sight of, far ahead of us, all shimmering in the fierce sunlight, the city of Dhamar itself. For the last hour and a half of the road we proceeded over perfectly level ground, strewn with sandy dust, and, though showing signs of cultivation, boasting scarcely a blade of anything green. As we neared the city we obtained a better view of the place, so twisted and turned had it at first been by the steaming vapour rising from the heated ground.

Dhamar lies in the flat plain, the nearest hill of any size being Hait Hirran, a mountain rising some hundreds of feet above the surrounding country a couple of miles or so to the north of the city. Many high mountains, however, are visible, especially the range of Jibel Issi to the east, though it is a long way distant. This and its neighbouring mountains must be of great height, for Dhamar itself is situated almost exactly eight thousand feet above the sea-level. It is not a walled city, but is more or less defended by a series of small, and, for the most part, mud-built forts. Three minarets dominate the town, one of them sadly out of the perpendicular, as it was struck by a cannon-shot during one of the many wars it has been its lot to witness.

A narrow street, twisting and turning amongst open drains, ruined tombs, and apparently objectless walls, leads one into the city. Here there are signs of more wealth, many of the houses being well built of stone, while a wide open square gives quite a handsome appearance to the place.

It is on to this square that the Government offices

look, and before we had half crossed it our mules were stopped by a number of Turkish soldiers, under whose guidance we proceeded to visit the Kaimakam of the town.

Alighting at a large gate leading into a yard and

Mosque and minaret at Dhamar.

garden, we entered a house, built in European style and with glass windows, and, ascending a staircase, found ourselves in a large room. Divans surrounded the walls, and a few shabby chairs and a table or two stood about the place. Seated at one end of the room, drinking coffee and smoking, were four or five Turkish officers in clean bright uniforms. As I entered one of these rose, and, walking to meet me, shook hands with me, and led me to the divan, at the same time calling to a servant for cigarettes and coffee. My guard, who had come with me from Yerim, presented a letter that had been intrusted to him by the Kaimakam of that place, which was immediately opened and read. The officer then told me I was welcome, and we conversed for about half an hour on general subjects. He could not understand how I had ever attempted or succeeded in getting through the country between Kátaba and Yerim, and laughed considerably when I told him of my adventures. He was, in fact, as were those with him, most polite and kind, and the one or two calls I paid to him, and he to me, during my stay, will always be remembered by myself as most pleasant.

Before leaving the Kaimakam I obtained his permission to take up my residence in the house of Saïd during my stay in that town; for the latter had insisted on my not going to a khan, but spending the few days we had determined to stay here in his father's house. This favour was readily granted me, and mounting my mules once more, Saïd, full of impatience, leading the way, we crossed the big square, and winding in and out amongst the narrow streets, finally drew up at a large three-storeyed detached mud-brick house, which Saïd, almost dancing with

MY QUARTERS AT DHAMAR.

delight, pointed out to me as "*el-beit betaana*"—
"our house."

Saïd received quite an ovation on his arrival, being
kissed and hugged in turns by all manner of strange
people : an old grey-bearded father followed his grey-
haired mother; brothers, sisters, cousins, children,
aunts, swarmed out of that house like ants, until one
believed that every available inch of the place must
be taken up by living people, and I began to feel
quite nervous as to where room would be found to
put myself away. At length the greetings were got
through, and the male portion of the relations turned
their attention to my mules, which were quickly unpacked and the baggage carried indoors. Then Saïd
approached me, and having run his hand through his
wavy black curls, as was a habit of his, bade me enter.
As I stepped into the doorway with him he greeted
me in true Yemen fashion, and with all the demon-
stration an Arab loves so much—and I believe in his
case it was genuine.

Climbing to the top storey of the house, we entered
a large airy room, the proportions and decoration of
which fairly astonished me, for from the outside, although the house was large, it had a poor enough
appearance, being built entirely of sun-dried mud-
bricks.

The guest-room, for such the chamber evidently
was, measured some thirty-five feet in length by
fifteen wide. One end showed a bare floor of cement,

but the other was richly carpeted with rugs and striped cloths, while divans, thick woollen mattresses, ran round the walls. The room was evidently not in use, which was reassuring, as I feared vermin. A number of handsome bronze brasiers, and strange bowls and coffee-pots, were piled up in one corner, while another was occupied by a pile of cushions, principally covered in European cottons, and happily tolerably clean. Sunk into the walls were alcoves, in which scent-bottles and sprinklers, cups and saucers, and many other things in which the heart of the Oriental delights, were standing. But of all the pretty things with which the room was filled, the windows were certainly the most lovely. Except for two or three that closed with wooden shutters from the inside, they did not open, the place of glass being taken by alabaster. The effect of the light falling through the semi-opaque stone was soft and luxurious, a rosy yellow in colour. The slabs used for these windows vary in thickness, so that the light is regulated, and though in this particular instance they were of uniform depth, in other places I saw them richly carved in relief, so that the background was a monotone of yellow ; but where the carving, principally geometric designs, was, a much deeper tone of colour was reflected, owing to the thickness of the material being greater. Such, then, were the quarters we took up in the house of Saïd el-Dhamari.

KARIAT EN-NEGIL.

CHAPTER VII.

DHAMAR TO SANAA.

ALTHOUGH the city of Dhamar boasts of a considerable antiquity, it displays none of the more remarkable points of the interest of age, and except that a large portion of the place is in bad repair, it might have been built but a few years ago. There are no walls to the city, and necessarily no gates. The absence of this has led the inhabitants to extend the town in many directions, with the result that it occupies a much larger space than would be necessary for the population it contains. This, however, has not prevented the streets from occupying the narrow limits the Oriental loves to give to the passer-by, and in the bazaars especially only two or three people could possibly walk abreast.

Ibn Khaldun, in his geography of the Yemen, makes no mention of Dhamar, but this can scarcely be looked upon as meaning that the town did not exist in his day—in fact, it is more probable that

JTY-T

his failing to notice the place was due to an omission, as the neighbouring fortress of Hirran is also left without mention, though from the remains existing there it is very probable that it was a site and fortress of no little importance in far earlier times than that of the native geographer; and El-Janadi, in his account of "The Karmathians," speaks of the capture of Hirran by Ibn Fadl about the year 293 A.H., and as the fall of the fortress was only one item of the leader's successful march to Sanaa, it is very probable that the event was considered one of no little importance. Several of the other early Arab historians make direct mention of Dhamar itself.

A few hours after my arrival in the city I sauntered out with Saïd to the bazaars, to purchase a few little luxuries in the way of food and fruit, for so far we had lived during our journey upon the bare necessities of life. Although at times a considerable crowd thronged us, we found the people extremely polite, and what little inconvenience we were put to˙was owing entirely to the curiosity of the inhabitants. The bazaars boast but little beyond their natural picturesqueness, which in many places is most noticeable. The shops are the usual little one-storeyed box-like dens of the Eastern world, and the trades are divided up into separate streets and quarters. Here, as elsewhere, the Jews have an entirely separate town, situated to the east of the city, from which it is divided by a large open space.

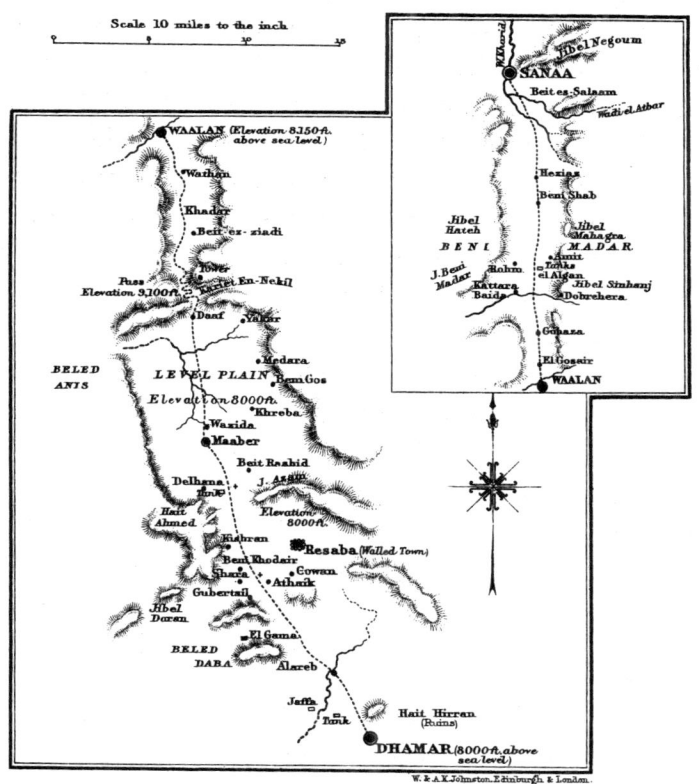

Scale 10 miles to the inch

WAALAN (Elevation 8,150 ft. above sea level)
Watham
Khadir
Beit-ex-ziadi
Bowl
Menzel En-Nekil
Pass Elevation 9,100 ft.
Danf
Yakar

J. el Negoum
SANAA
Beit-es-Salaam
Wadi el Athar
Bezias
Beni Shab
Jibel Hateh
BENI
Jibel Mahagra
MADAR
Anait
J. Beni Madar
Itahte
Rohm
el Afgan
Kattara
Baida
Jibel Sinhanj
Dobrehera
Gohaza
El Gossair
WAALAN

BELED ANIS
LEVEL PLAIN
Beni Gos
Elevation 8,000 ft.
Khreba
Madara
Waxida
Maaber
Beit Rashid
J. Assin
Delbana
Elevation 8,000 ft.
Hait Ahmed
Kudhran
Beni Khodair
Shara
Cowan
Athaik
Resaba (Walled Town)
Gubertail
Jibel Duran
El Gama
BELED DABA
Alareb
Jaffa
Tank
Hait Hirran (Ruins)
DHAMAR (8,000 ft. above sea level)

W. & A.K.Johnston, Edinburgh & London.

ROUTE MAP—DHAMAR TO SANAA
BY W. B. HARRIS

Near this great square is the principal mosque of the
town, a walled enclosure, with three large gates facing the city, and a handsome, though damaged,
minaret. In one respect, however, it is in better
order than that of another of the mosques, for it
still maintains its upright position, whereas the
other is sadly out of the perpendicular, owing to
its having been struck by a cannon-ball. A third
mosque of considerable size is within the bazaars,
but none of them possess much claim to architectural beauty, being built in the simple and un-
decorative Arab style, native cement and mud-
bricks being the principal materials used in their
construction. Prettier, certainly, are one or two of
the Shereefian tombs, with their white domes and
arcades of arches. One of these, lying on the
extreme south of the city, near where we had
entered the town, is really charming, with a small
garden in front of it and a huge shady tree for the
pilgrims to the sanctuary to rest under. Near here,
but standing separate from the town, we saw the
ruins of the Turkish barracks, which had been destroyed by the Arabs on their capture of Dhamar
from the Turks a few months before.

At sunset we returned to Saïd's house to spend
the evening in a family party, the members of which
varied between the ages of seventy or eighty and
grimy babies of a few months old. However, it
was an insight into Arab life, and was rendered

by no means unamusing by Saïd's wonderful lies
about Aden, his earthly paradise.   He fairly took
the breath away from his relations with the startling untruths he told, but I scarcely believe that
they gave him credence; and probably had he kept
to the strict truth, and only told about the forts
and troops and good government there, they would
equally have taken it for exaggeration.   Perhaps
after all he pursued the best course, and possibly
by knocking off some ninety-nine per cent for the
native love of story-telling, they arrived at about
the right result.

We were up with the sunrise, and enjoyed the
luxuries of a Turkish bath.   Fortunately the windows to admit the light were very small, otherwise
we should, I think, have seen much that was not
tempting; but one forgot any possible disadvantages
in the luxury of soap and hot water.   From the
"hummum" we proceeded to a *café* in the principal
square, and perching ourselves cross-legged under
an awning in front of the coffee-shop, joined in
the swim of conversation over "hubble-bubble"
pipes.   A handful of troops were drilling before us
in the square, poor dishevelled creatures, many
without even a boot on their feet.   There were
perhaps a hundred and fifty in all, and I was told
that of the four hundred who had been sent to
garrison the place after Ahmed Feizi Pasha's successful relief of Sanaa two or three months before,

these were all that remained, sickness having carried off the rest—starvation probably. The officers seemed as disheartened as the men, and appeared to lack all interest in the drill. Many of the soldiers were smoking cigarettes, but no one seemed to take any notice of it; and after an hour or so the soldiers wandered off in different directions, without apparently being dismissed. It was sad to see their poor wan faces, thinned and paled with sickness and hunger.

Although crowds now and again collected round me, it was surprising how polite every class of native was to me, and I do not once remember, during all the time I was in the Yemen, except on one or two occasions from the guards of my prison at Sanaa, a word of abuse. The Yemenis are the aristocracy of Islam. Wild in appearance, their manners are perfect, and though their nature now and again leads them to violence, they are as a rule gentle and hospitable, and as my travels proceeded, the more I saw of them, especially the inhabitants of the mountains and the plateau, the more I liked them. Nor did I find any difference with the townspeople, and many a kind word of welcome was said to me now and again.

Much as I wanted to push on to Sanaa, I had promised Saïd to stay three days at his house at Dhamar, and to tell the truth, I was by no means sorry of a pretext to rest in such comfortable quarters. Many a visit I received there. I think that there

could not have been a single Turkish official in the
town who did not at some time or another come and
see me, and although they seemed always to be sus-
picious as to the objects of my travels, they were
charmingly polite. Nor were the Turks my only
visitors, for many an Arab merchant in long robes of
silk came and spent an hour or so over coffee and
tobacco, and on one occasion I was honoured by the
visit of a local Shereef, first cousin to Ahmed ed-
Din, leader of the late rebellion, but who, wisely, had
not taken part on either side, preferring before entering into the affair to see who was going to win.
Saïd's people thought a great deal of the visit of this
Shereef, and personally I found him charming. He
was a man of perhaps some thirty years of age,
extremely handsome and beautifully dressed. He
seemed well educated, and had travelled a little, and
the hour he spent with me I shall always remember
with pleasure.

But of all the insights that I obtained into Arab
life during my time in the Yemen, the most interesting was the dinner-party given by Saïd in my honour.
About seven o'clock our guests commenced to arrive
—and what guests! The first to come were half-a-
dozen Arab tribesmen, with long wavy black hair and
a scarcity of clothing—in fact, their entire costume
consisted of a turban and a dark loin-cloth, from the
latter of which appeared the handles of their silver
daggers. Strange lithe beautiful creatures they were,

with limbs that would have been worth a mint of
money to an artist to paint from. A couple of merchants followed a few minutes later, their servants
carrying their silver hookahs. Natives of the same
country, it is extraordinary what a difference is apparent between the townspeople and the tribesmen ;
and our merchant friends were fat and heavy, boasting little of the grace of their wilder countrymen, and
in place of the scanty clothing, wrapped in long silk
garments of gaudy hues, and wearing white turbans
on their heads. More of the tribesmen followed, each
as he entered placing his long spear against the walls
in the corners of the room, till the place wore quite
the appearance of an armoury. Then came the
musicians, natives of the Hadramaut, wilder and
longer-haired than the Yemenis present, and bearing,
in place of spears, strange richly painted instruments.
More and more guests, until our room, big as it was,
was filled.

What a night it was ! One of those nights in a
lifetime which can never be forgotten. The cool dim
light of the swinging alabaster lamps, the flashing
spears heaped together in the corners, the wonderful
dark crowd of swarthy men, the steam of the brewing
coffee issuing from strange jars, the rich dark carpets
and gaudy cushions, the murmur and the blue curling smoke of the pipes—ay, a dinner - party in
Dhamar is worth seeing ! And then the soft music
and singing of the musicians, whose tall beautiful

figures moved slowly here and there as they played strange melodies! It seemed like some dream :—no wild African feast, merely the echo of the long-past glories of Arabia!

Then they brought us great dishes heaped with food, for the most part our old friend the antiquated goat, and we dipped our fingers into copper bowls of rose-water and ate together. Then coffee and pipes, and the bitter herb *kat*, and music and dancing. And the cool night air blew in through the windows and sent the filmy smoke circling here and there, and now and again ruffled the raven locks of one or other of our guests, who lay recumbent and silent, expressionless and beautiful, listening to the tales of love that our musicians, with strange monotonous dancing, sang to the strains of their painted guitars. We were back again in the days of Haroun el-Rashid, and all the hurry and scurry of modern life seemed lost and gone.

At length I brought out my electric machine, and, the guests joining hands, felt, for the first time in their lives, a shock. They smiled, and asked for more. Then one was brave enough to hold the handles by himself. I turned it on full, and fairly whizzed the wheels round. With a scream the man jumped into the air, and then apologised. Silently, one by one, our guests arose, and shaking me by the hand with the compliments the Arab knows so well how to bestow, bade me good-night. Then, taking their spears in their hands, they walked slowly to the door, until fairly outside, when they flew down the stairs at a pace that was positively dangerous, and from the window I could see them tearing down the street at a break-neck run. Such was the effect of a small electric machine at a Dhamar dinner-party. The following morning we paid a visit to the tombs of the family of a Turkish general, Ahmed Rushti Pasha, who had himself fallen near Lohaya in the beginning of the rebellion. The enclosed garden, with its mosque and tombs, tells of a sad story, for the family of Ahmed Rushti were assassinated by their house being blown up with gunpowder some few years since. However, as the story is to be found in the chapter on the Yemen rebellion, I shall not refer to it more particularly here. The tombs are situated without the city, on the west side. An acre or two of land are enclosed with high walls, in which stands a summer-house, where the bereaved Pasha was wont to come and sit ; but this, like the tombs themselves, was sacked by the Arabs during the rebellion, and little but the outside walls and the graves remain to-day. Passing back through the town we visited the Jews' quarter, which, unlike the Moslem city, is walled, the gates being locked every night from the outside. Miserable squalor and dirt existed on all sides, although the Jews themselves seemed well to do, and their houses airy and large. They are built almost entirely of mud-bricks, plastered inside and

out. This material forms a hard surface, and seems
to be very durable.

Our last day was spent in visiting the old fortress
of Hirran, lying a mile or two to the north of Dhamar ;
and well worth the trouble and heat I found the
expedition, for Hirran boasts many antiquities.
Passing through the north quarter of Dhamar, one
emerges into the dusty plateau, across which the
road continues for a couple of miles or so. Hirran is
clearly visible from Dhamar itself, the dark rocky
hill standing out black against the light soil. One
reaches the place near the south-west point of the
jagged rock, where are some old tanks sunk in the
solid stone, and of very considerable size. Keeping
still to the west side of the hill, we shortly reached
the scene of an old cemetery, the flat rock being
honeycombed with graves. These were often sunk
to the depth of twenty feet and more, and generally
measured some seven feet in length, and two to three
in breadth, but one or two were circular. They did
not point in any direction, but lay scattered about
the little elevated rocky flat in which they were sunk,
some east and west, some north and south. Besides
the empty ones, there were a great many visible
which had apparently escaped the hands of man, nor
could I find out why or when those that had been
dug out had been spoiled. An old goatherd, the sole
inhabitant of Hirran, told me that he had always
remembered them thus, and during his lifetime had

never seen any one digging in the graves, though

Hirran.

lately some of the larger cave-tombs further up the
rock had been searched for treasure, but only a few

coins and beads, he said, had been found with the bones.

The hill of Hirran is double-peaked, each point rising to some hundreds of feet above the level of the surrounding plain. These peaks lie almost due north and south, the rock taking a curving form between them, so that the whole forms a sort of crescent, which was formerly defended by a huge wall, still

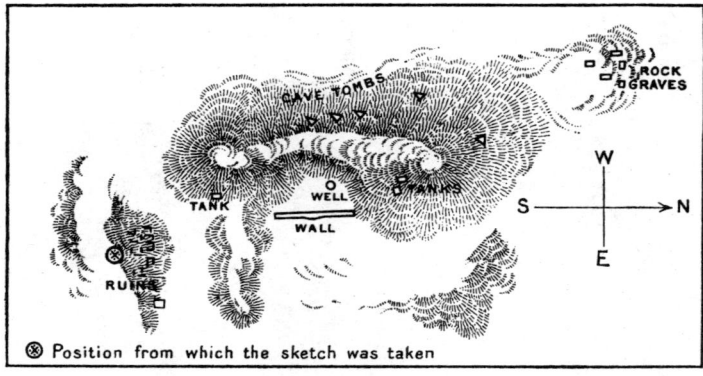

Cave-Tombs, Hirran.

remaining, joining the lower slopes of the two extremities on the eastern side.

Like the graveyard, the cave-tombs are situated on the west side of the hill, at a spot where the steep precipice, which rises to the summit, is joined by the lower boulder-strewn slopes. Although we entered all of the caves that are to-day open, there were signs of numerous others which the collection of falling material from the precipice had so blocked that considerable digging would be necessary to procure an entrance.

The first cave-tomb which I visited consisted of a circular chamber with a domed roof; the room measured some twelve feet in diameter, and the highest point of the roof was five feet eight inches from the floor. To the left of the entrance was an alcove three feet deep, three high, and four in length. The door was three feet wide and over five feet in height, but the walls were lower in the chamber.

A little higher up the side of the precipice we were able to gain entrance to a second cave, which I call Cave II. This excavation formed two oval chambers, partly divided from one another by a buttress running out from the solid rock. On both sides of this partition, and on the main walls facing it, were ledges cut in the rock three feet above the ground; in

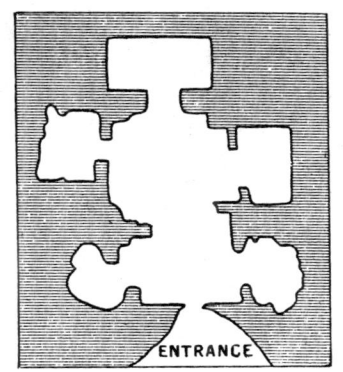

Ground plan of Tomb III.

the dust of one of which I found a few bones and an engraved bead.

Cave No. III. was perhaps the most important I visited, and showed signs of more careful excavation than any of the others. A doorway led one into a circular chamber, off which to right and left two

small rooms opened out.   This circular entrance-hall
led, opposite the door, into a still larger chamber,
into which in turn opened two alcoves and a room,
all of them four-sided.   On the left and immediately
in front the doors were raised above the ground and

Interior of Tomb III., Hait Hirran.

nearly square, the floor of the alcoves being level with
the lower part of the openings.   On the right, however, was a chamber level with the floor, entered
through an archway.   The two alcoves showed evident
signs of having at one time been closed up, for in

the lintels of rock were visible holes which may either have held a door or been used for joists to strengthen any masonry which may have been arranged to fill up the opening.

Cave IV., again, to the south of the others, presented quite a new feature, the face of the precipice being

Entrance to Tomb IV., Hait Hirran.

cut to form a large square chamber, in the back wall of which a doorway opened into the tomb. Below this window, a foot or two above the ground, ran a series of five holes drilled a short way into the rock, and which seems at some time to have held the supports of a platform or seat. Apparently the whole outer chamber was lined with plaster, and may have been once separated from the face of the precipice by masonry. The window or aperture opening into the tomb was situated three feet from the ground, and was two and a half feet in height and two feet three inches in breadth. The interior consisted of an alcove six feet in length, two feet wide, and three in height. Here, as in Cave No. III., I found bones amongst the accumulation of dust, but nothing else.

The fifth cave consisted of one large room, some sixteen feet by eight, at each end of which were ledges in the rock eight feet long by eighteen inches wide. The door leading into this cave-tomb was three feet six inches wide, and the roof inside five feet in height. The rock here was strewn with small chips of rock, and I found no signs of bones.

All these caves showed signs of having been opened, and my old guide the goatherd said that such was the case. Asking him how Moslems reconciled themselves to breaking open tombs, he replied that they were the tombs of "unbelievers," and that had they been Mahammedan graves no one would have dared to have touched them. This he exemplified to me by pointing out some tombs on the summit of the rock, in which Moslems are supposed to be buried, and it was quite apparent they had been left untouched.

Following the hill to its southernmost extremity, I climbed by a difficult ascent to a tank cut in the rock where water was formerly collected. To reach

this spot, so difficult and slippery was the path, I had
to go barefooted, a by no means pleasant task, as the
stones were so hot as to blister my feet. Descending
again, we proceeded to the site of the former "fortress," formed by the two eastern points of the hill
being joined by a great wall. This, however, showed
signs of early Arab work, being built of the peculiar
cement which is typical of Arab construction. This
wall is of enormous height and width, being some
hundred and fifty yards long and twenty feet high,
and one could drive a carriage and pair anywhere on
its summit. The only one dating from Arab times
that I have seen to equal it in size is the great wall
attributed to Mulai Ismail at Mequinez in Morocco.
Within the wall is a deep well, the upper portion of
which is built, the lower part sunk into the solid
rock. Above the northern end of the great wall are
a series of three tanks, reached by a roughly cut
stairway. Still ascending, one arrives at the summit,
where are the five Moslem tombs I alluded to, enclosed
in low stone walls, and the remains of much old
building, of which it is difficult to gather any distinct
idea, to such a state of ruin has it fallen. At all
events, the enormous amount of broken pottery, some
of gorgeous colour and fine design, speaks to the size
of the place.

From the summit one gains a fine view of the
surrounding country,—a great flat plain broken by
ridges of dark volcanic rock, like that on which we

were standing, until in the far east a tall range of mountains appeared on the horizon. Below us to the south lay Dhamar, almost as yellow as the plain itself, for there is but little green in its neighbourhood, although it is said that in the rainy season the whole country entirely changes its aspect. To the east of Hirran, and immediately below it, lie the remains of an old city, the loose stone walls of the houses still standing to the height of a few feet above the ground. Altogether the place must have been one of great importance in early times, and I regretted much that I was unable in my hasty visit to find any inscriptions. However, I was able to take the notes given above before a mounted Turkish soldier appeared on the scene, sent by the Kaimakam to watch my movements, and who begged me politely to return. Fearing that any suspicion on the part of the Governor toward myself might prevent my continuing my journey to Sanaa, I stated my readiness to comply with his request, and bidding adieu to the old goatherd, once more mounted my mule and returned to the town.

I was able to learn but little about Hirran in Dhamar, or in fact anywhere, except that it was once the centre of a great trade, a sort of caravanserai for the goods of Sanaa and the north, the kingdom of Saba or Sheba, and Aden. This is the only early tradition the natives seem to have concerning its former wealth and its being a centre of trade in very

early times, and this tradition has led me to a conjecture—it is nothing more—that Hirran may be the
site of the Haran of the Old Testament. The places
mentioned in the same verse are, I believe, all in
Southern Arabia, and have all been recognised, Haran
alone remaining undiscovered. It is more than
possible, judging from the similarity of names and
the report of its former importance in trade, that
they may be one and the same place.[1]

During the afternoon I paid a farewell visit to the
Kaimakam, which was returned an hour later, when
he promised me a couple of soldiers to see me safely
to Sanaa.

The following morning we left Dhamar. There
was, of course, a great leave-taking of Saïd, and just
as they had done on our arrival, a long string of
relations, illustrating all the seven ages of man, with
many of the intermediary gaps filled in, streamed out
of the house to bid him farewell. Good simple people
they were, though the younger members of the family,
when away from their parents' eyes, were importunate
in their demands for *bakshish*. The road led us to
the west of Hirran, close to the large tanks I mentioned as having seen on my ride to that place, and
then on over the dreary plain. Leaving the large-
walled village of Jaffa to our left for a time, we saw
but little signs of life.

---

[1] " Haran, and Canneh, and Eden, the merchants of Sheba, Asshur,
and Chilmad, were thy merchants."—Ezekiel xxvii. 23.

The early morning effect upon the flat plateau was one of great beauty, in spite of its dry arid appearance. A dull warm haze hung over the more distant desert, for such it really was at this period of the year, through which the far-away mountains shimmered in the heat, turquoise-blue in colour. As we proceeded the cultivated land became very sparse, the soil for the most part consisting of sand and stones, until, passing through a narrow gorge of rock, we entered a great circular plain enclosed by low rocky hills on all sides, no doubt the crater of some long-extinct volcano. From this point one catches a glimpse of Jibel Doran, a range of mountains of great elevation, which terminate in a strange sugar-loaf peak, unequalled in curious form by any I have seen elsewhere in the world, with the exception perhaps of "The Needle of Heaven" in the I-chang gorge of the Yangtze-Kiang, some eleven hundred miles up that river.

At a small *café*—half a cave, and half built of rough stones—we spent an hour or two during the hottest part of the day. Quite a number of men and camels had arrived before us, and in spite of the fact that scarcely a blade of anything green was to be seen, the surroundings were by no means unpicturesque. Joining in with the caravan-men, a cool corner was found for me in the cave, and our mid-day rest passed quickly and pleasantly enough. Far above us, perched on the summit of

JIBEL DORAN—EARLY MORNING.

a hill, was the large village of Athaik, its tall
towers dominating the surrounding plain and giving
the place the appearance of some old feudal castle.
A descent led us to a slightly lower portion of the
plain. The soil here was richer, but I noticed that
there was no cultivation, a fact that was explained
to me to be owing to the rebellion, which had deterred any investment in crops that were bound to
fall a prey either to the Turks or independent rob-
bers. To our left we could see the walled town
of Resaaba, but wishing to push on to Sanaa, and
as it did not lie in our road, I did not visit it.
There is but little of interest, I was told, to be
seen within its walls. It is, in fact, rather a very
large village than a town, and bears all the char-
acteristics of the villages of the Yemen plateau.
Again, another reason deterred me from penetrating
there; that I felt it advisable to give as wide a
berth as possible to any places where I might be
likely to run up against Turks and Turkish authorities. To have so nearly reached Sanaa, and then
be turned back, would indeed have been a disappointment.

Several times along the road we passed the deep
rock-cut tanks that even to-day form the water-
supply of the passing caravans. One that we
stopped to drink at as evening was approaching
bore rough designs of men on horseback, and inscriptions in the Himyaric language cut in the

plaster that lined the rock walls. Like so many
of these tanks, a flight of steps led to the water's
edge, at the summit of which was a smaller pool,
to be filled by hand for the beasts of burden to
drink from, and, like the main reservoir, circular in
form. The mountains we had seen all the afternoon
far ahead of us were now growing nearer, and as
evening drew on we found ourselves in a large open
valley, semicircular in form, and closed at the far
end by steep broken crags. The soil here was well
cultivated, though, as we were still nearly nine thousand feet above the sea-level, the young crops had
not yet begun to show, and the place looked dreary
and burnt up. That the soil must repay cultivation
is evident from the great number of wells distributed
over the country. At many of these, men, women,
and camels were engaged in drawing water. A
couple of tree-trunks form uprights to a beam laid
across their tops, over which the rope that supports
the skins in which the water is raised passes. At
the other end of the rope, men, women, or some
beast of burden is harnessed. Owing to the great
depth of these wells, and the size of the skins used
as buckets, the weight to be raised is very great,
and the labour of raising it proportionately so. But
the natives have discovered a means by which the
work is lessened, while at the same time their
irrigation is rendered more practicable—namely, by
building the wells upon the summits of mounds.

A long sloping path leads from the high mouth of the well to the level of the surrounding fields, so that the drawer, harnessed to the end of the rope, is assisted by the centre of gravity, instead of being dependent upon his, her, or its personal strength. This raising of the wells above the fields also renders easy the carrying of the water in little dikes to whatever spot it is needed. The skin, on reaching the well's mouth, empties itself into a trough from which the water pours into the irrigating channels. The fact that these channels consist of only small ditches adds much to the toil and labour, as the thirsty soil sucks up a large quantity of the fluid before it reaches its destination. However, labour is cheap, and a man, so long as he possesses a donkey, a camel, or a wife to work his well, can sit and smoke and look on himself.

At length we drew up at the village khan of Maaber, our resting-place, and climbing a rough outside staircase, found ourselves in a clean white-washed room, cool and airy, where our carpets were quickly spread and coffee on the boil. The people were very inquisitive, and at last I was obliged to give peremptory orders that no one was to be allowed to enter my room. But this did not seem to be of much avail, and eventually I posted a guard outside the door, armed with a long stick. The village is a poor enough place, built of mud-bricks, with a little stone masonry showing here and there.

The people seemed poor and dirty, and there was little or nothing of interest to be seen. Very different are these villages of the plateau to the well-built and fortified towers of the country we had passed through to the south of Yerim, nor were the people of this part half so clean or genial or handsome as the wild mountaineers.

Early the next morning we were on our way again, the road continuing over the dusty plain. A mile or two from Maaber we witnessed some skirmishing between the Turkish troops and the hillmen of Jibel Anis, one of the last tribes to hold out, and one that probably will never surrender to the Turkish Government. The country inhabited by this tribe consists of wild inaccessible country, into which the Osmanli troops are powerless to penetrate. The battle we witnessed was not apparently a very bloody affair, for it consisted principally in a small field-battery of the Turks firing into a few hill villages, from which a desultory and ill-aimed fire was kept up by the Arabs. This was the first active sign we had as yet seen of the rebellion ; for although Turkish garrisons were to be found in Dhamar and Yerim, their reconquest of these cities from the Arabs had been accomplished almost without bloodshed. For a time we stayed and watched the little battle, listening to the sharp cracking of the rifles and the louder tones of the field-guns, until, as it was apparent that the Turks had no idea of trying to climb to the villages

KHADAR.

or the Arabs of descending to the level, we continued our journey. The plain ends in an abrupt line of high rocky mountains, over which we could see our path twisting and turning in serpentine coils. Entering a narrow gorge, we passed close under the grandly situated village of Kariat en-Negil, its every rock crowned by stone towers—a striking and wild-looking place. Here it is that the old pilgrim-road from Aden and the Hadramaut probably joins the track I had travelled on. We had left the old road at Lahej, whence it continues *viâ* Ibb, our route lying more to the east. I have mentioned elsewhere this great pilgrim-track, founded by Huseyn ibn Salaamah in the fifth century A.H., and there is no further need of description here. Suffice it to say that at every night's *nzala*, or resting-place, was built a mosque, while tanks refreshed the weary with water by the way.

A tremendous climb takes one to the summit of the pass, where there is an old round tower, now used as a watch-house by the Turks. The path is extremely steep, and, though roughly paved, so slippery that all riding up was impossible, while the rarefied air made the climb by no means an easy or a pleasant one. The summit I found by observation to be nine thousand one hundred feet above the sea-level, about eleven hundred feet above the city of Dhamar.

A steep descent and an hour's ride along a broken valley brought us to the large village of Khadar, where we rested for an hour over pipes and coffee. The place is a picturesque one, though greatly lacking in vegetation. The upper portion of the village is situated on the summit of a precipitous hill, and is walled, while every available peak holds the usual tower-house. The few buildings that stand near the road are for the most part caravanserais and *cafés*. The inhabitants are almost entirely Jews, who, like certain tribes of their co-religionists that I have seen in the Atlas Mountains, are cultivators of the soil and agriculturists. A small mosque, the only whitewashed building in the place, shows, however, that there must be some Moslem inhabitants in Khadar.

A wild group were seated at the door of one of the *cafés*, Arabs and camels from Mareb, whence they were bringing salt. Our mutual curiosity in each other led to conversation, and I found them good fellows on the whole, though rougher in manners than the Yemenis I had as yet come in contact with.

Two hours after leaving Khadar we reached our night's resting-place, Waalan, the best-built village we had as yet come across. The size and solidity of the houses was astonishing; and when, on being led up a staircase and along a wide passage into a beautifully clean room in a handsome khan, the change from the quarters we had as yet found on our journey in the other villages, almost took one's breath

VIEW FROM WAALAN.

away. Our chamber, which commanded a fine view
of several surrounding villages through large windows
opening down to the ground, was well whitewashed,
the doors and window-shutters being handsomely
carved of polished dark wood, and with a ceiling of
the same material overhead. The change from what
we had been accustomed to was a most pleasant one,
and we soon made ourselves comfortable. A dear
old lady, and a very tolerably clean one, waited upon
us, and insisted on cooking our dinner, a task usually
shared by Abdurrahman and Saïd—and very well she
did it too.

This appearance of cleanliness and civilisation was
a sure sign that we were nearing the capital, and I
turned in to rest that night with a feeling of satisfaction, for only a few hours' ride lay between us and
Sanaa.

Four hours of heat along the valley of the Beni
Matar, and we reached the large village of Estaz,
where we rested for an hour or two in a large but
dirty *café*. There is certainly but little to see in the
place, though Turkish soldiers were more common
here than elsewhere, and the curiosity of their officers
would not allow of my being left undisturbed even for
the brief space of the hour or so we stayed there.
They must needs come and call and ask all sorts of
absurd questions. Estaz, however, boasts one superiority over much of the Yemen plateau, a river of
running water that flows by many channels through

gardens, the greenness of which was most pleasant
after days of travelling over yellow plains.

Before mid-day we were off again, and turning a
corner could see far away across the level ground,
shimmering white and yellow in the steaming heat,
the city of Sanaa.

With a thrill of satisfaction I urged my mule on to
its quickest paces, and a couple of hours later found
us entering the city by an old broken-down gateway,
near which a company or two of troops were drilling.
Signs of the fighting were common enough.   Some of
the little towers erected as forts by the Turks outside
the walls were in ruins, and half an hour earlier we
had passed all that remained of the village of Dar es-
Salaam, the "house of peace"—ill-fitting name!—
where the Arabs had made their last strong stand
against their Turkish enemy, and which they only
left when driven forth by the Turkish artillery playing upon the houses of the village.   Little remains
to-day but broken walls and tumble-down towers.
In many places one could see exactly where the shot
had hit, and one tower was drilled through, the torn-
up flooring and rafters showing what havoc the ball
had accomplished.

At length we were in Sanaa.   The road had been a
difficult and a dangerous one, but this was all forgotten now.   In spite of warnings and repeated efforts
to dissuade us from so rash an undertaking, we had
been successful, and it was with the keenest satisfac-

tion, though not without some doubts as to how I should be received, that I watched my little caravan enter the city.

Passing through a narrow street with high houses on either hand, we drew up at the door of a great caravanserai, a four-storeyed building of which the rooms all looked out on to balconies overhanging a large *patio*. The place was in wretched condition, and the ground-floor, which served as a stable for camels, horses, mules, and donkeys, looked as though it had never been cleaned out. Here I paid off my men, with the exception, of course, of Abdurrahman and Saïd. I had made a bargain with a caravan-man in Aden to send me through to Sanaa, and this bargain he had carried out in every particular, in spite of all manner of dangers and difficulties; and it was with much satisfaction that I paid the worthy fellows the remaining half of the sum agreed upon at Aden, and sent them on their way with more *bakshish* than had probably ever been in their possession before. Our parting was almost a sad one : from the day they had joined me we had shared the same food and the same room at the khans, and though it was under three weeks that they had been with me, I felt as though I had known them ages, and shall always remember with pleasure the trustworthy way in which they saw me through the country, and how, weary as they must at times have been with the long marches, they maintained their tempers throughout, and were always ready to do me some little service, however far removed it might chance to be from the routine of their work.

A saunter through the bazaars brought us to the quarter in which the Government buildings are situated, and in a few minutes more I found myself in the residence of his Excellency Ahmed Feizi Pasha, Governor-General of the Yemen and Commander of the Seventh Army Corps. I was almost immediately ushered into the general's presence. He was seated on a divan at the end of a handsome room, surrounded by quite a number of his staff. His Excellency received me pleasantly, and after exchange of salaams, a chair being fetched for me, he began to ask me what had brought me there. I thereupon presented him with my passport, vizéd by the Turkish Consul-General in London, and made out for the "Ottoman Empire," which had been issued to me by H.M. Foreign Office the day before I left London to visit the Yemen. Being unable to read English, Ahmed Feizi Pasha sent for an Armenian who spoke and read French, and the wording of my passport was explained to him. Suddenly his Excellency's manner quite changed, and he became very red and irascible, asking all sorts of absurd questions, which he did not give me time to answer. First, I was not an Englishman at all; then I was an officer sent from Aden to map out the country, and assist the Arabs in the rebellion;

THE AUTHOR BEING EXAMINED AND HIS PASSPORT READ IN THE PRESENCE OF AHMED FEIZI PASHA,
GOVERNOR-GENERAL OF THE YEMEN.

until at last I almost became bewildered as to what I was, or rather what the Pasha imagined me to be. Abdurrahman, good Moslem that he is, was an Englishman in disguise. No Arab, the Pasha said, ever spoke Arabic with such a foreign accent; and as to Morocco there was no such country, and no such person as Mulai el-Hassan, its Sultan, for he knew well enough that all North Africa was under the French. At length he insisted on his saying the Mahammedan belief, to assure himself that he was in truth a co-religionist. Abdurrahman's indignation was intense, especially as Saïd happened to be present; for with a true oriental love of exaggeration the Moor had been telling the Yemeni wonderful tales of the greatness and power of his country and its Sultan, and it pained him to find that the Turkish Pasha had never heard of either, and Saïd's smile and look were anything but reassuring to his pride in his fatherland.

At length, in a burst of anger, Ahmed Feizi called to a couple of officers, and his remarks being translated to me by the Armenian, I learned that I was to be kept in security for the present. A hand was laid on my shoulder, and I was gently led away, leaving the handsome old Pasha as scarlet as a tomato. In the large anteroom I was handed over to a guard of four soldiers, who conducted me through the streets to a guard-room, situated above the prison yard, where I was soon ensconced, the door banged and locked, and a sentry posted on the outside. My baggage, which I had left at the khan, was sent to me a little later. Meanwhile, Abdurrahman and Saïd were strictly cross-examined by the Governor-General, and as the account the first had to give of himself did not seem satisfactory, he quickly followed me to jail. That Saïd was a Yemeni there could be no doubt, but he suffered a like fate—I suppose for keeping such bad company.

I spent five days in prison at Sanaa. The room was clean, and I was decently treated, being only once roughly handled. Wishing to speak to an officer in the courtyard, I proceeded to leave my room, the door of which was kept open by day, when I was rudely pushed back by the sentry.

The first night I was allowed to sleep alone and in peace ; but on the succeeding three, two non-commissioned officers shared the chamber, dirty things in uniforms, which wore the look of never having been taken off. However, they were good-hearted fellows, and both spoke Arabic well.

My meals I was sent out to get for the first day ; but after that, all leaving the place was forbidden to me, except to take exercise in charge of a guard of soldiers. On the whole I had little to complain of, except that the water and sanitary arrangements were both very bad—so bad, in fact, that on the last night I was taken with violent fever, as also were Saïd and Abdurrahman, who by no means shared such good quarters as I did, being housed in a large dirty room, where chained prisoners were their companions. This, however, was changed on my representing that both were suffering from fever to the

The Author in prison at Sanaa.

Governor-General on my second interview. On this occasion I found his Excellency more reasonable, and once or twice he even laughed, being apparently much amused when I told him how I had got over the frontier in the disguise of a Greek. But the

Pasha's merriment did not bring about any change in my condition, and I was taken back from his presence to the same prison as before. I told him at this interview that one of my reasons for visiting the country was to correspond for the 'Times,' and he thereupon entered into a long political statement as to the rebellion and its reasons. His Excellency asked me what we should do in India in a like circumstance, and I replied that I thought the matter could be best solved by a total disarmament of the Arabs. While agreeing with me, he acknowledged such a task an impossibility with the troops under his command, and said he was earnestly hoping for further reinforcements from Constantinople. From his manner, and what I could gather about Ahmed Feizi Pasha, he seems to be a man of great personal courage and perseverance, besides possessing an extraordinary amount of diplomacy and skill in dealing with the Arabs, learned, no doubt, during the time that he was Governor of Mecca; and in spite of the fact that he saw right to put me in prison, I cannot but admire the thorough character which the general seems to possess. His surroundings showed that here, at least, some regard was shown for the common soldiers, and all wore boots, not to say fezzes. Here, too, their uniforms were not in rags, nor did they seem to be on the eve of starvation. There seemed, too, in Sanaa, more organisation than I had seen elsewhere. I asked the Pasha why I was kept in prison, and he replied that my presence was not entirely satisfactory, and that he had ordered me to be lodged in the guardroom lest the Arab population might do me harm.

I can quite imagine that to the jealous Turk the unexpected arrival of an Englishman was by no means a pleasant surprise. Up to this time all truth concerning the rebellion had been withheld, and the sole matter that the press had been able to obtain was from official sources at Constantinople. Therefore any chance of the truth leaking out, and the general public being made aware how very nearly the Osmanli Government had lost the southernmost of its Arabian possessions, would prove far from acceptable to the authorities. On this account Ahmed Feizi's bearing toward myself is explicable, nor do I complain very much of it. Not so, however, with the action of H.M. late Secretary of Foreign Affairs, who laid all the blame of my imprisonment upon myself, and entirely ignored the fact that my passport,—demanding that I should be allowed to pass without let or hindrance, and that I should be afforded every assistance and protection of which I might stand in need in the Ottoman Empire, and which had been vizéd by the Turkish Consul-General in London,—bore his own signature, which, if it were not lithographed, might have been worth the sum paid for the document that bore it, as an autograph, but was certainly entirely useless for the purpose for which it was supposed to be affixed. Although

298 DHAMAR TO SANAA.

I made my journey through the Yemen with the knowledge and consent of the late Sir William White, then H.M. Ambassador at Constantinople, I was informed, in one of those elegant despatches of the Foreign Office, that I had entered the Yemen on entirely my own responsibility, and must bear the results of my actions myself! and that if the Turkish Government saw right to put me in prison and give me such bad water to drink that fever was the result, they really could not hold any one responsible for it beyond my own person. My question as to whether the wording of my passport was of any value, or merely a form that meant nothing, they entirely ignored, and to this day I have been unable to obtain a reply. Suffice it to say that with all its seals and titles and stamps, a British passport does not seem to be of much value in the Ottoman Empire; nor when it is absolutely disregarded is any one blamed by the Foreign Office except the unoffending bearer, who may have been so dazzled by its splendour as to believe that it might be of service to him. However, what with making treaties and doing their duty in society, it can be easily understood that the time of the officials is too much occupied to attend to such an unimportant question as the imprisonment of an Englishman, even though by such an occurrence every word and sentence of a paper to which H.M. Secretary of State appends his signature is disregarded and abused.

CHAPTER VIII.

SANAA, THE CAPITAL OF THE YEMEN.

THE city of Sanaa is situated in a wide valley, at an elevation of seven thousand two hundred and fifty feet above the sea-level. Although the town lies almost altogether on the flat bottom of the valley, a mountain, Jibel Negoum, rises abruptly on the east—so abruptly, in fact, that the old fortress and castle which form the citadel of Sanaa are perched on one of its spurs, from which the main peak rises in rocky bareness to a very considerable height.

The town is in form a triangle, the apex being formed by the *kasr* above-mentioned, and the base by the wall of the garden suburb Bir el-Azab. There are three distinct quarters within the outer walls : the first or east quarter that of the Turks and Arabs, where are situated the bazaars, the Government buildings, and the principal native houses; the second the Jews' quarter, separated from the last by a wide strip of barren ground, part of which shows signs of once having been a cemetery; and thirdly, this suburb of Bir el-Azab, where many a villa stands within luxurious gardens of fruit and other trees, enclosed with high walls. In spite of the fact that Sanaa is situated only between the 15th and 16th degree of north latitude, and so well within the tropics, there are very few signs to be seen of anything approaching tropical vegetation, and one is surprised at first, until the great altitude of the place is taken into consideration, to find that nearly all our English fruits flourish there. Although, of course, by day the sun is intensely hot, it is quite a common occurrence to experience frosts on winter nights. Yet in spite of lying at so great an elevation above the sea, Sanaa is subject at times to serious droughts ; and although in the rainy season a torrent of water pours down the river-bed which runs through the centre of the town, in the dry periods of the year water is procurable only from wells sunk to a great depth in the solid rock. The water drawn from these wells is said to be very fresh and good. As is the custom in so many parts of the East, it is a marketable produce, and is carried about in skins by water-bearers, and sold at so much per skin, or even per cup. Yet in spite of water being a thing of money value, it is extraordinary how clean the general population of Sanaa seem to be, with the exception of the lower-class Turks, who, to judge from their appearance, one could believe never to have even heard of its existence. However, happily they are in the minority.

The whole town of Sanaa is surrounded by a wall

built for the most part of mud-bricks dried in the
sun, though in many cases the towers, which at
regular intervals protect the walls, and on most of
which the Turks have mounted small guns, are of
stone. The city is entered by four principal gates,
one lying to each point of the compass. Although
extremely badly built, and capable apparently of with-
standing no armed force, the walls of Sanaa formed
a sufficient protection to the city against the wild
Arab hordes by whom the place was infested in the
autumn and winter of 1891. Had the Arabs been
possessed of any artillery, instead of being armed
with only a few matchlock-guns and rifles and their
spears, no doubt the city would have fallen. Yet
it has been found by proof, especially in the several
bombardments of Mokha, that walls and fortifications
of sun-dried bricks are by no means as easy to form
a breach in as it might be supposed. However, in
these days of shells they would offer but poor resistance, although when fired at with shot the missile
merely buries itself in the clay, without doing any
appreciable damage. To further fortify the place, the
Turks have at regular intervals built, some few
hundred yards outside the walls, towers, somewhat
resembling our martello towers of the south coast.
Here, as they have done upon the main wall, they
have erected small guns which proved of great use in
the Arab attacks upon Sanaa. These towers, by being
built within easy range of one another, and being ex-

posed to no more serious fire than that of matchlock-guns, are said to have played terrible havoc amongst the natives, as a handful of Turks in each, with one piece of artillery and a dozen or so rifles, were able to pour a telling fire into the flanks of the Arabs as they approached the city walls.

But the strongest point in the fortifications of Sanaa is the old fort on the spur of Jibel Negoum, the walls of which are solidly built of stone. Where necessary, the Turks have repaired and strengthened it. It was opposite to the gate of this fort, which serves as the Turkish arsenal, that I was lodged during my stay in Sanaa; and I was not a little amused to notice that the guns by which the walls are protected point ominously into the city. It is no doubt by the constant view of these cannon, whose gaping mouths point direct at the Arab quarter, that revolt and revolution against the Osmanli forces was held in check within the city, when all the rest of the Arab population, with but few exceptions, had risen up in arms.

A fort, but not nearly so large or strong, protects the city to the west, lying close to the gate by which the highroad to Hodaidah and the coast leaves the town. Both this edifice and that at the east end of Sanaa contain the remains of old palaces, but to-day they have fallen into disrepair. No longer the fountains splash their crystal waters into the clear air; no longer the pavements re-echo with the bells and anklets of dancers : now nothing is heard but the rough voice and rougher tread of the Turkish troops upon the marble floors.   There is, in fact, but little to tell of the former grandeur of Sanaa.   No doubt, within many of the houses there must be beautiful courts and gardens ; but of these I saw little or nothing, for although I visited the Turkish Governor-General, Ahmed Feizi Pasha, in one of the old palaces of the Imams, the place has been so changed and decorated and spoiled that it resembles to-day a huge barrack rather than a palace.   The walls have been whitewashed, the great staircases are dirty, and the steps worn away by the nails of the soldiers' boots ; and even in the great rooms in which Ahmed Feizi Pasha resides, or does his business, the simple old Arab taste has been changed for decoration of *Louis Quatorze*, by no means bad of its kind, some of the wall-painting being far above the average, but still sadly out of place.

Of the remains of the old palace and temple of Ghumdan, reached by some sixteen hundred steps, nothing but a heap of ruins remains to-day.   Yet what a strange great place it must have been, with its four walls painted different colours, and its centre tower seven storeys in height, each diminishing in size, until the highest of all was floored with a single piece of marble.   At each corner of this little summer-house was a marble lion, the open mouth of which exposed to the wind seemed to emit roaring.   Strange

fancies they had, these old-world Yemen people ; and
it must be regretted that the old palace and the
adjacent temple dedicated to Zuhrah, supposed to be
the Venus of Arabia, should have incurred the fanatical wrath of Othman, the third Caliph, and by his
orders have been destroyed ; for had it been left to
die a natural death, there is little doubt that, in the
situation and climate it enjoyed, there would have
been at least some of it left to-day to tell of its former
splendour.

Although one cannot see the interior of the Arab
houses of Sanaa, a fair estimate of their size can be
gained from the outside ; and even to us English,
who are used to great houses, many of those of Sanaa
appear immense. It is impossible to describe the
style of architecture in which they are built, for it
is a style that exists nowhere else. It is purely and
essentially Yemenite, though in some cases gateways
and windows are found of Byzantine and Gothic form.
There is one house at Dhamar, built of red brick and
faced with white stone, with a stone porch, that, were
it set down in an English country district, would pass
for Elizabethan. The house, too, forms an E, and
although I could find out nothing about its history,
it seems impossible that the strange building could
be an accident ; and I am inclined to believe that it
must have been erected by one of the many renegades
who, in the middle ages, sought their fortunes in the
wealthy cities of Arabia.

At Sanaa I saw no houses of this kind, the style of architecture, with the exception of the decoration of doors and windows, being more or less uniform. Many of the larger houses are built of stone and brick and cement, the lower two storeys perhaps being of well-squared stone of various colours, arranged so as to form designs, the upper portion being of brick covered with a hard cement that takes a fine polished surface, not unlike the material used in Cairo, and corresponding to the *tabbia* of Fez. Many of the upper storeys are built overhanging the streets, but this is not carried out to nearly such a large extent as in many of the oriental cities ; while the *musher-ibeyeh* work of Cairo is rare here, its place being taken by long narrow windows filled in with stained glass in designs. From the outside the pattern is often inappreciable, as the chips of glass are simply stuck into the plaster framework. From within, however, only such of the glass is exposed as fits in between the solid pattern, and the designs are often exceedingly fine. The same can be seen in the tomb and mosque of Kaït Bey, one of the tombs of the Caliphs at Cairo, and again some specimens of the work exist in the museum of Arab antiquities in the same city. What carved wood there is used for window-screens does not in the least resemble that of Egypt, but is arranged in geometric designs, much more in the style of Chinese and Japanese workmanship, with which some of the designs are identical.

A word must be said here on the extraordinary quantity of Chinese and Japanese pottery to be found in the Yemen. There is scarcely a *café* by the roadside where one will not find that the cups have come from the far East, and yet I found that but very little enters the country to-day. I believe the origin of the presence of this extraordinary amount of oriental pottery is to be traced to the last few centuries, when Aden was the great mart of exchange between the East and Europe. With great wealth in the cities of the Yemen, a very appreciable quantity of the goods brought to Aden would be taken into the interior, and the care with which pottery and antiquities are treasured by the natives of the country would explain their existing until to-day. There is little doubt that should the Yemen ever be opened up, and Europeans be able to travel with safety and comfort, that it will become a field for the curio-hunter such as has not been known since the days when the Egyptian antiquities began to be unearthed. Coins, gems, inscriptions, sculptures, old Persian and Arab antiquities, embroideries, arms, brass and copper work, manuscripts, carpets, oriental pottery and glass— the Yemen is full of them, and as yet her treasures are almost untouched.

Although many of the streets of the town consist of narrow byways, turning and twisting in every direction between the high walls of the houses, there are parts that are by no means badly laid out, and

one or two of the main streets are quite wide
thoroughfares, in which the few carriages which
Sanaa boasts are able to pass each other. The most
important of these streets leads from the square
into which the Government buildings look to the
bazaars. It is only a few hundred yards in length,
it is true, but still it is sufficiently wide, and the
shops on either side sufficiently good, to compare
favourably with many in European towns. The
"square" itself is a large oblong open space, faced
on the east by the old castle and the large much-
bedomed Turkish mosque, and on the west by what
were once the palaces of the Arab rulers, and to-day
form barracks and Government offices. At one end
of the square an enterprising Turk has built a large
café, where the officers and the few Greek shopkeepers love to congregate, and from the large doors
and windows of which float clouds of pale-blue tobacco-
smoke, issuing in curling clouds from the *shishas* of
the smokers. It is from this point that the main
street leads off to the bazaars, and in the few hundred
yards of thoroughfare are to be seen the best shops,
kept either by Turks or by Greeks, in which every
imaginable article can be procured, from tins of sardines and inferior Turkish cigarettes to photograph-
frames and musty chocolate creams. One or two have
large glass windows in which the goods are exposed
to view, but they have a dingy dusty appearance,
and seem to tell that trade is not bright. There,

too, is a small restaurant, where all the favourite
Turkish dishes can be obtained, some of which are
by no means to be despised; while bottles of Greek
and native wines standing on shelves tell that the

Turkish officers in a café at Sanaa.

Turks of Sanaa do not keep too strictly to the tenets
of Islam with regard to drinking.

Issuing from this street, one emerges into the
bazaars, and here one sees Sanaa proper, not as it
has been altered and changed to suit Turkish tastes.
Of the many scenes that the city presents to the

traveller, the bazaars are perhaps the most interesting; for here one loses all idea of more modern times, and is thrown back, as it were, into the past. The bazaars have never changed. From time immemorial there have existed the strange box-like little shops, filled with much the same objects, and tended by people who, from the distance that they are separated from the outer world, have changed but little. Just as they dress to-day, so have they dressed since the word of Islam was first heard in the land. The only change, perhaps, noticeable to the casual observer, is the scattering of Turks and Turkish soldiers, whom now and again one passes in the narrow streets. The shops are all of one storey, the floor being raised about two feet above the ground, but not projecting on to the street in the little platforms one is so used to in Egypt and elsewhere. Here the seller sits cross-legged amongst his goods in the shadow of his mud-brick shop, gazing in front of him into the sun-lit yellow street and beyond into the shop opposite. A little awning or covering of wood often projects above the opening, sufficient to give a patch of shade large enough to shield the purchaser from the sun's hot rays.

As is the custom throughout the East, each trade has a number of shops, or often a whole street, put aside to its special business. The workers of arms, the jewellers, the second-hand shops, the sellers of silks and cottons, the crockery and china vendors,

each has his own special quarter; while the vegetable
and fruit bazaar is an open space, where, under rough
little awnings, supported on poles and canes, the
market produce is exposed for sale.

Particularly interesting amongst the shops are those
of the jewellers and makers of arms. The walls of
the former are hung with silver necklaces and bangles
and anklets, many of which are of very beautiful design. Some of the necklets particularly are extremely
lovely, resembling in workmanship the finest and best
Greek and Etruscan work, with none of the rough-
ness apparent in the jewellery of so many oriental
countries. The favourite design seems to be single
chains supporting pendants of various shapes and
forms, from discs of fine filigree-work to solid pear-
shaped globules of metal. The bracelets are generally
bands of worked silver, though some, like the necklaces, are decorated with small chains and hanging
pendants. But the greatest skill of the jewellers of
Sanaa, who are rightly renowned for their workmanship, is exhibited in the dagger-sheaths, many of
which are of rich silver-gilt, and even, at times, of
gold. Perhaps the most lovely, however, are of plain
polished silver inlaid with gold coins, principally of
the Christian Byzantine emperors; others, again, of
delicate filigree, which the natives line with coloured
leathers or silks. But more than even the sheaths of
these *jambiyas*, as they call their daggers, the natives
value the blades. Antique ones are generally con-

sidered the best, and the people declare that the old
art of hardening the steel has been lost.   Be this as
it may, there is no doubt that the modern blades are
of no mean workmanship, and great prices, for the
Yemen, are paid for good specimens.   The two parts
of the dagger are nearly always sold separately, and
a Yemeni, having found a blade to suit him, has a
sheath made according to his taste and wealth.   The
early European visitors to Sanaa speak of the jewelled
arms worn by the Imams and their companions ; but
I saw only one specimen of these in the bazaars, a
silver-gilt sheath studded with rough pearls and turquoises, for which the shopkeeper was asking some
forty pounds sterling, without the blade.   Another
art long lost, but of which examples are still to be
procured, is the application of silver to copper and
brass.   This kind of work usually takes the form of
boxes of one of the latter metals, covered with inscriptions in Kufic or other Arabic characters in silver.
The later forms of this work are very inferior to the
earlier, and the silver is apt to peel off.

   One of the great institutions of Sanaa are the
khans, or caravanserais, of which there are a considerable number, the greater part being situated near the
gates of the city.   These buildings vary in size, but
some are very large, though nearly all in bad repair.
They usually consist of large houses three and four
storeys in height, open to the sky in the centre.   The
lower floor forms stabling for the animals, while a

number of rooms of various sizes open out on to the balconies which surround the court on the upper storeys. The hire of these rooms is very small, something like twopence a night, and as many as like to crowd into it do so. There is nearly always a *cafe* attached, where cooking can be done, either by the visitors themselves, or, if more extravagantly inclined, by the servants of the khan. Assembled round the gates of these khans are to be seen the tribes-people from every part of the interior—bringers of salt from Mareb, the modern Saba or Sheba; of coffee from the northern districts; of indigo and grain and spices from wherever the soil is suitable to their growth. Caravans from the Hadramaut and Yaffa discharge their goods here too, to reload their camels with the produce of the largest city of Southern Arabia.

The population of Sanaa, although there is no official census to base one's calculation upon, probably numbers some forty to fifty thousand people, of whom twenty thousand are said to be Jews. These, as has already been stated, have a quarter entirely to themselves; and although many hire shops in the bazaars, and are daily engaged in the town in attending to them, or in carrying on their respective trades, at night retire to the *ghetto*, with the exception of a few who are servants, and who sleep in their masters' houses. There seems to be no more oppression of the Jews in the Yemen than there is of the Arabs. They are free to carry on whatever trade they will;

to attend their synagogues and schools, and, in fact, seem very little interfered with by the Turks. They, of course, pay their regular share in the taxation, as is only right they should; and if it be exceptionally heavy in their case, it is so also in the case of the Arab inhabitants—though naturally the Jews, as to nature born, cry out a great deal more than the natives.

The *ghetto* is quite separate from the Arab city. The houses are built almost entirely of mud-bricks, but look clean and comfortable, though the habit of throwing all their refuse into the streets is by no means a pleasant one for the passer-by. However, in this they are little worse, if at all, than the Arabs, whose drain-pipes project well over the middle of the narrow streets, through which generally flows an open drain. The passer-by has to be careful to keep near the house-wall, or he will run the risk of coming terribly to grief. There are said to be more than twenty synagogues in the Jews' quarter, and over seven hundred boys attending the schools. The whole male population is supposed to be able to read; but the females attend entirely to their house-work, or the sewing of garments, and all education is neglected in their case.[1]

The Jews of the Yemen are believed to have come from India, and, as far as is known, there are none remaining of the old Jewish stock of pre-Islamic

[1] General Haig, in the Royal Geographical Proceedings, August 1887.

times. Although much despised by the proud Arabs,
they are seldom treated with violence or even rough-
ness, and what little persecution there can be said to
exist consists almost entirely of the jeers of small
boys, and even this is rare.

One cannot help noticing and admiring the extremely pleasant manners shown by the people of
the Yemen toward Europeans. With the exception
of the lower classes there is no crowding; and even
when curiosity leads the people to congregate round
a stranger, there are no rude remarks, much less any of
the ribald cursing which distinguishes the attitude of
the Moors of Morocco toward Europeans. This trait
in the character of the people of the Yemen adds
very largely to the pleasure of travelling, and many
a kind word was said to me on my journey by
"warriors" of the fiercest aspect, and many a pleasant smile and "God-speed" followed me as I rode
away from the villages and towns. In fact, with a
very few exceptions, I never heard a word of unpleasantness spoken either to or of myself. There is apparently less religious fanaticism towards Christians
than exists between the two sects of Islam repre-
sented in the country—the Zaidis[1] by the Arabs,
and the Sunnis by the Turks.

Through the centre of Sanaa flows at times the
river Kharid. However, the river - bed is dry
except in the rainy season, when a huge torrent

[1] The Zaidis are a division of the Sheiya sect.

pours down its course, often doing considerable damage to the adjacent houses. A bridge spans the river at one spot, and from here a good view is obtained both up and down the stream, the high yellow banks of which are crowned with tall houses, built in the peculiar style of architecture common to the place.

Beyond the Jews' quarter, and to the extreme west of the town, is the suburb of Bir el-Azab, of which mention has already been made. Here the roads are wider, and pass between the high walls of the gardens, over the top of which can be seen the leaves and blossoms of the fruit-trees. Two villages also form country residences for the inhabitants of the city—Jeraaf, about two miles to the north, and Raudha, the same distance farther on. Shortly before my arrival at Sanaa the rebels had succeeded in blowing up with gunpowder the Turkish barracks at the latter place, together with some five-and-twenty soldiers.

With the exception of the Turkish mosque, all the others seem to be in bad repair, owing, it is said, to the Osmanli Government having seized most of the mosque property, the sole means of adding to and keeping in order the building themselves. The great mosque is a huge square building surrounded by a high wall, and boasting two tall minarets of curious construction. It was here that Ibn Fadl, the leader of the Karmathians, in the year 911 A.D.,

carried out one of those acts of licentious cruelty
with which the history of the East teems.   Having

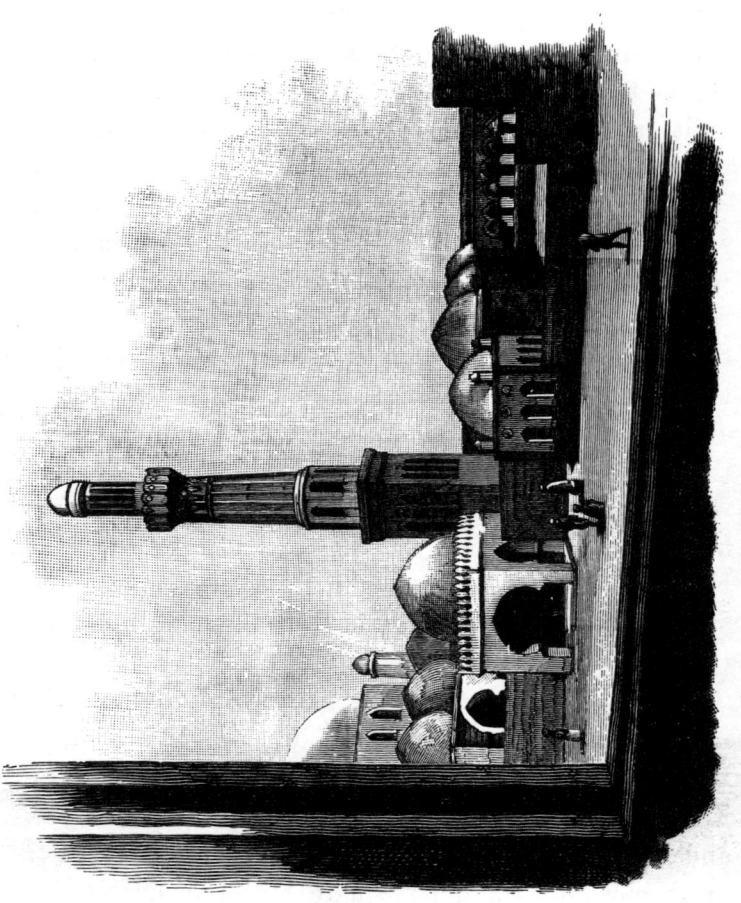

Turkish mosque at Sanaa, as seen from the prison window.

in that year successfully installed himself at Sanaa,
from which on two previous occasions he had been
ousted, he caused the great courtyard of the mosque

to be filled some three or four feet deep with water, into which were driven naked all the young girls of the city. From his seat on the minaret he gazed upon them, and such as pleased him he dishonoured. The height of the water, however, discoloured the walls, and for centuries told the tale of the brief power wielded by this licentious usurper.

But of all the sights offered by the city of Sanaa, the population presents the most interesting. Everywhere some strange figure meets the eye : here it is some wild tribes- man with bronzed skin and raven-black locks, girded with his loin-cloth of dark blue cotton ; there some merchant from the Hejaz, slow and stately, with strange glassy eyes that speak of *hashish*, robed in striped silks, and whose turban, so white it is, literally seems to sparkle in

Turkish soldier.

the sunlight. Again it is some ill-fed, ill-clothed Turkish soldier, with only one boot perhaps, and that scarcely more than a shadow of its former self, with face unshaven and sunk with illness ; and as one is

still watching him, there rattles past a shabby
victoria, in which is seated some fat Pasha or
Bey, with hideous black-cloth clothes richly sewn
in gold lace ; and one knows that as often as not
his clothes, his carriage, and his horses are bought
with the money that ought to feed the soldiers, for
but a small proportion of the pay of the troops ever
reaches them.   Then, again, a woman passes, wrapt
head to foot in coloured garments, the veil of
coloured stuff just transparent enough to allow
her to grope her way, for so do the women of Sanaa
hide their charms ; and here, there, and everywhere
are the " gamins," the same all over the world,
though their blood and their language be different,
—little monkeys all, and in Sanaa rebels to the very
heart.

Of all the cities of the Yemen, there is none that
can boast the antiquity of Sanaa.   Tradition says
that it was founded by Ad, the ancestor of the tribe
of Adites, who were destroyed by a miraculous hot
blast of wind for refusing to listen to the voice of the
Prophet Hud.   A second tribe, that of Thamud, met
with a like fate for disregarding the Prophet Salih ;
only in their case it was a terrible voice that called to
them from the skies that caused their deaths.[1]   There
is only one drawback to this tale—namely, that long
after the destruction of the Adites we find them
attacked and conquered by a descendant of Yarub,

[1] The Koran, *sura* vii.

brother of Hadramaut, and son of Kahtan. He was apparently more successful than the miraculous hot wind, for they were evidently entirely wiped out on this occasion, and we find no more mention of them in history. But there is another interest belonging to the Adites—namely, that they were of the autochthonous stock of the Yemen, and therefore probably one of the original Semitic people who afterwards spread over Arabia and founded the Arab races, and who have, with the propagation of Islam, wandered far into Asia and Africa. The original name of Sanaa was Azal, Uzul, or Uwal, the latter of which means "primacy" in the Arab tongue. The authorities appear to differ as to which was really the first name, and it seems not improbable that Azal or Uzul was the original title, which, being incomprehensible to the later races, they changed to the Arabic Uwal—a word that described not only the antiquity of the place, but also bears a strong resemblance to its original name. This is, however, merely a conjecture.

Although Saba seems in the days of the Sabæans to have been a more important place than Sanaa, there is little reason to doubt that the latter was in existence ; and amongst other authorities Ibn Khaldun states that Sanaa was the seat of the Tubbas or Himyaric kings for centuries before the time of Islam. This alone, apart from the traditions of far greater antiquity, of which we have no reason to doubt the truth, shows that probably two thousand

years ago the city of Sanaa was a flourishing community, the seat of the government of powerful kings,
who were living in a state of civilisation and culture.
But the question of the antiquity of Sanaa is not one
that can be entered into at any length here, and interesting as is the subject, space does not allow of
carrying it further.

There are one or two episodes in the history of
Sanaa that cannot be passed over without some slight
mention. The first is the erecting there of a Christian
church by Abrahá el-Ashram, Viceroy of the Yemen,
under the Abyssinian King Aryat, for the building of
which the Emperor of Rome is said to have supplied
marble and workmen. Abrahá, who was a fanatical
Christian, hoped by the erection of this wonderful
structure, of which unfortunately we have but few
details—and such as do exist are absurd—to change
the goal of pilgrimage from the Kaabah at Mecca,
which, it must be remembered, was an object of
veneration long before the time of Mahammed, to
Sanaa. Failing to entice the Arabs, he attempted by
force to bring them to his church, which eventually
led to his famous attack upon Mecca in 570 A.D.,
and in the total destruction of his army by pebbles
dropped from the claws and beaks of birds.[1]

At the time of the introduction of Islam into the
Yemen, we find the government in the hands of
Budhan, or Budzan, the Persian Viceroy, who, how-

---

[1] The Koran, *sura* xv.

ever, embraced the new religion, and was confirmed by Mahammed as Governor of the Yemen—a post he held until he died. Within a year or two of the death of Mahammed himself, Islam was firmly grafted in the country, owing, it must be added, to the indomitable courage and energy of Mohajir, who, on his triumphal march to the Hadramaut, secured the leaders of the party dissentient to the rule of the then Caliph Abou Bekr, and, sending them prisoners to Mecca, planted the Caliph's rule firmly in Sanaa.

Although the Christians of Nejran continued such for a period, the enthusiasm of the people for Islam swept them along in its tide, and idolatry and Christianity soon became extinct in the Yemen—the third Caliph, Othman, destroying almost the last vestige of the former by razing the temple of Zuhrah at Ghumdan, the remains of which and of the Christian church of Abrahá are visible to-day in a heap of ruins at and near Sanaa respectively.

From this period the history of Sanaa has been a troubled one. Constant warfare with foreign princes, and assassinations and rivalry fraught with bloodshed between the local rulers, help to make up as dark a page of history as can be imagined. Yet in spite of this, the city has been always an important and flourishing one, renowned for its manufactures, its trade, and its wealth. With every disadvantage accruing from a constant change of government, it managed to survive; and not only to survive but to increase, until toward the middle of the seventeenth century it reached unparalleled prosperity under the then powerful Imams. But as they sank in power, so did Sanaa lose its prosperity. Its fate seemed drawn along with that of its Imams; and as ruler after ruler lost more and more of his territory, so the glories of the capital diminished. Yet there was now and again a flicker in its death-throes; but never did it last above a few years, when once more the steady decline would commence.

How it ended is well known; for, broken in spirit and harassed by the surrounding tribes, Sanaa offered no resistance when the Turks, in 1872, entered the place; and the city, which had nobly held her own in so many encounters, almost welcomed the stranger into her midst. Had the inhabitants been aware at that time how their action would lead to their oppression, there is but little doubt that they would have hesitated in their invitation to the Turkish forces, already firmly established on the coast, to come and take over the reins of government.

MENAKHA, FROM THE NORTH.

CHAPTER IX.

SANAA TO MENAKHA.

As long as I live I shall never forget my departure from Sanaa. In the cold grey dawn, the temperature little if anything above freezing, worn out with a night of raging fever that still throbbed in my veins, I was lifted on to my mule at the door of the *conak*, and, with a couple of soldiers to accompany me, sent upon my way. Weird and wretched everything looked. The houses, that only the day before had struck me as beautiful in their strange oriental architecture, now looked like pallid ruins, depressing in the extreme; while the few hurrying persons we passed seemed but shadows in the grey light of dawn.

On through the bazaars with their closed shops; on by narrow streets and byways, over which the tall houses seemed verily to hang suspended; across the bridge that spans what is at times a roaring torrent but was now but a dry bed; across a wide open space and through the dirty Jews' quarter, and the garden suburb of Bir el-Azab; then out under the great town

gateway with its strange towers, on which a shivering
sentry or two kept guard, into the open country. A
long level road leads one from the city across the
surrounding plain, a road as good as one could expect
to find in England. Then a range of bare hills seems
to block the way, and one begins to climb up and up
by the winding twisting track, until the summit is
reached. Looking back, a fine view of Sanaa was
obtained, lying on the spur of Jibel Negoum, backed
by still higher mountains. To right and left extended
the valley, until some way off to the north one could
see the town of Raudha, where not a month before
the rebels had blown up the Turkish barracks and
some twenty-five soldiers with gunpowder. From
this spot one could obtain a better idea than we had
as yet been able to do of the size of Sanaa, as it lay
mapped out below us, a great flat-roofed city, dull
yellow and white, upon still yellower and whiter
plains, the only break in which were the gardens at
Bir el-Azab.

At the summit of the ascent a plateau is reached
scattered with villages, now all more or less knocked
down by the Turkish artillery, after the road from
Hodaidah had been forced, and the Arab Shereef,
Sid esh-Sherai, dislodged from Hajarat el-Mehedi, a
spot a few miles farther on. Over the plateau the
road proceeded tolerably straight, though the going
was by no means good, in spite of the fact that the
track was a wide one. But its repair had evidently

been neglected for a time, and it was strewn with stones.

After the sun had risen it became very warm, but it was a change for the better from the miserable cold of the early morning, and, weak as I was from fever, I was glad to get off my mule for a time and stretch my limbs by walking.

At the *café* of Metneh we stopped for our mid-day meal. A large, low, stone building forms the caravanserai, both for man and beast. The place is roughly built, one storey in height, the roof being supported on arches and stone columns, round the bases of which are little raised platforms, on one of which we spread our carpet and rested for a time. The *café* was nearly full of Turkish troops, poor, ill-fed, and ill-clothed fellows, but the very acme of good-humour. It was amusing to hear them discussing my presence with some Arab merchants who happened to be there at the same time. The conclusion they arrived at was that the presence of a Christian in the country foretold the downfall of the Yemen, and the sooner they, the Moslems, cleared out of it the better. It was flattering certainly to hear one's self considered of such vital importance to a country the size of the Yemen ; nor did the fact that I was a prisoner in the ѩands of a Turkish guard seem to lessen their opinion of me. On discovering at length that I spoke Arabic, we joined parties and lunched together, and very polite they all were. The group was a strange one, representing in the Arabs the rebel party, in the Turks the conquerors and oppressors, and last, but not least, in my humble self the future of the Yemen (for so they deemed my presence to foretell). Yet we were a merry band, and shared the same hubble-bubble of peace, and parted with protestations of profound respect and friendship for one another.

One of the pleasantest recollections of the Yemen that I bore away with me is, and always will be, the hours spent in these wayside *cafés*. Then more than at any other time one saw the people as they really are. Then all restraint was thrown aside ; there was exhibited none of the suspicion we habitually show to fellow-travellers ; and often we unburdened our aims and ideas to one another, the Arabs and I. As I write of it I long once more to go back, to sit cross-legged on the floor and sip the beverage of coffee-husks from the tiny Japanese and Chinese cups the Yemenis love so much, and listen to the patient murmur of the hubble-bubble amongst a group of half-naked Arabs.

Leaving Metneh in the afternoon, we pushed on through Bauan, with its strange market, toward our night's resting-place. The road still continues to ascend, and is in most parts very rough and bad, rendering travelling by no means pleasant. However, any unpleasantness from this was amply repaid by the magnificent view that from time to time met our gaze. The track was leading us along the summit of a mountain-top, which to the north looked straight down into a great valley thousands of feet below. What a wonderful valley it was, full of coffee-groves, and luxuriating in all the glories of gorgeous vegetation, amongst which banana-leaves could be plainly distinguished, waving their great green heads! Amongst all this verdure, clinging as it seemed to the mountain-sides, were villages, each crowned by its *burj* or fort, the whole perched on some overhanging rock. On to their very roofs we seemed to look. Often on the road I would rest for a few minutes to gaze in wonderment on this entrancing scene, until, as evening came on, filmy mists rose from the valley, and concealed from view all but the opposite mountain-peaks, torn and rugged, which rose above the sea of iridescent cloud like great cathedral steeples. What a land it is, the Yemen! What a world of romance and history lies hid in those great mountain valleys! What tales the little, sparkling, dancing rivulets could tell, for often, I wot, their limpid waters have run red with blood! Night fell, and the scene became one of still grey silence, weird and strange.

After reaching an altitude of ten thousand feet above the sea-level the road began to descend, and we passed once or twice through villages, crowned by their strange towers, until at length Sôk el-Khamis, our night's resting-place, was reached. There are several of these villages in its vicinity, and one we passed was occupied by Turkish troops, whose riotous laughter and singing jarred on the peaceful sounds of night, the humming of the insects and the soft hoot-hoot of the rock owls.

We stopped at one of these strange tower-like buildings, and my guard informed me that this was our halting-place. After repeated knockings at a heavy wooden door we were admitted into a yard, and from thence entered the house—the way led by a dirty mountaineer in little else but a sheepskin coat, who, with a small oil-lamp, lighted us up a flight of stone stairs into the guest-chamber. A poor enough place it was, and none too clean, its ceiling blackened by the fumes of charcoal-fires, its floor of rough stones and mortar, the ups and downs of which a carpet ill disguised. This was, however, the sole accommodation, and our host plaintively asked us to make ourselves as comfortable as we could, while he went off to search for provisions, adding that the Turkish garrison at the neighbouring village had exhausted the supply.

So we spread our carpet, and Abdurrahman and Saïd, and the Turkish and Arab soldiers who formed my guard, sat down together over a charcoal brasier, in which bubbled one of the common narrow-necked earthenware pots in which they brew their drink of coffee-husks, and smoked our hookah in peace, sharing alike in its cracked amber mouthpiece. We were all tired, and talked but little; but Saïd now and again would burst into song, and very well he sang, too, the plaintive melodies of the country.

Presently our host returned with a scarecrow of a fowl and some leathery bread, which was all the good fellow was able to raise, and it was not long before a rather too savoury dish of rancid butter and chicken-bones—for there was little else—had usurped the place of our coffee-pot on the brasier. What jokes we made about that poor chicken! After all, we agreed, it could not be anything but thin after having lived through the late rebellion. However, we ate it all right.

The view as we left Sôk el-Khamis the next morning was almost as lovely as that of the day before. As the night-mists rose at sunrise, range after range of mountains loomed up before us, peak above peak, until in the far west one great mass overtopped all the rest.

The road descends steeply, winding the while, in parts showing signs of the repairs of the Turkish engineers, in others merely a foothold on the mountain-side. Numbers of blue rock-pigeons fluttered hither and thither in the morning sunlight ; but lovely as they were, I was enticed to shoot a few, for, after all, one fowl is not sufficient food for eight persons, and there seemed every likelihood of our faring as ill at our next halting-place as we had done the night before.

At one spot we passed one of the most lovely scenes I had as yet seen in the Yemen. Half-way down a steep slope, wooded with forest-trees, was a

tomb and fountain, the clear cold water tumbling
into a deep tank.   Away behind a peak of the mountain rose bare and rocky into the blue sky, its lower
slopes covered with trees, its summit crowned with
the ruins of a village which the Turkish artillerymen
had destroyed, leaving little but the walls to tell of
its existence.   The domed mosque, a tiny place,
glistening white against the foliage, and the sound
of the running water, added a charm to a scene of
perfect peace and loveliness.

At length the descent was accomplished, and we
entered a desolate valley, keeping to the rock-strewn
river-bed, now almost dry, as being better than the
road, which here is almost indistinguishable, winding
and turning amongst great boulders, which appear to
have fallen from the steeps above.   An hour or so
later we passed under the strange fortress of Mefhak,
grandly situated on a pinnacle of rock some five
hundred feet above the valley; and, leaving a large
encampment of Turkish troops on our left, once more
began to ascend.   For a while our way led through
the loveliest of little valleys, which seemed like the
greater one we had been passing through in miniature.
On either side walls of rock some fifty to a hundred
feet in height rose precipitously, but, sheltered from
the sun, a number of varieties of wild-flowers had
taken root, and the place was a fairyland of colour.
Great clusters of jasmine hung over the precipices,
while on every side bloomed acacias and aloes.   A

gorgeous flowering-tree, bearing pale-pink blossoms, edged the narrow water-course, just as if it had been planted there by the hand of man.

An hour more and we drew up at the caravanserai of Ijz for our mid-day rest. Very hot it was; but the proprietor of the *café*, a wounded Turkish soldier, full of grievances and very dirty, amused us much, mumbling and grumbling as he leaned over the fire to cook my coffee and the men's drink of coffee-husks. Although coffee in very large quantities is exported from the Yemen, it is drunk only by the Turks and the richer classes, the poorer contenting themselves with, and preferring, they say, the boiled husks.

We spent only an hour or two at Ijz, as I was anxious to push on to Menakha before dark; and accordingly in the heat of the early afternoon we said good-bye to our old host and the handful of Turkish troops who had joined us in our meal, and mounted our mules once more.

As our road proceeded it increased in magnificence, entering the heart of the mountains, on the summit of one of which the town of Menakha is perched. This river lies at an elevation of somewhat over five thousand feet above the sea. Quite suddenly the valley comes to an end, and we commenced one of those steep ascents to which we were almost becoming accustomed now. The path is little but a boulder-strewn track in the mountain-side, and one could not help wondering how our little mules would ever

accomplish the climb.   Dismounting at the foot,
Abdurrahman, Saïd, and I raced ahead, scrambling

Gorge near Menakha.

and tumbling over the rocks, and nearly frightening
the wits out of a descending caravan, who probably

had never seen the like of us before ; for although Saïd was in the Yemen costume, Abdurrahman wore the there unknown dress of the mountaineers of Morocco, while I was in riding-breeches, and flannel shirt, and a red fez cap. Great proud-looking fellows the caravan-men were, and they watched us with a startled stare, evidently putting us down as lunatics. However, our laughter at their surprise so amused them that they became quite friendly, and would not let me go on till I had shaken each singly by the hand, which I was only too pleased to do. Up and up we toiled, leaving the mules to follow with the muleteers. Every here and there are springs which the natives have aided by building tanks, and now and again we would stop to drink and bathe our faces and hands.

Almost suddenly we reached the summit, after a climb of over two thousand five hundred feet up the execrable zigzag path, and the little town of Menakha lay before me.

I determined to wait here for my soldier-guards, whom we had left a long way behind us ; so we threw ourselves down, panting and hot, upon a ledge of rock, and gazed at the scene before us. Wonderful, stupendous it was ! Around us on all sides the bare fantastic peaks and perpendicular precipices, on the edge of one of which we were perched, and up the face of which we could see the path we had climbed winding in and out. Below us, far, far below, like little ants, we could see our mules and men toiling up. A thread of river, the Wadi Zaum, was distinguishable down the valley, the few green thorny trees which grew along its banks being, with the exception of some stunted brushwood and a few aloes and creepers, the sole vegetation in view. A very entrance to the "Inferno," gloomy and dark. The rays of the setting sun lit up in contrast to all this the roseate peaks of the mountains, many of which, thousands of feet above us, were crowned with strange villages and towers. At length our mules caught us up, and mounting again for the few yards that yet remained between us and Menakha, we made our entry into the town, drawing up at the principal Government building, where the Kaimakam resided.

My guard of Turkish soldiers had been intrusted with letters to the governors respectively of Menakha and Hodaidah, and no sooner was our missive presented than I was shown into the presence of the Kaimakam. I found him pleasant, as nearly all Turks can be when they like, and an hour or so passed very cheerily. Meanwhile he had given orders for a room to be prepared for me within the precincts of the Government offices, and on leaving him I was shown to a large, comfortable, airy chamber on the ground-floor, with a window looking over a sort of drill-yard, beyond which was a fine view of the mountains, the opposite spur of which, at an altitude of some hundreds of feet above the town, was crowned with a Turkish fort, near which some artillerymen were drilling.

It should have been mentioned already that the road we had been following from Sanaa was almost identically the line taken by the Sanaa and Hodaidah telegraph-wire, which, like all provincial Turkish telegraphs, is, I believe, worked by the Government, from a representative of whom one is obliged to obtain permission before making use of it. This permission had been refused me at Sanaa. At Menakha there is quite a pretentious office.

After leaving the Kaimakam I went for a stroll in the town, followed of course by a guard, who, how-ever, did not in the least interfere with my actions, and in whose presence I was venturesome enough to sketch, without calling forth any sterner reproof than that if they were caught allowing me to draw they might get into trouble, so that I had better creep behind a rock and make any sketches I wanted from a spot where I would not be seen.

Of all the places it has ever been my lot to see, Menakha is the most wonderfully situated. The town is perched on a narrow strip of mountain that joins two distinct ranges, and it forms the watershed of two great valleys—that up which we had proceeded on our arrival, and the second to the west. So narrow is the ridge on which the town stands, that the walls of the houses on both sides seem almost to hang over the precipices ; and there are spots—for instance, near

the military hospital—where one can sit and look
down absolutely into the two great valleys at the
same time. Curious and wonderful as this is, the
grand effect of the scene is doubly increased by the
extraordinary peaks which rise above the place—enormous pinnacles, for no other word can express their
fantastic shapes and forms. Great, bare, rocky crags
they are, perpendicular, and ending, like sugar-loafs,
in points, on which, in several places, the natives
have built their strange towers. How they ever
ascend or descend seems incredible, or from whence
they obtain their water-supply.

The town of Menakha is quite a small one. It contains, perhaps, some five thousand inhabitants, without counting the very considerable number of Turkish
troops stationed there at the time of my visit. The
houses are well built of stone, some of them four
storeys, and many three, in height. The Government offices and the military hospital and barracks
give the place quite a European appearance, for
they are all built in modern Turkish style, with glass
windows and flat roofs.

The bazaar is tolerably well supplied with the nec-
essaries of life, though at the time of my visit meat
and vegetables were scarce, on account of the influx
of troops. There are, too, several large shops, one or
two kept by Greeks. I was surprised, in passing
through the town, to be accosted in excellent English
by one of these shopkeepers, who, he told me, had

been a servant to an Englishman in Suakin for some years. I went with him to his store, where everything was purchasable, from sardines to port wine, and spent half an hour or so talking with him. He was evidently an intellectual man, and seemed well up in the affairs of the Yemen. He had been present at the taking of Menakha by the Arabs, and its recapture by the Turks; but his property had been respected in both cases, and he had suffered little if any loss.

The great altitude at which Menakha is situated —some seven thousand six hundred feet above the sea-level — renders it liable to sudden changes of temperature; and two hours after we had arrived in blazing sunshine, clouds gathered over the town, obscuring the view, and the temperature fell to below 50°. We managed to procure a charcoal brasier, over which my men and I huddled, our circle being joined by a couple of charming Turkish officers, both of whom spoke Arabic well.

About eight o'clock I was taken suddenly ill with fever, which did not leave me until ten the next morning, by which time I was so weak that I could only stand with assistance, and accordingly travelling was out of the question. The Kaimakam made no difficulties about my remaining another day, and did all in his power to make me comfortable. During the afternoon I had sufficiently recovered my strength to crawl out and seek the shade of a hollow in the rocks, where my men lit a little fire and brewed coffee. The spot we had chosen looked directly into the great valley that runs west from Menakha, far down which we could see. Away below us, tier above tier, were the terraced coffee and banana groves ; while the rocky precipices, here bare and frowning, were in other parts hung with creepers, while in every crevice some strange flowering aloes had found room to grow.

Amongst this mass of verdure, far, far away below us, lay villages, their flat roofs upturned, as it were, to us, who were so high above them, looking like the squares on some fairy chess-board. Away down the valley a silvery thread of light told the presence of a river, fed by a hundred little streams, which, issuing from the rocky slopes, leaped and danced to join the larger stream below. Beyond, again, all was haze and mountain-peaks, faint as a cloud and inexpressibly lovely.

Wild-flowers and ferns, especially maidenhair, grew in abundance round our little nook in the rocks, in which we were shaded from the sun's rays by an overhanging crag. The whole scene was so framed by shrubs and creepers and flowers, a mass of blossom and green, that one lost the effect of distance ; and, in the clear air, it seemed but a step from our resting-place to the bottom of the valley, and a step more to the far-away peaks.

But it is not on account of its gorgeous scenery

that Menakha has become an important place. Rather it is owing to its great strategical position; for it dominates the two parts of the highroad from Hodaidah to Sanaa, from each of which it is roughly equidistant. It is, no doubt, on this account, and to the practical advantages it offers, owing to its fine position for keeping up a line of communication between the capital and the coast, that a considerable number of troops are stationed and some forts erected there.

It played by no means an unimportant part during the rebellion; and although this has been referred to elsewhere in a chapter dealing with that subject, it may be as well to mention the facts here. Menakha was one of the first Turkish strongholds to fall into the hands of the Arabs. The governor was taken prisoner; numbers of the troops were killed in the rebel rush; and what remained of its military population were sent to the leader of the rebellion at Sadah. It was not, in fact, until after the battle fought near Hojaila, on the road from Hodaidah, at a spot where the Tehéma ends and the mountains commence, that Menakha was retaken. To Ahmed Feizi Pasha belongs the credit of the wonderful march from Hodaidah to Sanaa, in which the Turks dragged their guns by execrable roads over passes ten thousand feet in altitude; and it was upon this triumphal entry of the new Governor-General of the Yemen that the town once more came into the possession of the Turks, being deserted by the Arabs before the arrival of the Osmanli troops. Had the native horde only been better officered and possessed better arms; had they destroyed the road more successfully than they did, and stood firmly to their impregnable position at Menakha,—there is little doubt that the capital could not have held out, and that the Yemen to-day would have been in the hands of the Imam Ahmed ed-Din. At sunset, as had happened the evening before, the place became wrapt in cloud, and the temperature fell to such an extent that even in our room, with a fire, we suffered considerably. However, one can bear the cold, provided one is free from fever; and, tired and weary after a sleepless night, I lay like a log, and, in spite of the cries of sentries and the occasional blowing of a bugle, did not awake until grey dawn was creeping up, and my men were loading the mules.

CHAPTER X.

MENAKHA TO HODAIDAH.

THE road from Menakha to the coast leads one for the first few miles along the mountains on the southern side of the valley, gradually ascending the while, until, an hour or so after leaving the town, an altitude of eight thousand feet above the sea-level is reached. At this spot a spur in the mountain is crossed, near to which is the remarkable village of Kariet el-Hajra, a rock crowned with tall stone houses, many of which are built in the strange fashion of towers. A precipice surrounds the village on every side, the lower slopes of which are cultivated in terraces. The place has the appearance of being a large and important one, and from its position must be exceedingly strong. The country immediately surrounding this spot is very beautiful, there being an abundance of water and no lack of trees, while the terraces and fields were, at the time of my visit, green with young grass and crops, and gorgeous with wild - flowers. Leaving Hajra on the right, the road begins to descend, and

soon another village, more extraordinary than that we
had already passed, came into sight. This is Attara.
From an expanse of terraced slope rises a single
pinnacle of rock some hundreds of feet in height,
split perpendicularly into two divisions. On the very
summit, on which there is only just room for it to
stand, is a large building, apparently a house and
tower. Although unable to see the track by which
this, to the eye, apparently unscalable position is
reached, my men informed me that there is a stairway cut in the solid rock, by means of which the
inhabitants ascend and descend. Close nestling under
the pinnacle is the rest of the village, built tier above
tier on the steep mountain-side. The path by which
we were descending zigzags down until one arrives in
a sort of amphitheatre, of which the village forms an
apex. The ground here is richly cultivated with
coffee-trees and bananas, growing upon terraces. In
one place the jungle seems to have gained possession
of what was originally cultivated land, and appears
in a mass of euphorbiæ and other strange trees and
plants. Here, too, jasmine grows in wonderful
abundance, the whole air being filled with its sweet
fragrance.

Zigzagging down the mountain-side, we arrived
before mid-day at the *café* of Wisil, wonderfully
perched on the very edge of the precipice. The place
is poor enough, but a few shady huts of grass and
mats have been erected round a little terraced garden,

THE VILLAGE OF EL-HAJRA.

over the wall of which one gazes far down into the valley beneath. Here under a shady tree we spread our carpet and refreshed ourselves, revelling in the magnificence of our surroundings. This resting-place was situated at an elevation of a little over four thousand five hundred feet above the sea-level, so that since the morning we had descended some three thousand feet.

From this spot is obtained perhaps the most extraordinary view of the terraced mountains we had as yet obtained. These surrounding ranges are celebrated for their coffee, principally Jibal Masar and Safan, both of which lie to the north of the road. Away above the terraces the mountains rise in perpendicular precipices, and nearly every peak is crowned with one of the curious towers already described.

The view from Wisil was the last we were to see of its kind, for we were fast leaving the mountains behind and descending to the plains, or Teháma, and even from here the change to the country was appreciable, for far away to the west the great mountains became lower, and the horizon was bounded with rough barren hills, very like those we had seen around Jibel Menif, when we left the desert beyond Lahej. A weird old lady served us with coffee and food at our resting-place—a parchment-skinned grinning old hag, half clothed in torn dark-blue rags, with a lot of what looked like dirty bandages wound round her head ; but she was a cheery old gossip, and Saïd took

advantage of her to exhibit his wit and sarcasm, much
to her amusement as well as our own.

View near Wisil.

Poor Saïd! The wear and tear of the last month
had worn him a bit. Fever had paled his skin, and

left him thinner than he was when he had started from
Aden ; but no weariness, no fever, had caused him to
pay less attention to his personal charms than before,
and his curly locks were as soft and silky and glossy
as ever, although his loin-cloth and sash told tales of
travel. Still, in all our hardships he had been ever
bright and gay, and as we neared civilisation once
more, and there seemed some chance of his seeing his
paradise—Aden—again, his eyes regained their former twinkle, and his laugh grew more cheery than
ever. With Abdurrahman it was different, and the
strain and exertion he had been through had told on
his more delicate constitution. Brought up in the
bracing mountains of Morocco, where frosts are common, and even in the daytime the heat is never oppressive, he had felt severely the sudden changes of
the tropics. All his gaiety had left him, and he
scarcely spoke. It was with difficulty that we could
rouse his spirits, try hard as we did, Saïd and I. Almost every evening, in spite of arsenic and quinine,
fever would seize him, and he would lie awake of a
night, tossing and moaning in a way that was pitiful
to see and hear.

Leaving Wisil, the road descends, by a zigzag track,
the steep mountain-side. Here were apparent one
at least of the advantages of the Turkish occupation
of the Yemen, for the road was wide and in good repair, supported by a stone embankment, and planted
on either side with mimosa-trees, which no doubt help

in some degree to prevent the floods which the heavy rainfalls occasion from washing the stones away, and which will eventually prove no small advantage to the traveller by their shade. At length the bed of the water-course was reached, down which the road proceeds, roughly and unpleasantly, over great boulders and stones that tired our poor little mules, and necessitated our proceeding on foot. Thick vegetation, principally trees of the mimosa type, fringe the edge of the river-bed, which, except for an occasional pool or spring, contained no water.

On and on, until the gorge narrows and enters a defile, merely the water-course and walls of rock on either hand, some eighty feet perhaps in height. Here was a sight that caused us an hour or so of amusement and laughter, for the precipices were the haunt of hundreds of apes and monkeys, which scampered away at our approach, and sat chattering and grinning at us from their perches. So tame many of them were, that we were able to approach within fifteen or twenty yards of them before they would seek refuge in the nooks and crannies of the rocks. My men were eager to shoot one or two, but I would not allow it, as it was a real pleasure to watch the funny creatures in their antics, and to listen to their squeaking and chattering. In some cases the larger apes were carrying their young in their arms, and handling them as carefully as a woman does her child. Even Abdurrahman awoke from his melancholy, and laughed heartily at the strange creatures, which bounded from rock to rock, or showed their rows of chattering white teeth from some hole in the cliff.

Continuing along the bottom of the valley for some little way farther, we turned eventually from the water-course, and climbed a bare rocky hill to the north of the river, and, crossing a small plateau, descended to the village of Hojaila, which we reached an hour or two before sunset.

At this point we had said farewell to the mountains, for although the foot-hills extend farther into the Teháma, beyond Bajil in fact, we were to see no more of the greater ranges. But not only is Hojaila the finishing spot of the mountains, but the people entirely change, becoming from that point Arabs of the plains, dwelling in mud and thatch houses, and different in appearance and habits.

We had passed during the day's march through a part of the country the inhabitants of which need investigation, and about which I, unfortunately, can say but little here. These are people of a religious sect who called themselves Makarama, but of the origin of which, except that their belief is said to be of Indian extraction, I have found it impossible to discover anything. These Yemenis are in language and appearance like their Moslem neighbours, although several names in the vicinity tell of India. Principal amongst them is the "Dar el Hinoud," or Indians' monastery or house, farther on in the Teháma. Of their belief but little was to be ascertained. It is summed up, however, in two lines of poetry, of which I was able to obtain the translation :—

" God is indiscoverable, by day or by night.
   Do not worry about anything, there is neither heaven nor hell."

Professing these strange tenets, there is this sect on the highroad from Hodaidah to Sanaa. As to their observances, the only man of their belief I met with would say but little, while the Moslems, although uninfluenced by the fanaticism one would expect to find, are careless. They have, I was told, the old Judaic observance of the scapegoat, and a particular night in the year in which they shut themselves into their houses, and are said to practise incest. This, however, may be possibly the Moslem idea of what really takes place. Were this to be absolutely depended upon, the fact might point to a Karmathian origin, for Ibn Fadl allowed the drinking of wine and this practice ; but then it is scarcely likely that a Karmathian superstition should survive in a belief which is in direct contravention to Islam. It is known that in certain Phœnician rites incest was allowed, and the practice of a certain nightly annual feast in which the houses are illuminated might point to the worship of Adonis, certain remains of which, I am informed, are found amongst the mountaineers of the Himalayas. My information on this sect of the Makarama continues that

TURKISH CAMP OF HOJAILA.

they are at times visited by natives of India, who
prize the charms that they are in the habit of
writing; and most probably their orgin may be
found in that country, for Hodaidah has always
been largely frequented by Indian traders.

Hojaila is but a small place, more a collection of
huts than a town, as it is elsewhere described, though
at the time I passed through it was augmented by a
large Turkish camp, pitched near the *jimerouk*, or
custom-house. There seems, with the exception of
this building, a large, low, square place, to be no
other of importance, though the Sheikh resides in a
house two storeys in height, painted red and white
in bands, which stands a curious landmark on the
edge of a steep incline leading down to the river-
bed. A few trees are scattered about the place, and
under these were lolling Turkish soldiers, while the
tents, and sentries passing and repassing, gave quite a
martial appearance to the otherwise dreary scene; for,
with the exception of these trees and the oleanders in
the river-bed, the country was dull and sun-dried.

Only a short rest was allowed me here, although
we had been travelling, almost without interruption, since the early morning. However, as I was
entirely in the hands of the Turkish guards who
had been sent to see me to Hodaidah, any attempt
at expostulation was out of the question. Another
advantage, too, was to be gained by pushing on—
namely, the moonlight night.

We had left behind us now the high elevations
and watered valleys, and nothing but plain and
desert lay between us and Hodaidah, some eighty
miles distant, over which, although the month was
February, travelling by day is torment. So an
hour or two was all the time we spent in the
café at Hojaila, and as soon as the sunset glow
was dying away we loaded our little mules again
and set off.

From sunset until near dawn we plodded on over
the plain, the broken rocky hills showing up on
either side in the clear moonlight, which was sufficiently bright to allow us to see that a considerable
portion of the country we were passing through was
under cultivation.

How balmy and warm the night was! and had it
not been that one was tired and weary with the long
ride from Menakha, it would have proved most enjoy-
able. As it was, one could not help admiring the loveliness of the still moonlight, and the silence, broken
only by the thud of our mules' feet upon the sand and
the humming of the insects in the air. Every now
and then we would pass a caravan of camels, slow-
gaited and patient, which seemed to grow out of the
moonlight like spectres, only to vanish again into the
darkness.

As dawn grew near we reached Bohay, situated to
the north of Jibel Damir. It is a poor little place;
but the rest in a mat *café* was inexpressibly refresh-

ing, for out of the last twenty-four hours we had been
nearly twenty on the road.

Stretching ourselves upon the string couches, which
do not seem to be in use anywhere out of the Teháma
and the southern plains, we were soon wrapped in
sleep. But at sunrise my guards woke me, and we
made a start again. But our march was happily to
prove only a short one, and three hours later we drew
in sight of Bajil, where at length I was promised a
well-earned rest.

Bajil is quite a little town, its population number-
ing probably some 3000 souls. Except for a large
Turkish fort, built for the most part of squared stones,
and a few houses of the same material, it consists of
mud-and-thatch and mat houses, enclosed by high
hedges of dry mimosa and acacia thorns in the form
of zarebas. The place is prettily situated, lying at
the foot of Jibel Obaki, the surrounding plain being
cultivated with millet of two varieties, the *dokhn* and
the *durra;* while a good water-supply allows of the
growth of a considerable number of trees, principally
acacias, which render the place a veritable oasis.

The *café* here, except for those of the towns and
that at Waalan, was the best we had come across;
for although it only consisted of a series of mat-huts
built round a large yard, everything was so clean and
so tidy that it was a real pleasure to rest in the shade,
all the more so as by this time the rays of the sun had
become fierce in their heat.

We engaged one of these mat-houses for our private use, and unloading our mules, settled in for the day. What rendered our stay at Bajil more refreshing than it otherwise would have proved was the presence of an excellent *masseur*, under whose skilful hands one's limbs lost all their weariness.

As soon as the cool of the afternoon allowed, I sauntered out for a stroll through the little town. There was but little to see, it is true; but a Yemen village always presents sights which, if not exactly pretty, are generally of interest. A wedding-party was in full swing, guns were being fired off, tomtoms rendered the air hideous with their sound, and shrill pipes added to the confusion. The crowd of women who filled the open spaces between the zarebas, that answered for streets, were attired in holiday garments, and a gay throng they were; for, in spite of their dull-blue clothing, they had succeeded in tying them-selves up with handkerchiefs and scarves of all colours, until they resembled rainbows. Here, as elsewhere, it seems to be the lot of womankind to do the hard work, and I stood for a time to watch them filling their pitchers from the wells. The manner in which the water is drawn is the following. A framework of wood is built over the mouth of the well, a solid beam passing from side to side; over this cross-beam runs the rope, to the end of which is fastened a bucket. Owing to the great depth to which the wells have to be sunk, these ropes are necessarily of enormous length, and the only means by which the weight can be supported is by a couple of the women harnessing themselves to the end and running at a gentle trot until the bucket has reached the surface, where it is emptied by a third. One well, the length of the track passed over to draw the bucket to the surface I measured, was only a few feet under two hundred in depth. The labour is a severe one, but the women seem to take it as a matter of course. In southern Morocco, where much the same system is in use, camels or donkeys are harnessed in their place.

The only building of any size or importance in Bajil is the Turkish fort. It is a great square place, with circular towers jutting out here and there, and is built almost entirely of cut stone and bricks. Though useless against artillery, it would prove impregnable to Arab hordes, armed only with spears and matchlock-guns. A few ill-dressed Turks were lying about under the shade of some acacia-trees, and half-a-dozen field-guns, none too well kept, stood near the door; but the place offered no other signs of things military, and wore the weary appearance of orientalism.

This was all that there was to be seen in Bajil, so I retraced my steps to the *café*, where I found our mules being loaded preparatory to a start. A number of Turkish officers from Sanaa had arrived during my absence, and we instantly struck up an acquaintance, as we were proceeding over the same road to

Hodaidah. They had been invalided from the steamy Tehàma, and had been in hospital at Sanaa. Their recovery told a tale of the magnificent climate of that place, for they assured me that they had left Hodaidah a couple of months before almost dead of fever.

At four o'clock we made a start, our two little caravans uniting. The road continues over the desert, which is here dotted with mimosa-bushes and tufts of long grass. It was the delight of the Turkish officers to throw matches into the latter, and as night came on we left a track behind us of fiery stars and heaps of black ashes. There was no danger of the fire taking too large dimensions, as the tufts of grass were sufficiently far removed from one another to prevent the flames spreading.

It was the last of our desert marches. A glorious night, the sky a blaze of myriads of stars, the desert like a silver sea. Quietly and quickly our little mules glided on. Every now and again a caravan of slouching camels would pass by us with a dozen or so wild Bedouins in charge, on the heads of whose spears the moonlight played and flashed, but they soon vanished into the night. One could scarcely believe that this cool plain, fragrant with the sweet scent of mimosa, its fragrance increased by the heavy dew, was in the daytime a howling desert, where the sun scorched everything to death save the thorny bushes and the coarse grass tufts, and the camels and

GATE OF A WALLED VILLAGE IN THE YEMEN.

their Bedouin drivers; but even they scarcely ever travel by day. Wonderful as were the sights and the grandeur of the mountains of the Yemen, I think these night-rides over the desert have fixed themselves more upon my memory. Tired as we often were, one could not but wonder at the glories of the starlit heavens, and revel in the fragrance of falling dew and mimosa.

Before midnight we reached a *café*, merely a few little huts in the desert, but welcome nevertheless, and with shouts and cries we woke the owner, who lit a lamp and showed us into his best accommodation, a roof of grass supported on long canes. However, one could need no more ; for it kept off the chill of the dew, and allowed the breeze, which every now and again stirred, to cool the hot night air.

I shall never forget that last night in the desert, —Turks, Arabs, Moors, and Englishman squatting on carpets, sharing a common pipe in a dimly lit *café* in the desert. Coffee and supper were cooking, and one could hear the bubbling of the coffee-husks in the earthen pot that was preparing for our men. And then they brought our supper, a couple of desert fowls that tasted as though they had tramped a century over the sand, so tough they were. A rest of an hour or two was all we were allowed, and long before daylight we were off again. The desert here takes the form of sand-dunes, in parts covered with scanty scrub, in parts bare yellow sand, broken only

by the hideous lines of crooked telegraph - posts.
There were no signs of a road, not even a track in
the sand, for the slightest breeze destroys the marks
left by those who have gone before. But our men
knew the way well, and just a little after seven
o'clock, when we were beginning to suffer severely
from the intense rays of the sun, a cry proceeded
from our foremost man, who stood spear in hand, a
silhouette against the burning sky.

Hodaidah! There it was at last, dancing in the
shimmering heated air of the desert,—turned, and
twisted, and indistinct, but Hodaidah nevertheless!
As we neared the town the scene became quite
picturesque. Here an old Turkish fort, half in
ruins, stood out yellow from the white sand; there
the remains of some aqueduct in which no water
flowed. Then we entered palm-groves, whose greenness after the desert was refreshing, under the shade
of which nestled the clean grass-and-mat huts and
zarebas of the Arab and Indian inhabitants.

Still on; past many a pretty country-house of
the Arab merchants, surrounded by gardens, until
at length we emerged into the great market-place
that lies without the walls of the town proper,
above which rise the houses snowy white, tier upon
tier in strange disorder.

Passing under a great gateway, the upper part of
which served as barracks, we proceeded by narrow
streets to our destination, a large *café* kept by a

Greek. Here I engaged a room, and sending my Arabs and Turkish guards to forage for themselves until I had rested, we carried our scanty baggage to an upper chamber, the windows of which looked out on one side to the sea, and on the other to the principal street I settled myself in.

But the fatigue of my march from Sanaa had been too much for me, and in an hour my fever had returned, and I was lying, almost unconscious, tossing from side to side. Saïd and Abdurrahman likewise were attacked, and suffered as much perhaps as I did. But our journey was over, we had finished with the mountains and plains of the Yemen, and our goal was reached.

CHAPTER XI.

HODAIDAH.

THE earliest mention that one finds of Hodaidah in Mahammedan history is its capture by El-Ghuri, Sultan of Egypt, in A.D. 1515. In the native historian's account of the invasion of this wild horde of Circassians, Kurds, and other strange peoples, the town is mentioned by the name of Jadidah,[1] the new (town), although this by no means can be taken as a proof that the city had only been founded shortly before that period—for Jadidah, as the name of a city, is common all over the East, and every place was probably at one time "new," though the title may long ago have become inappropriate. This tends to prove that it was probably not until the Red Sea trade had reached a flourishing condition, although at that time entirely in the hands of the natives, that Hodaidah sprang into existence.

Being situated on the sea-coast, and only a little to the south of the country of the Asir tribes, it has not

[1] Kay's Omarah, p. 237.

escaped from attack from both quarters. Principal amongst these, perhaps, was its capture by the Asir chief, Abd el-Hakal, in 1804. In the interests of the Wahabi belief, which he, like so many of his tribe, had embraced, he made an organised attack upon the northern Tehàma. His people, buoyed up with the fanaticism of their new tenets, devastated whole districts, and held the entire Yemen in terror. Four years later, however, Hodaidah was once more restored to the then reigning Imam of Sanaa, Seyed Ahmed ibn Ali Mansur.

From this time, for a space of some four-and-twenty years, we find Hodaidah thriving under the impetus given to trade by the European merchant-ships, which were at this period crowding to the Red Sea; and its lot seems to have been a peaceful one, until the arrival there in 1832 of the dreaded Turkchee Bilmas, by which nickname Mahammed Agha was generally known. Marching overland from the Hedjaz, he encamped close to the city, while his vessels, which had proceeded by sea from Jeddah and Yembo, blockaded the port. On being refused provisions by the governor, he commenced to open fire upon the town walls, whereupon the place capitulated. However, the energetic Mahammed Agha did not remain there, but, leaving four hundred men under the command of Agha Murshid, he marched on Zebeed.[1]

The Egyptian Government abandoned the Yemen

[1] Records of the Bombay Government.

in 1840, eight years after the taking of Hodaidah by Turkchee Bilmas, and it was arranged that this portion of the country at least should fall into the possession of the Grand Shereef of Mecca. But another claimant stepped forward in the person of Huseyn ibn Ali, Shereef of Abou Areesh, who with the Asir tribe, whose assistance he had been able to obtain, took the field with twenty thousand men;[1] and the very day that Hodaidah was abandoned by Ibrahim Pasha, the Shereef's troops, under the leadership of his brother, Abou Taleb, took possession of the place. Notwithstanding the recognition of the Shereef Huseyn's power did not last long; for the Asiri, ever ready for plunder, occupied the town, and only released the merchants, whom they had imprisoned, on their paying large ransoms.

In 1849 a great change was destined to take place in the government of the Yemen, and the Turks, proceeding from Jeddah, occupied Hodaidah, the Shereef of that town obtaining a subsidy from the Ottoman Government in return for his handing over the place. This pension, however, he never received; and accordingly, in 1851 he started to report his case to the Sultan at Constantinople. But sudden death cut short his career on the road, and there is little doubt but that he was murdered.[2] The leader of this Turkish expedition, Tufieh Pasha, became governor of Hodaidah and the surrounding country.

[1] Playfair's Yemen, p. 146.   [2] Ibid.

It was shortly after this that a treaty was drawn
up between the Imam of Sanaa and the Sublime
Porte, in which the principal clauses were that the
Imam was still to continue to reign, but that he
should be considered as a vassal of Abdul-Mejid, the
then reigning Sultan of Turkey; that the revenues
were to be equally divided between the Sultan and
the Imam; and that Sanaa should be garrisoned by
Turkish forces. Although the sequel of this story
belongs rather to the history of Sanaa than to that of
Hodaidah, it may be given briefly at this point, as it
follows as a sequence upon this treaty of Hodaidah.
Returning with the Imam, Tufieh Pasha arrived at
Sanaa, and the change in government was made
known to the inhabitants. What, however, seems
particularly to have fired them to opposition was the
substitution of the name of Abdul-Mejid for that of
their Imam Mahammed Yahia in the prayers. Being
of the Zaidi sect, one of the many divisions of the
Sheiyas,[1] this naturally affected them more than any
temporal changes could have done, and before midnight they had cut to pieces a large proportion of the
Turkish troops, who, although they had taken possession of one of the city forts, were unable to make
any resistance. At length, wounded, and with only
a handful of men, Tufieh Pasha bought a permit
to return to Hodaidah, for which he paid twenty
thousand dollars, and retired to that spot, where he

[1] See chapter on " The Influences of Islam in the Yemen."

died of his wounds and exhaustion. Mahammed
Yahia, the unfortunate Imam who had entered into
this treaty with the Turks, was secretly assassinated,
—Ali Mansur, already twice deposed, being installed
in his place.

But a still more horrible tale is yet to be told
regarding Hodaidah. In 1855 some sixty thousand
men of the Asir tribe marched against the place with
the idea of sacking it. They deferred the attack,
however, owing to the presence of British ships of
war ; but the inhabitants, owing to all communication with the interior being cut off, had reached a
condition of great misery, when cholera broke out
amongst the Asiri, no less than fifteen thousand
dying before they reached their homes.

But to return to Hodaidah as I saw it in February
and March of last year—1892.

Hodaidah lies on the north-east side of a large bay,
and somewhat sheltered by a promontory on the
north-west. The town is a large one, and contains
probably between thirty and thirty-five thousand inhabitants, though at the time the author was there the
number was swelled by a large addition of Turkish
troops. The place is a flourishing one : the bazaars, of
which more anon, are well supplied ; the houses solidly
built, and high. Its one great drawback is its feverish climate, the few Europeans and the natives alike
suffering at certain periods of the year. After a rainfall, for instance, or in the winter when the westerly

winds are blowing, fever attacks the place like an epidemic.

With this short description I may revert to my personal experiences of Hodaidah.

As soon as my attack of fever had worn off sufficiently to allow of my going out, accompanied by my guards, I proceeded to the Governor's residence. He received me most politely, a chair was at once got for me, cigarettes and coffee brought in, while his Excellency perused the letters which my soldiers had brought from the Governor-General at Sanaa. This over, he bade me welcome, and we had a pleasant chat, conversing in Arabic, of which his Excellency knew less than myself, so that at last we found that things went more easily when a Greek entered who spoke French.

The Governor's first question to me was worth recording. He was a little nervous at first, and for a minute there was an awkward silence, which his Excellency broke by asking, "Did you fight in the Crimea?" I replied that I was not born until some ten years after that war was over. However, I found the question had a purpose, for on the Governor's breast hung the English Crimean medal, which he handed me to examine with great pride. After this episode conversation was carried on more easily, and finally I obtained his Excellency's permission to continue residing in the upper chamber of the *café* until I should depart. Very different were the Govern-

ment offices here from the gorgeous apartments of
the Governor-General at Sanaa.   Here there was only

A Street in Hodaidah.

a small bare room with a
few chairs, none of which
were in very good re-
pair.   An outside staircase
of rickety steps leads to
the first storey of the building, where the principal
offices appear to be situated, the lower portion serving

as a store.   A constant flow of gaudy officers and ill-clothed soldiers passed and repassed.   I had several interviews with the Governor during my stay of a week in Hodaidah, and on every occasion found him polite and amiable, although he refused to allow me to continue my journey by land, as I had hoped to have done, *viâ* Beit el-Fakih, Zebeed, and Hais.

On my return to my quarters I found a couple of Turkish soldiers calmly seated in my room, one of them on my bed, and smoking my cigarettes.   Although I was prepared to be watched, I was not at all inclined to put up with this intrusion, and with the aid of Abdurrahman, Saïd, and a boot, soon put them to flight.   I at once returned to the Governor to explain the matter to him, and on my way to his apartment was accosted in the most polite manner by an officer, who begged me not to report the matter, saying that if I liked to pay him a couple of dollars he would see that the guard was removed.   But what with annoyance and fever, I was not in a mood to pay anybody anything, so went straight to his Excellency and told my story.   The old man and his officers burst into fits of laughter, explaining to me that the guard had only been put there for me to pay something for their removal, and that the whole thing was a "plant."   I begged him to send for the officer who wanted *bakshish*, and speak to him, so that I should not be put to the same annoyance again, and this he willingly did.   Nevertheless, in spite of

the fact that I was left in tolerable peace, I soon
found that my every movement was watched, but
never interfered with. This last was no doubt
owing partly to the good offices of one who showed
me great kindness and hospitality in Hodaidah,
Dr Ahmed, a native of India, who ably represents
H.B.M. Government as Vice-Consul there. I cannot speak highly enough of my appreciation of his
and his English wife's many acts of kindness toward
me ; and although, owing to ill health, my recollections of Hodaidah are none too cheery, I shall always
remember how anxious Dr and Mrs Ahmed were to
render pleasant my stay. A doctor of Glasgow Uni-
versity, Dr Ahmed made his name in Assam in the
Indian medical service, and was only a short time ago
appointed Vice-Consul at Hodaidah; and it is to be
hoped that the skilful way in which he carries out
his by no means easy duties there, and keeps firmly
rooted in that town a feeling of respect between the
British and Turkish Governments, will shortly obtain
for him a post in some more healthy and important
place.

The *café* in which I had taken up my quarters
faced the sea on one side, and the only wide street in
the town on the other, that which lies along the sea-
board, from which it is only divided by the Government offices and huts of *areesh* or reeds. From my
window on the second storey I was able to watch the
people passing and repassing, and many an hour was

spent thus in idleness. But if this street offered scenes of character, how much more so did the bazaars! and there, when I was well enough, I used to sit talking to the Arab shopkeepers and sipping coffee. Good intelligent fellows many of them were, and always ready to waste half an hour in listening to tales of Egypt and Morocco, and even of my journey in the Yemen. What sights the bazaars offer! All the nationalities of the world seem to crowd there—strange weird people in every stage of clothing, from almost nakedness to rich robes of striped silks. Unlike the bazaars at Aden, those of Hodaidah are roofed in from the sun, the fierce rays of which yet find cracks and crannies in the wood and mats to creep through. But their brilliant light falling upon some stall of fruit perhaps only tends to throw into deeper shadow the rest of the crowded street. In the cool of the afternoon I would saunter round and take up my station on the little shop-platform of a seller of books, and spend an hour or two with him. A wizened little old man he was, a native of Zebeed; but he was good company, and would put aside all ideas of business when he saw me coming, and would point out the strange figures amongst the passers-by, and tell me whence they came and who they were. Jews, Indians of all kinds, Persians, Arabs, Egyptians, Bedouins, Abyssinians, Turks, Greeks, negroes, and a few Europeans, would jostle each other in the narrow ways.

From the bazaars to the town walls is but a step.

Passing out of the fortified gates, of which there are several, one issued on to the large open space, the *sôk* or market, which we had crossed when we entered the town. Here garden produce was offered for sale, generally exposed on the ground, though a number of little mat-and-reed huts contained small shops. The larger of these flimsy structures serve as *cafés*, and one or two as Parsee theatres. The largest of the *cafés* was a constant resort of mine, and of an evening I would sit, accompanied by Saïd, who, in spite of his fever, had polished up his dress—what there was of it—and his raven locks. So beautiful had he become that little groups of the female sex would come and joke with him; and though he treated them with a certain amount of haughty indifference, he was by no means unappreciative of their attentions, and had a knack of being out after dark. There one would see the Turkish officers in gold-lace, with their glass hookahs in front of them, lounging away the afternoon hours. There, too, were the merchants, gorgeous in silk raiment and turbans, talking business over coffee and tobacco.

The remaining streets and places of Hodaidah offer but little attractiveness. The streets are narrow and the houses high, and except now and again for a richly carved doorway, there is but little of interest to be seen.

The greatest disadvantage to Hodaidah, after its

feverish climate, is the exceedingly poor water-supply; for although there are some brackish wells in the neighbourhood, all pure water has to be brought from a distance of some miles. It is carried in skins and barrels on the backs of camels and donkeys.

Near these wells, under the guidance of Dr Ahmed, I spent a pleasant afternoon in a beautiful garden belonging to a certain wealthy Arab, whose fortune was made, it is said, by purchasing the right of collecting taxes from the Ottoman Government. This, in the hands of an unscrupulous and hard man, means a very considerable income, and the garden in question was a proof that the old Arab evidently throve. The road from the town passes along sandy lanes and amongst palm-groves until the open desert is reached. Continuing over this for a mile or so, one reaches the wells, while green trees peeping over the high garden walls break the monotony of sand and scrub.

Immediately on our arrival the gate was thrown open, and we entered a veritable paradise—a walled garden many acres in extent, and filled with gorgeous trees and shrubs, which the owner is said to have collected from all quarters of the tropics. Irrigation was carried on by water-wheels and wells, and streamlets flowed in every direction. Under the shade of the large trees summer - houses had been erected of trellis-work, over which jasmine and roses and many a creeper, the name of which I did not

know, climbed in luxuriance. In these divans were
arranged, and one could enjoy the sight of the
flowers in cool shade. Wonderful they were, those
shrubs and trees and plants, hung with great masses
of bloom of every colour, while here and there tall
lilies raised their stately heads. The trees were full
of birds, and the garden was sweet with the scent of
the flowers and the hum of the insects' wings.

Long into the moonlit night we sat there, until the
chill dew told us it was time to seek more secure
shelter. Yet in all their loveliness there lurks poison
in this paradise, and nearly all our party suffered
from fever in consequence of our visit.

But few Europeans live in Hodaidah, with the exception of the Greeks. The wife of the British Vice-
Consul was the one English lady in the place, the
only other British subject, excepting natives of India,
&c., being a Maltese gentleman, agent for a British
firm. A few Americans, however, are to be found,
the trade in skins to America being an important one.
Of the other nationalities there are perhaps in all
half-a-dozen representatives.

During my stay the port was visited by a small
Turkish gunboat, the captain of which, whose name
I never discovered, paid me a call. He had been
educated at the Naval College at Constantinople, and
spoke English remarkably well. He was tired of his
berth, he said, his weariness being materially added
to by the irregularity of his pay. In this respect, he

added, he was better off than most of the Turkish soldiers in the Yemen, for they received none at all. Although at Hodaidah the condition of the troops seemed fairly good as regards food and clothing, we had found at more than one place in the interior the soldiers bootless and payless, and receiving as rations only two loaves of bread a-day, one of which they usually ate, the other being exchanged for tobacco. A piastre or two to a soldier won as genuine thanks as ever one heard. It meant little luxuries which his heart longed for, cigarettes and coffee, and which for weeks very likely he had been unable to attain to.

At length, after seven days of fever, a steamer arrived in the port, and I saw means of getting to Aden. Saying good-bye to Dr Ahmed on the rickety little pier, down one of the supports of which I was obliged to clamber in order to reach the rowing-boat, as the steps had been washed away, or never built, I forget which, I shook off the dust of Hodaidah from my feet, and in an hour or so was aboard an English steamer, having a yarn with an English captain and mate.

In a few days we were back once more in Aden, arriving on the very day on which quarantine from the Red Sea ports was removed, so that I was only detained half an hour on the hulk Hyderabad, in place of the seven days I had feared I would have to undergo.

The welcome I received from all friends here was very kind, and many a laugh we enjoyed together over my adventures in the Yemen.

. . . .

Just as my journey was then concluded, so is my account of it finished now. A year has passed since I left the country, and yet its every detail is as clear to me as if it had all happened yesterday. As I lay down my pen I conjure up in my mind the desert-rides under a myriad of brilliant stars; I feel upon my cheek the soft balmy southern breeze; I see again our little party hiding in the gullies, and creeping on by night over the terrible rough roads of the mountains. Once more, warned by an unknown friend, I escape by night from Beit Said; once more, but this time with a smile, I spend five days a prisoner in the *conâk* of Sanaa. Once more I pass through the great valleys and descend to the desert, and I shudder over the remembrance of nights and days of fever—a fever that clung to me for months. Yet my recollections of the country are ones that I shall always treasure; and in spite of dangers and sickness, in spite of long marches and days in prison, the Yemen will always be for me, at least, Arabia Felix.

APPENDIX

GENEALOGICAL AND CHRONOLOGICAL TREE OF THE IMAMS OF SANAA,

SHOWING THEIR DESCENT FROM MAHAMMED.

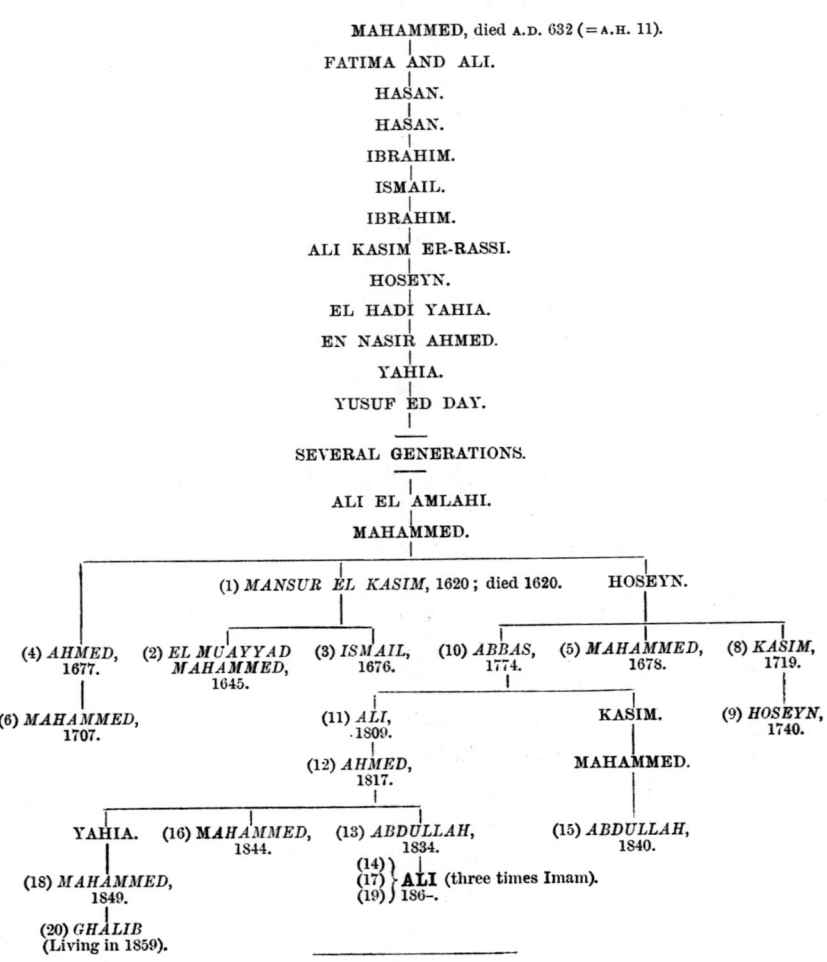

MAHAMMED, died A.D. 632 (= A.H. 11).

FATIMA AND ALI.

HASAN.

HASAN.

IBRAHIM.

ISMAIL.

IBRAHIM.

ALI KASIM ER-RASSI.

HOSEYN.

EL HADI YAHIA.

EN NASIR AHMED.

YAHIA.

YUSUF ED DAY.

SEVERAL GENERATIONS.

ALI EL AMLAHI.

MAHAMMED.

(1) *MANSUR EL KASIM*, 1620; died 1620.   HOSEYN.

(4) *AHMED*, 1677. (2) *EL MUAYYAD MAHAMMED*, 1645. (3) *ISMAIL*, 1676. (10) *ABBAS*, 1774. (5) *MAHAMMED*, 1678. (8) *KASIM*, 1719.

(6) *MAHAMMED*, 1707. (11) *ALI*, 1809. KASIM. (9) *HOSEYN*, 1740.

(12) *AHMED*, 1817. MAHAMMED.

YAHIA. (16) *MAHAMMED*, 1844. (13) *ABDULLAH*, 1834. (15) *ABDULLAH*, 1840.

(18) *MAHAMMED*, 1849. (14) (17) (19) } **ALI** (three times Imam). 186-.

(20) *GHALIB* (Living in 1859).

Note.—The parentage of the seventh Imam Mahammed ibn Hasan is not known for certain. He died in 1708.
The names in italics are those of the Imams of Sanaa. The numbers within parentheses refer to the order in which they reigned. The numbers after the names are the probable dates of their deaths.

A LIST OF THE IMAMS OF SANAA,

GIVING THEIR FULL TITLES.

Note.—This list is compiled from Niebuhr's table, as given in Sir R. L. Playfair's 'History of Yemen,' with one or two corrections from native authorities.

1. Mansur El-Kasim El-Kebir.
2. El-Muayyad Mahammed.
3. Ismail El-Metawakil Al' Allah.
4. Ahmed El-Mejd Billah.
5. Mahammed El-Mehdi Hadi.
6. Mahammed El-Mehdi.
7. Mahammed En-Nasir.
8. Kasim El-Metawakil.
9. Hoseyn El-Mansur.
10. Abbas El-Mehdi.
11. Ali El-Mansur.
12. Ahmed El-Metawakil.
13. Abdullah El-Mehdi.
14. Ali El-Mansur.
15. Abdullah En-Nasir.
16. Mahammed El-Hadi.
17. Ali El-Mansur.
18. Mahammed El-Metawakil.
19. Ali El-Mansur.
20. Ghalib El-Hadi.

PEDIGREE OF THE
REIGNING ABDALI SULTAN OF LAHEJ.

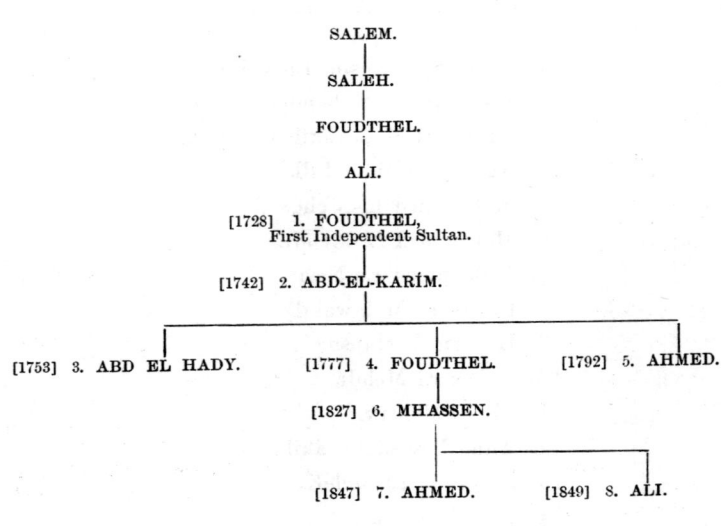

Note.—The dates are those of their succession according to Playfair's 'Yemen.'

INDEX TO PROPER NAMES.

Koreish, 45, 46.
Kos, Bishop, 46, 75.
Kudaah, 31.
Kufa, 50.
Kurds, 358.

Lahej, 16, 20, 21, 24, 60, 65, 115,
  132, 151, 161, 167-169,
  171, 172, 177, 179, 180,
  181, 242, 243, 287.
  ,, Wadi, 176.
Laing, Prof., 36.
Lakhnia, or Lakhtiaa, 41.
Lebanon, Mt., 85, 88.
"Liars," the, 49.
Lisbon, 128.
Lohaya, 10, 13, 64, 100.
Lokman, 38, 145.
Ludovico de Barthema, 128.
Lumley, Captain, 12.

Maaber, 111, 285.
Maadi Karib, 44, 45.
Maala, 136, 143.
Madeira, 231.
Mahammed, 36, 44-49, 52, 53, 57,
  77, 82, 83, 94, 255,
  320, 321.
  ,, Agha, 65, 131, 359,
        360.
  ,, Ali Pasha, 17, 64, 65.
  ,, el-Meccawi, 66.
  ,, ibn Ziad, 51.
  ,, Rushti Pasha, 96.
  ,, Yahya, 67, 361, 362.
Mahdi el-Fakih Saïd, 17.
Mahmoud, 43.
Main Pass, 143, 158.
Makarama, 347.
Makulla, 131.
Malik, 31.
Mamlooks, 55, 65.
Mamun, el-, 51.
Mansur, el-, 54.
Mansur el-Kasim, 57.
  ,, ibn Hasan, 87.
Mareb, Saba, or Sheba, 23, 36, 37,
  38, 40, 126, 143, 280, 288, 312,
  319.
Masar, Jebel, 343.

Mashonaland, 28.
Mavia, 25.
Mecca, 4, 13, 18, 22, 43, 45, 46, 63,
  64, 66, 93, 205, 296, 320, 360.
Medina, 4, 63, 64, 93.
Medinet el-Asfal, 24.
Mefhak, 330.
Mehdi el-Mentether, 67.
Mehdi, Senussi el-, 90.
Melh, el-, 187.
  ,, Sailet, 188.
Menakha, 78, 104, 109, 331, 333,
  336, 337, 339, 340, 341, 350.
Menes, 35.
Menif, Jibel, 181, 343.
Mequinez, 246, 297.
Meruan, Beni, 100, 105.
Meryeille, Mons. de, 148.
Metneh, 325.
Middleton, Admiral, 130.
Milne, Captain, 133, 181.
Minæans, or Maïn, 32-36, 38, 39.
Mjisbiyeh, 196.
Mohajir, 321.
Mokha, 10-13, 55, 56, 59, 61, 63-66,
  68, 130, 138, 301.
Morocco, 4, 81, 91, 123, 153, 156,
  171, 201, 246, 255, 293, 314, 345,
  353, 367.
Mosailma, 48, 49.
Moulas, the, 77.
Mrais, Jibel, 202.
Mshareg, 102.
Muavia, 50.
Muayyad, Mahammed el-, 59.
Muir, Sir William, 77.
Mundah, 236.
Munkat, 243-245.
Munsoorie Hills, 149.
Mustain, el-, 52.
Mustansir, el-, 88.
Mutawakil, el-, 52.
Mutazilites, the, 89.
Muza, 6, 11.
Muzaffer, el-, 54.

Nadir, 230.
Nebuchadnezzar, 30.
Negoum, Jibel, 106, 107, 110, 224,
  298, 299, 301.

384 INDEX TO PROPER NAMES.